BURNING RAGE OF A DYING PLANET

THE FBI VS. THE EARTH LIBERATION FRONT

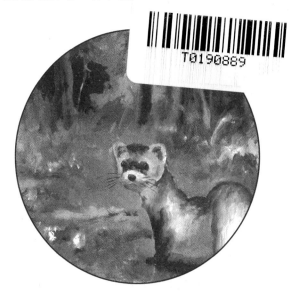

CRAIG ROSEBRAUGH

MICROCOSM PUBLISHING

Portland, Ore | Cleveland, Ohio

BURNING RAGE OF A DYING PLANET
THE FBI VS. THE EARTH LIBERATION FRONT

© 2004, 2024 Craig Rosebraugh
© This edition Microcosm Publishing 2024

Second edition - 3,000 copies - July 9, 2024

ISBN 9781648412073

This is Microcosm #849

Edited by Lex Orgera

To join the ranks of high-class stores that feature Microcosm titles, talk to your rep: In the U.S. **COMO** (Atlantic), **ABRAHAM** (Midwest), **BOB BARNETT** (Texas, Oklahoma, Arkansas, Louisiana), **IMPRINT** (Pacific), **TURNAROUND** (UK), **UTP/MANDA** (Canada), **NEWSOUTH** (Australia/New Zealand), **Observatoire** (Africa, Europe), **IPR** (Middle East), **Yvonne Chau** (Southeast Asia), **HarperCollins** (India), **Everest/B.K. Agency** (China), **Tim Burland** (Japan/Korea), and **FAIRE** and **EMERALD** in the gift trade.

For a catalog, write or visit:
Microcosm Publishing
2752 N Williams Ave.
Portland, OR 97227
All the news that's fit to print at www.Microcosm.Pub/Newsletter.
Get more copies of this book at www.Microcosm.Pub/BurningRage.

Did you know that you can buy our books directly from us at sliding scale rates? Support a small, independent publisher and pay less than Amazon's price at **www.Microcosm.Pub**.

Library of Congress Cataloging-in-Publication Data

Names: Rosebraugh, Craig, author.
Title: Burning rage of a dying planet : the FBI vs. the Earth Liberation
   Front / by Craig Rosebraugh.
Other titles: New edition.
Description: [Portland] : Microcosm Publishing, [2024] | Summary: "A
   harrowing, captivating firsthand history of the rise of the radical
   environmental movement the Earth Liberation Front (ELF). Since 1997, the
   ELF has inflicted over $100 million in damages on entities they believe
   to be causing environmental destruction, mostly through brazen arson
   attacks on timber companies, ski resorts, and car dealerships. Former
   ELF spokesperson Craig Rosebraugh charts the history and ideology of the
   ELF and explores its tactics, successes, and limitations-examining the
   question of whether or not violence is justifiable, along with the
   short- and long-term political benefits and drawbacks of using
   violence"-- Provided by publisher.
Identifiers: LCCN 2023050215 | ISBN 9781648412073 (trade paperback)
Subjects: LCSH: Deep ecology. | Earth Liberation Front. | United States.
   Federal Bureau of Investigation. | Ecoterrorism—United States.
Classification: LCC GE197 .R67 2024 | DDC 364.1/317—dc23/eng/20240331
LC record available at https://lccn.loc.gov/2023050215

MICROCOSM · PUBLISHING

MICROCOSM PUBLISHING is Portland's most diversified publishing house and distributor, with a focus on the colorful, authentic, and empowering. Our books and zines have put your power in your hands since 1996, equipping readers to make positive changes in their lives and in the world around them. Microcosm emphasizes skill-building, showing hidden histories, and fostering creativity through challenging conventional publishing wisdom with books and bookettes about DIY skills, food, bicycling, gender, self-care, and social justice. What was once a distro and record label started by Joe Biel in a drafty bedroom was determined to be *Publishers Weekly*'s fastest-growing publisher of 2022 and #3 in 2023 and 2024, and is now among the oldest independent publishing houses in Portland, OR, and Cleveland, OH. We are a politically moderate, centrist publisher in a world that has inched to the right for the past 80 years.

Global labor conditions are bad, and our roots in industrial Cleveland in the '70s and '80s made us appreciate the need to treat workers right. Therefore, our books are MADE IN THE USA.

To those courageous heroes who have risked their freedom and lives for the benefit of us all . . .

To Elaine Close, who provided me with exceptional support and love . . .

And to Stu Sugarman, who always had my back.

CONTENTS

FOREWORD

I wish that, in the two decades since *Burning Rage of a Dying Planet* was first published, precautionary action had been taken, that you were reading from a solar powered train, traveling through fields of turbines and permaculture, towards a liveable future.

But it didn't happen like that. Instead, there's been an unprecedented expansion of fossil fuel–based energy infrastructure. The number of floods and instances of heavy rain have quadrupled since 1980 and doubled since 2004. Apart from a small blip during COVID-19, greenhouse gas emissions continue to rise even further into uncharted levels.

The climate and ecological emergency that the Earth Liberation Front fiercely attempted to slow is now our context. The consequences play out across the world all the time. We are living through the sixth mass extinction and dancing at the edge of climate apocalypse.

This new reality affects us all. The front lines of environmental disasters are felt hardest by global majority nations, but now, the houses of white people in Western countries are flooding and burning down too.

We share this page—at the beginning of this book—in a moment when many millions of people are waking up. People who have benefitted from systems of power that create climate change. People like me, and perhaps like you, too, are sick of our role in a system that works for a tiny minority whilst oppressing everyone else. We want the world to change. We feel the urgency with which our relationships to one another and our world must transform.

And if we—who tread so heavily on the earth—can reduce the environmental impact of our societies, the effect for the planet will be disproportionately good.

Yet the power of vested interests to kill political will and manipulate public debate is relentless. Even now, when the shit is hitting the fan, it is difficult to know what action we should take to lead us to a future where we stop burning fossil fuels and stop extracting beyond what this planet can give us. As Vanessa Machado de Oliveira wrote in *Hospicing Modernity*, "The mess we find ourselves in is unprecedented and we all have a lot of work to do!"

This is the context in which *Burning Rage of a Dying Planet* is re-released: a time when thought leaders within the environmental justice landscape are questioning the tactics of our movement. If nonviolent, creative protests have barely slowed the growth of fossil fuel infrastructure, then should we be considering more radical acts? The sort of action—industrial sabotage and arson—that Craig Rosebraugh presented to the mainstream media when he was the press spokesperson for the Earth Liberation Front?

In this context, I read Craig's account of a particularly brave moment in his life, and the life of the North American environmental movement, as a call to action. When he received communiqués from activists, he did everything in his power to get the word out about their actions. He tried to shift public consciousness by offering his take on why these anonymous people risked so much to challenge environmental destruction. He might not have done the acts himself, but he offered something essential to the activists by becoming the voice that interpreted their acts to a national, and sometimes global, audience.

Throughout my life as an activist, I've tried to stay ahead of the mainstream media. Whilst they're invested in depicting popular resistance as ridiculous, pointless, or criminal, we have to be disciplined about the images we create and the narrative our protests tell. Whether scaling the Houses of Parliament to drop banners in protest against airport expansion or declaring rebellion against the British government by bringing central London to a standstill for two weeks, I've helped to create iconic protest sites.

By curating the story that each protest tells, I've tried to stop audiences from feeling alienated and, instead, to help them feel excited by the possibility of uprising and the invitation for all of us to discover what gifts we have and to take part.

Because, although many of us would not go to the lengths that the ELF did, we can be inspired by the story of their uprising: their refusal to permit growth that threatens our planet's life systems. Their courage calls us to become part of a new story of human responsibility. It encourages us to step up and find our place in sorting out the mess we've made:

To examine our lives, acknowledge the sacrifices that others have taken, and commit to doing more. To get involved in a local environmental group. To contact an elected representative and be a pain in their ass. To organize our neighbors to do the same. To protest. To change so that our tread is gentler on the earth. To use less energy, drive less, fly less, eat healthier food without meat, and to encourage friends, families, and colleagues to do the same.

Right now, more than at any other time in human history, every decision we make matters. Every single action we take either moves us towards a future where we all can live or deepens the wound of a way of life that this one planet cannot support. Every time we find the courage to break with business as usual, we make the future of this planet more possible.

I don't think I will ever be the kind of person who can take the risks that Craig and the ELF took during the late nineties and the early aughts. But that doesn't mean I can't do more to participate in transforming this world from where we are to where we need to be. The world is on fire, and so I will try to walk into the footprints that Craig and many other brave people have created. To step out of my comfort zone and try, in my little corner of the world, to put the fire out.

Tamsin Omond

Writer and activist

PROLOGUE TO THE NEW EDITION

$\mathcal{E}$arly in 2001, I was approached over email by a man named Robert Eringer. The message was quite polite, contained just the right amount of flattery, and seemed like just another one of the many emails I would receive either praising or condemning me and the ELF or ALF. However, upon a closer read, what seemed to set this one apart from others was that Eringer wrote that he was a book packager[1] and had recently seen me speak. He believed that my story would make a fascinating and very marketable book, and he wanted to know if I was interested in discussing this potential with him.

Now by this time, I was admittedly fucking paranoid. Not only had I been arrested a dozen times by the police, but I had been subpoenaed to multiple federal grand jury investigations, had my home and office raided twice, my arm broken by the cops, experienced mysterious break-ins at my homes, been followed around the city and across the country by the FBI, been ripped out of a vehicle by the FBI and made to lay face down at gunpoint on a busy street in Florida. I also knew the Feds were monitoring my phones, emails, and physical mail. If that wasn't enough, not only was I occasionally approached by attractive, yet out of place, women wanting to take me out for a drink,[2] I also had been receiving frequent and serious death threats. So, yeah, I was extremely paranoid and didn't trust anyone.

My initial response to Eringer was to thank him for his email and decline his offer. I wasn't interested in writing a book about the ELF or my experiences at that time. In truth, I couldn't imagine how—with my incredibly busy schedule—I could carve

---

1 While a book agent typically represents a writer, assisting to negotiate and land book deals, a book packager (as Eringer defined it) finds people with interesting stories, helps put those stories into literary form and then assists in selling.

2 On a few occasions, at Earth First! gatherings or after public speeches I gave, I was approached by far too flirtatious and forward women seeking to become close with me. Foregoing my inner James Bond instincts to sleep with the enemy, I thankfully rejected these advances out of a well-founded fear that these were attempts by the government to get people close to me in order to obtain private information on the ELF or ALF. My FBI file contains an abundance of pages referencing "CI's" or confidential informants, let alone infiltrators.

out the better part of a year it could take to pen such a work. I also figured that if I ever was interested in writing such a book, I could do it on my own terms without the involvement of someone I didn't necessarily know and trust.

While Eringer responded that he understood, he didn't give up. Throughout that year, he proceeded to send emails "checking in" on how I was doing and asking if I had reconsidered his offer to potentially "package" a book for me. Most of the time I paid him little attention, with my focus more centered on the second raid on my home and business by the FBI in April 2001, and then my eventual controversial stepping down as a spokesperson for the ELF later in the year.

But Eringer persisted. Having removed myself as a media mouthpiece for the eco-saboteurs on September 6,[3] I finally began speaking to Eringer in late November and early December 2001. Attempting to vet him as much as I was able to at the time, I asked Eringer for more information about himself. I figured, since he was claiming to be a book packager with connections to major publishing houses, he would have previous book projects in which he was credited. Eringer complied with my request and sent some reviews of titles he had helped package, as well as others he had written himself.

By December of that year, I had agreed to meet with Eringer on January 7, 2002, to hear more about him and his proposal. In an email to me dated December 21, 2001, Eringer writes,

> Hi again, Okay, I've made arrangements—finally! I arrive on Monday Jan 7th; will stay two nights at the Governor Hotel, which supposedly is in the middle of everything. I suggest we meet for drinks and dinner at my hotel on Monday night, say six p.m. Will that work for you? R.

That night I met with Eringer in Portland and, while I was skeptical as hell of this guy, I listened to him compliment me and discuss his background and the potential of a book project. After hearing him discuss the numerous benefits a book might

---

3 I had no way of knowing that I was stepping down as a spokesperson for what the FBI had labeled the number one domestic terrorism threat in the United States—just five days before the horrific terrorist attacks of September 11, 2001.

have in getting the message of the ELF and ALF out to a wider audience, I began to take more of an interest. I went away from the meeting telling Eringer I was about to head to the East Coast, where I was conducting a series of lectures on the ELF and where I also had been subpoenaed to testify before a US Congressional Subcommittee investigating "ecoterrorism."[4] But I also agreed to create an outline of a proposed book for Eringer to review to see if we could move forward with the project.

After the hearing in Washington, DC concluded and I breathed a sigh of relief that I was not imprisoned for my noncooperation with the Subcommittee,[5] I spent some time creating an outline for a memoir of my time speaking for the ELF and ALF. I did hope that the project—if it moved forward— would provide more of an opportunity to explain the rationale of the ELF strategy and tactics as well as provide a greater understanding of the environmental crimes of some of the entities targeted by the group. I say *more* of an opportunity as, in the overwhelming majority of mainstream news stories about the ELF and its actions, the most I would be afforded was typically a quick sound bite, while the bulk of the stories would be focused on demonizing the group under the cliché "terrorist" labeling.

After creating a chapter outline and drafting a sample chapter of the book, I sent them to an overly eager Eringer, who quickly responded with praise and excitement. His next move was to invite me down for an all-expenses-paid meeting that he would host in Santa Barbara, California. In attendance would not only be me and Eringer, but a man by the name of Frank Martin, who Eringer told me was his editor colleague that lived in Chicago.

---

4 On February 12, 2002, I was forced to appear in Washington DC in front of a US Congressional Subcommittee on Forests and Forest Health. In front of the national media and a room largely full of paid seat fillers, the Committee—led by Rep. Scott McInnis (R-CO)—grilled me on anything and everything I knew about the ELF. I relied on my Constitutional rights to remain silent to 54 out of 56 questions and only confirmed the answers to two questions, my name and that I had submitted written testimony to the Subcommittee.

5 Under the law, I could have been held in Congressional contempt and imprisoned for up to one year for each question I didn't answer or for each response the Subcommittee did not appreciate. So, there was a potential that Congress could have imprisoned me for up to 54 years at the February 12, 2002 hearing.

The meeting was set for February 23, 2002, and I chose to drive down to avoid the added anxiety of flying. With the extreme and growing impact of the government repression against me resulting from me speaking out on behalf of the ELF and ALF, I developed a severe anxiety problem. As a result, I tended to attempt to avoid placing myself in situations that would heighten my anxiety, and flying was one of them.[6]

While I remained open about the idea of the book, I was skeptical of Eringer and now this Frank Martin. As a result, I convinced my sister Keri, who was living in Los Angeles at the time, to join me for the weekend in Santa Barbara. I hoped if nothing else, she would be able to provide added observation and feedback about Eringer and Martin to help me decide if I should run for the hills. So I drove to Los Angeles, picked Keri up, and we headed to Santa Barbara, checking into the hotel suite that Eringer had reserved. In his email to me on February 21, 2002, Eringer wrote:

> Hi Craig, Assuming you can receive email on the road . . .
> I've booked you a room at The Inn at East Beach at 1029
> Orilla Del Mar. This is opposite the beach a couple blocks
> from Stearns Wharf. R.

That night, and throughout the weekend, Eringer and Martin met with Keri and I, wining and dining us and sparing no expense. For most of that time, I sat back and said very little out of skepticism, while Keri tried to get to know Eringer and Martin better to see what information we could learn about them. Eringer seemed to take a particular liking to Keri and, by the end of our time together, was sharing one-hundred-dollar-plus bottles of wine with her and alluding to connections that might advance her art career. At the end of the weekend, Keri and I headed off, unsure of these characters but feeling confident they likely meant no harm. While I made the trek back to Portland,

---

6 While I never had a particular fondness for flying, during the 1990s, I was taking frequent air trips while organizing rallies and protests across the United States. It was during one of these flights that I watched one of the two engines on a small commuter plane ignite, causing the aircraft to become significantly unstable, descend rapidly with passengers screaming, and make a hard emergency landing.

Eringer and Martin were going to discuss moving forward and making me an offer.

Sure enough, within a couple of weeks, Eringer sent a message wanting to proceed with the project. In his March 8, 2002 email, Eringer wrote:

Hi Craig,

Good news: I have decided to go ahead and commission the book we discussed.

Hence, I agree to an advance of $5,000 on the basis that it will take approximately three months to write. You will write a minimum of 300 pages and cover the areas laid out in your proposal and those discussed while you were in Santa Barbara.

I will make these funds available to you in five installments of $1,000 each, based on your progress, final installment payable upon completion.

Frank will deliver the first installment of $1,000 as soon as it is convenient for him to visit Portland and commence the collaborative process.

Additional amounts of $1,000 will be paid as you write/upon Frank's satisfaction with your material.

If I market this book elsewhere, first monies will repay my $5,000.

Beyond that, I would receive a 15% commission on all revenues emanating from this book.

Okay?

R.

The plan was that I was to work closely with Martin, wherein I would draft three chapters at a time and, upon his review and acceptance, I would receive an installment of $1,000 and proceed to the next set of chapters. As the process began, Eringer told me he was moving to London and that, while he would still be in the loop on the project, Martin would be taking the lead in working with me on a regular basis. Shortly thereafter, Martin wrote via email to me,

Craig,

I want to meet with you for two days early next month to take care of the first phase of your business deal with R and to go over comments and questions I have about the content of the book. Please let me know what dates work for you.

R says he's 'constantly getting rained on in London and knows what it must be like to live in Portland.' Say hello to Keri for him.

Frank[7]

I told him I had a flexible schedule and asked if he would be coming to Portland for his proposed meeting. Martin responded,

Craig,

Yes, I'll fly to Portland. It is good to know you're flexible at the beginning of the month. I'll get back to you with dates as soon as I juggle a few things here and check flight availability.

Frank[8]

So on April 13 and 14 of that year, I met Martin in his hotel suite in downtown Portland. Like Eringer, Martin was personable and full of compliments and acted like it was an honor to be in my presence. I collected my first installment of $1,000 and proceeded to discuss the first few chapters with Martin before setting off to commence the writing process.

This working process would continue for the next nine months. Every three or four chapters that I would complete would be reviewed by Martin, and then I would be paid my next advance installment before continuing. Sometimes these installments would be sent via mail and other times hand delivered by Martin.

On one occasion, I met Martin at a hotel room in downtown Portland, where we worked for a couple of hours reviewing a set of chapters I had written. For the most part, everything seemed fine with the working relationship. The only oddity came with increased pressure from Martin and Eringer not only to finish

7 Email from Frank Martin to me on March 20, 2002.
8 Email from Frank Martin to me on March 20, 2002.

the book, but to ensure I included as much detailed information as I could about the ELF.

And then there was the time Martin visited me for a meeting at my home. It was September 2003, and I had just completed another few chapters of the book, which brought me up to being about three-quarters done with the first draft of the manuscript. As we had agreed, Martin arrived in Portland and, after checking into his hotel, proceeded to make his way to my house. Answering the door, I could see Martin was his usual charismatic self, eager to see me and to continue moving forward with the project. This time, however, he had brought me a gift. In his hand was an FBI baseball cap that Martin said he picked up at the airport, thinking it would be a comical present for me. I took the hat, thinking the joke was a bit bizarre, but paid it little attention. Yet months and even years later this gift would take on a new meaning.

On December 10, 2002, I finally finished the last set of chapters and sent the completed first draft of the manuscript to Eringer and Martin. I was extremely relieved as it had been a lengthy process, and I believed—since each set of chapters had, upon completion, been approved by Martin and Eringer—that my main task moving forward would be some minor editing. However, this proved to be wrong.

Initially, though, this was the impression I got from Martin. He wanted to schedule an in-person meeting for January 5 and 6, 2003, to review the manuscript with me and proceed with the minor editing. Yet, as December wore on, Martin informed me that both he and Eringer were not happy with the manuscript and that it needed a significant amount of work. I was told the meetings then scheduled for the first week of January would involve creating a plan to basically start from scratch with an entire rewrite of the manuscript. What I was told was missing was more in-depth information about the ELF and who the members really were. I found this troubling and extremely frustrating, as I had let Eringer and Martin know from day one that I did not have this information and, if I did, would certainly not include it in the book. Now, after working on this book for nearly a year, I would have to rewrite the entire manuscript.

This horrible news came simultaneously with other upsetting information from Eringer. Part of the deal I had with him was that while I was drafting the manuscript, Eringer would be shopping the title to publishers that he allegedly had contacts with and at some of the world's largest book fairs. As 2002 moved forward and I was busy writing the book, my inquiries to Eringer for updates on outreach to publishers were mostly ignored. When I did receive responses, Eringer would say that he was shopping but that no one had shown an interest. I began to feel increasingly uncomfortable with this as I couldn't imagine publishers having no interest in the first-ever book about the elusive eco-saboteurs. While at first I trusted Eringer's information on the progress of the publisher solicitation, I grew skeptical after his alleged ongoing attempts at shopping the title were unsuccessful.

Moving forward and preparing for the January 5 and 6 meetings with Martin, I was feeling pretty down about the project, but a part of me still trusted that perhaps their assessment of the manuscript was correct—maybe it did need a significant rewrite. I took a deep breath and promised myself I would see the project through.

That was on Saturday, January 3. By Sunday I was a basket case again, skeptical and unsure of why, after a year of writing chapters that were already approved, I would have to go back and do a complete rewrite? Why did there appear to be no interest in the book from the many publishers Eringer had allegedly contacted? These questions haunted me. As the night approached, I found my anxiety refused to allow me to sleep. Martin would be knocking on my door early the next morning, and I felt a heightened panic set in.

I parked myself in front of my computer and began searching the internet for any information I hadn't previously seen on Eringer and Martin. In a fatigue-ridden, sleepless daze, I poured over page after page, searching for something, anything, that would prove my paranoia was well-founded. At first, I saw the same listings of book titles Eringer had worked on and a few about Martin here and there. And then after perusing a series of additional pages, I found a listing that made my heart race, made my breath vanish, and sent me off to gather every weapon I had in my house.

The listing that caught my eye was for a Salon.com article entitled, "Send in the clowns: How Ringling Bros. minions tormented a freelance writer for years."[9] The article centered around a writer named Jan Pottker, who had obtained inside, potentially significantly damaging information on the Ringling Bros. Circus empire. She had written an article critical of Ringling's chief Ken Feld and the business that appeared in a 1990 edition of the now defunct *Regardie's* magazine.[10] As a result of the article, Pottker had received interest from several book publishers seeking a longer piece.[11]

The *Salon* article detailed how a man by the name of Robert Eringer approached Pottker claiming to be a book packager. He told her that he believed she had a compelling story to write, and he wanted to assist her with drafting the manuscript and getting it published. Sound familiar? Except in this case, Eringer was actually on the payroll of Feld Entertainment with specific orders to "obstruct Pottker's planned book about the circus." And obstruct he did. Over the course of the next few years, Eringer worked side by side with Pottker encouraging her writing, while all the time sharing the information with Ringling Bros. If that wasn't sinister enough, Eringer, through a series of memos written to Feld, argued that while it was his intention to monitor Pottker closely, the spying wasn't enough. Pottker needed to be distracted away from the circus story completely.

The planned distraction came in the form of commissioning a book on the Rockefeller family that Pottker would write after being convinced it would be more marketable than the circus story. While this particular book never was written, Eringer was successful in convincing—and paying for—a book to be written by Pottker on the Mars candy family. And guess where the financing for this book came? It came from none other than Feld Entertainment, which had a vested interest in keeping Pottker

---

9 Jeff Stein, Salon.com, August 31, 2001.
10 *Regardie's* was a Washington, DC business magazine published from 1980 through 1992.
11 Stein, Salon.com.

distracted so she would give up the story on the Ringling Bros. Circus.

As spooked as I was reading this article, it only got worse. Not only was Robert Eringer likely lying to me about who he was and his motives for having me write the book on the ELF, but the *Salon* article clearly laid out his direct connection to Clair George, former Chief of Covert Operations for the CIA. The two apparently met in 1988 and became close friends.[12] In the operation against Pottker, Eringer actually worked for George in their campaign to thwart any negative story being released on the circus. The two called their operation to derail her book "Project Preempt." For eight years, Eringer and George ran this campaign against Pottker as private contract spies hired by Feld Entertainment. Only after Pottker filed a lawsuit did this information finally become public, though still not easy to find.

By this time, I was used to dealing with the FBI, ATF, and other law enforcement agencies, and I grew to know what to expect, what their capabilities were, and the tactics utilized against historical social justice movements. The potential involvement of the CIA or individuals connected to the Agency was a different beast to consider—one that had me scared to death.

It is well known that the FBI has utilized dirty tactics to curtail the advancement of activist movements throughout its history. But with the CIA, no strategy or tactic is off of the table. This is an organization that has assassinated world leaders, made people disappear, and toppled governments. Silencing me would be akin to a simple morning warm-up exercise before the Agency got on to its more important work of the day.

I won't lie. I was shaking, and Martin was going to show up for the supposed editing session in just a few hours. *What if he knows I'm on to them? What if they were monitoring my internet browsing and saw me reading the* Salon *article? Who the fuck did they work for anyway?* I sat in my bed, cold from fear.

Hours of paranoid sleeplessness passed before morning finally came. I waited impatiently for 7:00 A.M. when I could

12 Robert Eringer's backyard neighbor in Washington was also former CIA Director Richard Helms.

call my attorney to seek advice on where I stood and what to do from a legal perspective. Taken aback by the story, my attorney advised me to do two things. First, under no circumstances was I to meet with Martin for safety concerns. Second, he asked me to come in early the next morning, January 6, for a meeting at the law office and to bring any and all evidence I could regarding this situation.

By 8:00 A.M., Martin was calling me. I answered and told him that I had come down with a bad flu and would be unable to meet with him. That didn't seem enough for him, however, as he proceeded to show up on my front porch, knocking at my door later in the day. I quickly hid out of sight and listened to Martin repeatedly ring the doorbell and knock over the course of many minutes. Finally, he gave up and appeared to leave, and I hoped this was the end of it.

Early the next morning, after another sleepless night, I snuck out of the house and drove to my attorney's office. I walked in with a small box of documents, including all of the email correspondences between Eringer, Martin, and me, as well as a copy of the *Salon* article. Sitting in a conference room with my attorney and an associate, I proceeded to tell them the story of Eringer and Martin and my involvement with them over the past year. They were both shocked. It is not everyday a lawyer has a client walk in with documented evidence of how they had been targeted by spies. They said they would review the documents I brought and get back to me, while also reaffirming their advice to stay away from Eringer and Martin.

Martin's calls and visits continued for the next few days. I ignored the constant phone ringing and kept a low profile, remaining out of sight—with weapons in hand—during each time Martin proceeded to visit the house. Finally, on Thursday, January 9, I received an email from Martin letting me know he had flown home to Chicago. I wasn't sure if I believed it, so I kept my guard up for the next few days, not knowing what, if anything, was going to happen next.

Within a week, my attorneys contacted me and let me know they had finished reviewing the materials and, while they had no idea who Eringer and Martin were working for, they appeared to be fraudulent. Their additional concern pertained to the rights to the manuscript. They worried about the possibility that, since I was paid four out of five installments of the $5,000 advance, that the manuscript could be considered a work for hire and, thus, owned by Eringer. To make matters worse, in my stupidity, I never had the original agreement with Eringer reviewed by an attorney, and it was quite simplistic and vague, especially over the rights to the manuscript.

Their suggestion was to send back the $4,000 out of $5,000 I had already received in advance monies to Eringer, along with a letter declaring the agreement to be void based on failure to meet contracted obligations[13] and potential fraud. In late February 2003, I sent the following letter to Eringer at the last known address I had for him in London:

Dear Robert,

It is with regret that I am writing to terminate our agreement and relationship relating to your marketing of my ELF book. Enclosed is my check in the amount of $4,000, returning the funds you advanced to me relating to the book. Our agreement was that I would prepare a draft of a book consistent with a proposal and book outline which I presented to you in February, 2002. You would take the draft book and shop it with publishers to get the book published. You were to receive a 15% commission on all revenues emanating from the book sales.

I presented the last chapter of the book to you on December 10, 2002, with the majority of the book being delivered far in advance of that date. To date, nothing has been done to market the book with publishers. Instead, you insisted I go through editing with Frank Martin, who is not a publisher. This exercise would be more appropriate with a publisher. I have serious doubts you ever intended to assist me in getting this book published.

---

13 As part of the deal, Eringer was supposed to be "shopping" the manuscript to his publishing contacts. Yet any proof of this was never provided.

Your continued requests for revisions to the book, which go far beyond the scope of the outline presented to you at our meeting in Santa Barbara, California, were not part of our agreement. Indeed, such revisions should have been made with input from the publisher or potential publisher of the book.

Because of your continued attempt to go beyond the scope of our initial agreement as to form and content of the book, and your lack of progress in marketing the book, I am terminating our business relationship and returning the monies you advanced.

Please return all copies of my manuscript at your earliest convenience.

Sincerely,

Craig Rosebraugh

While there was never a response to this letter, the check was cashed a few weeks later. Still uncertain if I would face any repercussions from Eringer and Martin, and whoever the hell they were working for, I began to shop the manuscript myself to publishers. Before long, I found a supportive team at Lantern Books in New York that got behind the book and, in 2004, the first edition of *Burning Rage of a Dying Planet: Speaking for the Earth Liberation Front* was published. Few people ever knew the story behind the writing of the book, and for the better part of fifteen years after, I still would be left wondering who hired Eringer.

•　　•　　•

The FBI has utilized infiltrators, informants, and even agents provocateurs throughout its controversial history. Where infiltrators are typically employed by the Agency to go undercover to obtain information on perceived bad guys and their groups, informants may be on the Agency payroll or just do-gooder citizens believing they are preventing crime by snitching on others. Agent provocateurs, on the other hand, also occasionally employed by the Agency, are not only usually undercover but also have the specific purpose of attempting to provoke perceived bad guys into doing something illegal.

These tactics utilized by the Feds originally gained the most prominence during the FBI's official Counter Intelligence Program or COINTELPRO. A covert program run by the Agency, COINTELPRO targeted left-wing groups from 1956 to 1971. Targets included the Communist Party, civil rights groups, the Black power movement, antiwar groups, the American Indian Movement, the Puerto Rican independence movement, and more.

It was on March 8, 1971 that seven individuals calling themselves the "Citizens Commission to Investigate the FBI" broke into an FBI field office in Media, Pennsylvania and stole over 1,000 documents. These documents exposed J. Edgar Hoover's COINTELPRO, which had been conducting widespread surveillance of American citizens. Public outcry led to the Agency officially ending COINTELPRO, yet in the decades to follow, and in my own personal experience, the FBI continues to utilize the same old dirty tactics.

•　　•　　•

In 2016, I completed a Freedom of Information Act (FOIA) request with the US Department of Justice in an attempt to acquire any and all records the FBI had on me. I was initially told that my file contained two thousand pages, of which I received a portion.[14] Unsatisfied with the Agency's response to my request, I filed a federal lawsuit against the DOJ for wrongfully withholding and failing to provide my FBI file.

The following year, in 2017, I prevailed out of court when the FBI admitted to my file containing 7,876 pages and agreed to a release schedule. Under the agreement, the Agency would process five hundred pages per month and release all that weren't completely exempt. Then, in 2018, I received another communication from the DOJ. The FBI, after additional searches, was now admitting to my file containing another 13,450 pages, bringing the total page count of my FBI file to over 21,000.

---

14 Many records are fully withheld by the Agency, which claims they meet the qualifications of one or many exemptions from release. The records that were sent are highly redacted.

Based on information contained within this file and a confirmation by an unnamed source, fifteen years later, I would finally learn the truth about Robert Eringer and Frank Martin. Beginning in 1993, Eringer was on the payroll of the FBI, working on covert missions for the Agency's counterintelligence department. Similar to the case of Jan Pottker, Eringer's plan on behalf of the FBI was to have me disclose anything and everything I knew about the ELF—including the secret identities of those involved—while ensuring any manuscript that I would write would never be published. Frank Martin, an FBI agent, was working with Eringer in this endeavor. While these bastards had me fooled for a year, I thankfully provided them with no information, inadvertently, that could have led to potential prosecutions of those committing ELF or ALF actions.

PROLOGUE TO THE ORIGINAL EDITION

*T*his book is the story of the Earth Liberation Front as I know it, having served as media spokesperson for the group since its first action in 1997 and until 2001. But in order to understand how I came to play my part in that story, you should know something of my early history.

As I began writing this story, on my thirtieth birthday, it occurred to me that no one—neither my family nor my friends, nor even myself—could have imagined that I would lead such a strange life. I certainly did not plan, nor could I have ever expected, the events I am about to set down here.

Before what I have come to refer to as my awakening, I led what I considered to be a typical life for a young American boy. I was raised in a working-turned-middle class family, the son of two hardworking and wonderful parents. In the almost cliché, 1950s-style suburb where we lived, I hung out with friends, played soccer, and of course spent as many hours as possible with my eyes glued to the television (isn't that the American way?). Growing up in the Pacific Northwest, I was also fortunate to have easy access to the natural world. Much of my childhood was spent in the fields and forested areas behind our home, innocent of growing threats to the environment, and of any other societal problems, for that matter.

Throughout my childhood and adolescent years, my parents, school, popular media, and culture instilled in me a pride in my country, my government, and everything that the United States represented. I was taught about the greatness of our country's past—our Constitution, the Bill of Rights, and the American tradition of being at the forefront of democracy and freedom. I vividly recall how proud I felt, standing in front of the stars and stripes with my hand over my heart before soccer games. Playing in Eastern European soccer tournaments on a US team as a high school student, I wore my USA labeled clothing with pride. The glares and hostility I noticed during my travels in the Eastern Bloc countries (Czechoslovakia, East Germany, Hungary) didn't faze me; I just assumed the anger was an expression of envy of US freedom and opportunity.

At that time, one of my primary goals was to become a soccer player, to be in the Olympics, and then to play in professional leagues. I was also interested in photography, advertising, and business, and I believed that going into business would best allow me to support myself and achieve happiness in the future.

Most people go through a rebellious stage, at some point: an uprising against forces (parents or guardians, school employees, counselors, or even the law) labeled by the rebel as oppressive, restricting, abusive, etc. For me, this phase began in 1990, when I graduated from high school and moved out of my parents' house into a Northwest Portland apartment. There, with exposure to new people, forms of education, and ideas, I found my horizons beginning to widen. It started with skateboarding, an activity that led to my involvement in the rebellious subculture of punk rock music.

Before my introduction to punk culture, I had not been aware that at least some of those spiky-haired, tattooed, pierced, deviant-looking people were actually intelligent and politically active. Many of the people I met had taken to this subculture as a political act of rebellion against a society that did not appear to provide a just and inclusive future for them. While negative forces such as drugs and alcohol are an inherent part of this lifestyle, my friends were involved first and foremost in political movements. Unlike the mainstream, overpopularized, and apolitical music that today is considered "punk" by many people, the tunes that drove my friends and me emotionally discussed social and political issues. Whether a firm antiwar message or a stance on animal rights, the environment, or human rights issues, bands such as Crass, Conflict, Chumbawamba, Subhumans, Culture Shock, Citizen Fish, and many others were as much a catalyst for my future action as anything else. At minimum, these musicians, often drunk and disorderly and singing redundant, clichéd lyrics, exposed me to the reality of social problems I hadn't known existed, and for this education I am grateful.

In addition to the education I was receiving from my new companions, college life at Portland State University and the current events of the day substantially contributed to my first awakening. George Bush Sr. had just thrust the United States into what became known as the Gulf War, and students were immediately presented with the question of whether or not to support that war, whether or not to get involved.

I did not find this decision easy. The absolutist support of my country and government with which I had been raised dictated that I wave the stars and stripes and unconditionally support this allegedly noble action to "promote democracy and freedom." Furthermore, as a freshman in college, then majoring in business, I pondered the wisdom of questioning the very government I might rely on in the future for financial success. Yet, as I began to look into the matter further, I found myself asking questions such as, *Why are we there? Why are we killing Iraqi civilians? What is the true motive behind the conflict?* After extensive research, through school and on my own, I concluded that the desire for natural resources and regional power was the primary motive behind the US military action.

As news slowly filtered into public consciousness from independent sources, I became increasingly horrified at the slaughter of Iraqi civilians by the US military. With social and political conflict staring me in the eye for the first time, I felt impassioned and invigorated. I had no choice but to act, to take a stand on something that concerned me. With NO WAR FOR OIL as my personal guiding statement, I joined the local antiwar movement, little guessing where this first political activity would lead me.

As my anger and disillusionment grew throughout the early 1990s, my antiwar activities took on various forms. In addition to living amidst the Portland punk culture, engaging in heated political discussions (most often over a forty-ounce Pabst Blue Ribbon, Olde English, St. Ides, or a nice toxic green bottle of kiwi-flavored Mad Dog), I also wrote lyrics and played percussion for a punk band called Unamused. (It's a sort of rule of thumb that the name of your punk band has to reflect in some way your negative view of society.) To me, the message of the lyrics was always of first importance and the music was secondary. Composing song lyrics allowed me to develop and express my reflections on the issues I was contemplating at the time.

In addition to writing political music and debating the antiwar issue with just about anyone I could find, I began to take part in local protests and rallies. These demonstrations against the war also provided my first exposure to the repressive agencies of the state and the police, who have the difficult job of trying to enforce the law even when it is unjust. With my sheltered suburban upbringing, prior to this interaction, I had had no particularly negative feelings toward the men and women in blue. Like firefighters, postal employees, electricians, and other professionals, they were simply people with a job to do.

Leave it to a direct shot of pepper spray in my eyes—from less than three feet away—to change my feelings. During one of George Bush Sr.'s visits to Portland, I was attending a massive protest when the police began attempting to clear demonstrators from various areas. (Bush and his New World Order were always met in Portland with a rambunctious crowd of angry protesters. It was during this time that Portland's active protest scene earned it the label of "Little Beirut" from federal officials.) As I saw friends and fellow protesters being hit with police clubs, sprayed with chemicals, and arrested for what appeared to be no reason, my anger skyrocketed. When a police officer came for me, I made a quick decision to not back down but to meet him face to face. Hitting me with his baton, he knocked me back a good five to ten feet. When I still refused to move, he came at me again and struck me in the stomach even harder. This time my anger got the best of me, and I shoved him back with all my strength. As he regained his composure, his hand went quickly to his waist. My immediate thought was, *This guy is going for his gun.* A second later, a black canister sent a heavy stream of pepper spray stinging into my eyes and face, knocking me to my knees. Immediately, other protesters, still unknown to me, helped me get to a safer location where I could allow the effects of the spray to wear off. Not surprisingly, my opinion of the police began to go downhill.

As my antiwar activism progressed, I also became involved with a local animal advocacy organization in Portland called People for Animal Rights. Through independent reading and early college courses, and inspired by the music I was listening to at the time, I had developed an interest in human society's relationship with the many animal nations. I began to attend meetings of People for Animal Rights to further my own education and hear arguments for the rights of animals. While I definitely felt out of place—a punk rocker in a fairly conservative animal rights group—I felt compelled to stay, inspired by the conviction of the many hardworking volunteers and the education I received from them. The more I learned, the more I felt compelled to involve myself fully in working for animal protection.

After attending numerous meetings, I decided to go to my first protest with this group, which happened to be against a meat processors' convention being held in Portland. I had recently adopted a vegetarian diet—a choice based on the education I had received from this organization and from political bands and influential friends—and so it felt righteous to be there on the street picketing, voicing my opposition. As I continued to learn about animal issues and to develop a personal moral response to them, I joined in many more protests and soon became an office volunteer with People for Animal Rights.

Soon I went from merely attending meetings and protests to organizing them. Over the next year, I found myself spending the majority of my time reading, organizing, planning, protesting—generally working on animal issues. I put school on the back burner, knowing I should be paying more attention to it but lacking the initiative and heart. What concerned me the most was activism, acting on my passions and fighting for my version of justice.

By 1995, however, I noticed that the group itself was in a slump. It had not been attracting many new members or volunteers, its activities had gone sharply downhill, and its effectiveness seemed increasingly compromised. Noticing this trend, five or six of the younger, more energetic and optimistic volunteers, including me, took it upon ourselves to try to assist in creating a more successful organization. Many of our ideas and attempts were met with reluctance by some of the more conservative and veteran members of the group.

One stumbling block was the fact that the more conservative and controlling members of the group would not take a stand in support of the controversial Animal Liberation Front (ALF). This was an organization formed in England in the late 1970s that liberated animals from abusive situations. I had first heard of the group in my early punk years, listening to Conflict and other bands on the Mortarhate label that participated in benefits for the ALF. In the early 1980s, ALF actions began in the United States, and shortly thereafter, they started to include the use of property destruction. For instance, if a group of people in the ALF rescued animals from a medical laboratory, they might also destroy lab equipment and records in the process.

In 1995, I came to the decision that I would philosophically support illegal activity such as civil disobedience and property destruction as long as it was nonviolent. I placed the ALF in this category and felt that People for Animal Rights should support the organization, which was noticeably active at the time. However, because the ALF was controversial and its actions were illegal, People for Animal Rights elected not to support it.

I was also feeling alienated from the animal rights organization because of my own growing awareness of the links between various social and political issues. Prior to this time, I hadn't really considered animal rights, human rights, and environmental protection as being connected in any way. It eventually dawned on me, however, that no single social or political issue is truly independent or isolated from other factors.

Most animal abuse, for instance, does not occur merely because humans have some sick desire to torture and kill animals. (Certainly some do, and, as the Animal Legal Defense Fund has pointed out, those who do are also likely to act with violence toward their families, co-workers, and others with whom they may be in contact.) Institutionalized animal abuse occurs not only for the sake of human convenience and perceived necessity but also out of an unhealthy desire for financial gain. This desire, I realized, lies at the foundation not only of animal rights abuses, but also of human and environmental problems. Are forests clear-cut out of an actual or perceived need? Is slave labor used by US companies overseas for any other reason than pure profit? Do automobile manufacturers really need to constantly create newer and larger automobiles? With this very basic connection in my mind, I began to feel that People for Animal Rights's single-issue focus was problematic.

So, early in 1996, four to six of the more active People for Animal Rights members, including me, became frustrated to the point where we left the organization and formed another, which we called Liberation Collective. We felt this new organization would provide us with the opportunity to link social justice issues together and to work without having to answer to more conservative, controlling interests—which also meant we could declare ideological support for more radical strategies and tactics, such as those of the ALF.

In 1996, Liberation Collective emerged as an energetic, positive force that drew increasing support from the local community. Our primary campaign became working to stop the feline research program occurring at a local hospital in what was considered to be one of the most progressive parts of Portland. But, attempting to keep in line with our mission of linking social justice movements, we also tried to spread the message that human, animal, and environmental issues are not separate. By handing out literature at local colleges and universities, cooking and distributing free food to the homeless, and organizing protests for the human and animal rights issues of the day, we tried, the best we knew how, to bring together various movements.

During this time, I was completing my bachelor's degree at Marylhurst University, where I took a profound interest in Gandhi and his work in South Africa and India. His philosophy of nonviolence as a catalyst for social and political change appealed to me. I quickly became a nonviolence proponent and attempted to work an ideology similar to Gandhi's into my own life's activities. The more I took part in civil disobedience myself, the more I favored it as a strategy in Liberation Collective campaigns. I became convinced that nonviolent campaigns held the only true chance of creating a just world.

Seeking to increase our strength as an organization, and to provide a healthy and comfortable living situation, several of us decided to form a collective household early in 1997. Josh Smith, Leslie Pickering, Vanessa Villareal, Casea Betts, and I moved into a house in Northeast Portland, an area where the rent was still somewhat affordable. The house was soon considered a primary location of Liberation Collective, and we even set up a small, makeshift office in an oversized closet. We also developed a growing library of books and videos on various social and political issues that we would use to educate ourselves and others who came over to visit or work. Sitting on the corner of Northeast Going and Cleveland Streets, the house quickly gained the nickname "the Cleveland House" (or "the Activist House," as we later learned others called it). We developed our own newsletter, a monthly publication that discussed our current campaigns, activities, and philosophies, and also provided information about historical social movements for public education. It was in this publication that we, as an organization, first declared our ideological support for the ALF. As a 501(c)(3) nonprofit organization, Liberation Collective could not take part in such illegal activity as rescuing animals and/or destroying property that is used to harm them. However, we did categorize the ALF as a nonviolent organization and, therefore, felt positive about declaring philosophical backing for the group. Strategically, we believed that the ALF, at minimum, had some value—rescuing individual animals and making the cost of animal exploitation just a bit higher.

None of us imagined that we would ever find ourselves actually publicizing ALF actions and championing them in front of the US news media—let alone that we might become the official voice of another underground liberation movement. The story of how this happened is tightly entwined with the course of my own evolution as an activist. If you have taken part in justice struggles—for humans, animals, or the environment— perhaps you will recognize some of your own experiences in the pages that follow. If you haven't, I hope you will finish this book with a new understanding—and feeling inspired and empowered to begin.

1

THE TELEPHONE RINGS . . .

*I*n March 1997, Liberation Collective organized a two-day program called Against Animal Testing—A West Coast Conference on Animal Experimentation. As part of the group's local campaign against the cat research at Legacy Health System (one of Portland's primary medical care corporations), the conference was aimed at educating activists and the general public on the problems associated with scientific and medical experimentation on nonhuman animals. In addition to the educational lectures, the conference would also be used to directly place further pressure on researchers at the local hospital to stop their feline testing.

Attempting to attract maximum attendance both from within Oregon and throughout the West Coast, the program consisted of presentations on the ethical and scientific reasons to oppose animal experimentation, information on our current local campaign, entertainment, and two large protests at the local medical facility. Free lunches would also be provided for the conference attendees by Food Not Bombs, an international group that cooks healthy, vegetarian food for homeless and low-income people. Liberation Collective was already involved with the organization; every week, members of our household took turns picking up the donated items from grocery stores, preparing the food, and serving it in a nearby park.

Organizing from our small office in the Cleveland House, none of us thought that in promoting this conference we would link Liberation Collective with illegal activities.

Our only concern was to attract as large an attendance as possible. To do this, we decided to send out brochures advertising the event to locations throughout the West Coast that we felt would be receptive. This included other animal rights and environmental organizations, and even human rights groups, as we were constantly trying to demonstrate to ourselves and others that we were a multi-issue organization and not just focused on animal advocacy. As the Cleveland House was large and would act as a staging site for the conference (where the food would be prepared and props and tools would be stored), the five of us living there at the time decided to open up our home as a free place to sleep for conference attendees coming from out of town.

The address was also advertised in our brochures and other promotional materials as a check-in point for everyone, both local attendees and those from other cities. This meant that the house's location and telephone number found their way to activist email lists throughout the country.

Clearly, in hindsight, we should have considered the possible repercussions of sharing our home address and telephone number so openly. During the weeks before the conference, we were too involved in the frenzy of preparation to think about what opening up our home to the public could mean. First, since the Liberation Collective organization had been slowly building a reputation as a group that took part in illegal civil disobedience and philosophically supported illegal direct action—such as the activities of the ALF—there was the possibility that opponents of our ideology would now know where to find us. Additionally, as the local police appeared to be looking increasingly into Liberation Collective at the time due to our advocacy and our role in civil disobedience protests in Portland, they now had a location that could be (correctly) perceived as a central organizing point for the group. Yet, as we rushed to get everything ready for the conference, we simply looked upon our home as one of the only possibilities for housing people. The conference, for all intended purposes, was a success. Of course, there were the typical minor problems that many activist groups face when attempting to organize events—too much work, too few people, lack of money and resources, and, in this case, the giant cat head puppet I had made for the protests turned out to look like more of a tiger-elephant mix with an overexaggerated tongue—but overall, with nearly a hundred people in attendance, we considered the two days successful. The lectures educated some, the protests placed a bit more pressure on the local health facility, and by using civil disobedience and having a small handful of people arrested during the protests, we garnered media attention that helped our message reach a wider audience.

Headed Down to Davis

A month after the conference, we received notice that a regional convergence was being planned for the last week of April in

Davis, California. The target of the two days of protests was the University of California at Davis, which houses the California Regional Primate Research Center (now called the California National Primate Research Center). One of seven regional primate centers in the United States funded by the National Institutes of Health, the location was chosen in part because it housed thousands of nonhuman primates for experiments and had been targeted twice by the ALF, who had burned two new buildings under construction. The site was also chosen for its symbolic value, as it had been the location of the first massive anti-vivisection protest in the United States back in the early 1980s.

As an added bonus, the protest organizers planned the convergence to begin the day UC Davis was hosting its annual Agricultural Day ("Ag Day" for short, otherwise known as "Picnic Day"). Many of the colleges and universities across the United States that specialize in agricultural studies hold an Ag Day or similar event to open the campus and the program to the public for informational and promotional purposes. UC Davis's Ag Day would feature open houses at the on-campus slaughterhouse and veterinary studies department, as well as a petting zoo. In addition, the school would sponsor demonstrations of animal training and a fistulated cow. The latter is a living cow with a surgical hole cut into its side and covered with a round piece of clear plastic. This hole, referred to as a fistula, allows students to insert their hands and other foreign materials into the cow's rumen to study the digestive/ruminating process. For anyone concerned with animal rights issues, Ag Day at UC Davis provided no shortage of objectionable practices.

, Wanting to increase our involvement with animal rights on a regional and even national level, we set out to mobilize activists in Portland to make the trip. We decided to take the Collective van, a big old Chevy model that we would pack with as many people as we could convince to join us. Jeff Morehead had recently purchased the van for the group, a generous gift that helped us carry out our weekly Food Not Bombs pickups and occasionally transport activists or materials to and from protests and other events.

The event was also important to me personally. Animal experimentation was the main animal rights issue that I had been studying on and off for years, and I knew the trip would provide some valuable education. This would also be a great time for networking with other activists from the West Coast, which I felt was a beneficial step if the movement was going to continue to progress.

Our van soon filled up with other activists, including Leslie and Kattie Louis. I had met Kattie toward the end of my time with People for Animal Rights, and she had been a key volunteer with Liberation Collective from the beginning, always demonstrating a hardworking ethic and a serious drive to make the organization a success. Kattie and I had also been romantic partners since early 1996. I was excited that she had agreed to go, not only out of a personal desire to have her close, but because I knew she would contribute needed energy to the action.

Two other people from Oregon, Josh Harper and Chelsea Lincoln, would also be joining us. Josh had only been involved in the group a short time but had demonstrated a sincere dedication to the cause and had grown into one of the most well-spoken Liberation Collective volunteers. I had first met Chelsea in 1996 at ELAW, an environmental law conference held annually at the University of Oregon. She had introduced herself to me at the Liberation Collective table and told me about an animal rights group she had been helping to start at the U of O called SETA (Students for the Ethical Treatment of Animals). She was soon making frequent trips from Eugene to Portland to attend and take part in our actions and events.

We also agreed to take four activists from a couple of different groups in Seattle: Northwest Animal Rights Network and Students for Animal Liberation (the main student group at the University of Washington). We met them at the Greyhound bus station in Portland, and the nine of us embarked on our mission south.

We figured it would take ten or so hours to get to Davis, a small college town just over an hour's drive from San Francisco. Of course, with an old 1970s Chevy van and nine bladders to contend with, it was 2:30 in the morning when we finally arrived in Davis, nearly fifteen hours after we had left Portland. We were supposed to be given a place to stay for the duration of the convergence, but in the early morning hours, we were unable to reach anyone.

As I had been one of the primary van drivers on the trip, I was exhausted and vowed to do whatever was necessary to find a place to sleep. The van was too small for the nine of us, and after arguing over where to sleep we agreed to see if we could get into the dormitories on campus. We gathered up some belongings and headed for the dormitory across the street, leaving the van parked in a strip mall parking lot.

The access door to the dorm was locked, but after waiting for a short while, we saw a student emerge, and we grabbed the door on his way out. Dazed and exhausted, we crashed in the nearest lounge, where the couches, tables, and heat felt like paradise. After a few hours, which felt like seconds, I was shaken awake by Leslie telling me that we had to go. Apparently the dorm monitor had been informed of our stay and demanded our evacuation. Some slept on the grass outside, others inside the van, and I found a nice refuge on the top of the van. (Okay, the metal roof was hard as hell, it was cold out, and I felt like shit from being in a van for fifteen hours with eight other people, but at that point, simply lying down seemed like a wonderful privilege.)

After scrounging breakfast at the strip mall the next morning, we set out for the pre-arranged convergence meeting point at 9:00 A.M. It was Ag Day, and we were going to do all we could to make sure UC Davis regretted exposing themselves and their objectionable programs to the public. At the small morning meeting, the plan for the day was set—to attempt to disrupt Ag Day as much as possible. No ground rules, just disruption.

We spent the day wandering among the crowd, getting in the occasional argument, asking frequent challenging questions of some of the display attendees, and generally trying to have a noticeable presence. While there is no doubt that the Ag Day attendees noticed all of us, dressed in our animal rights T-shirts, storming around the place as if we owned it, the main attention we received came from the campus police. It seemed everywhere we went, they were there behind us, trying to make sure we kept ourselves in line.

That night, we were again literally left out in the cold, as we could not find any place to stay. As the nine of us found our desired sleeping locations for the night, I crawled on top of the van again and into my sleeping bag. *Tomorrow is the big day*, I thought. I didn't know what to expect, but I looked forward to the opportunity to take out my anger and frustration in a protest against another one of the regional primate centers.

The plan for the next morning had been set. Everyone would meet at 10:00 A.M. at the John E. Thurman Veterinary Diagnostic Laboratory on the UC Davis campus, a site targeted in 1987 by the ALF, who had set a $4.6 million fire. Upon meeting there, a two-mile march would commence, ending at the California Regional Primate Research Center. What would happen when we got there no one exactly knew, but I could tell from the overall militant tone of the first day that confrontation was quite likely.

When the nine of us reached the meeting spot for the march, I dropped everyone off and went to locate a parking spot. Walking back, the sun was already hot and I knew the day was going to be a scorcher. I arrived back at the crowd to find that everyone was preparing to leave on the march. Signs and banners had been distributed, key people picked up their megaphones, and within seconds a commanding voice shouted out a message to start.

"LET'S GO! STICK TOGETHER!" I recognized the person taking control of the megaphone and the situation. I had met J.P. Goodwin at a Seattle Fur Exchange action in 1996. At that protest, his macho, bullying mannerisms—screaming, insulting, and physically intimidating people—had instantly turned me off. Even though his style annoyed me, in a strange way it appeared to be working.

"WHAT DO WE WANT?" Goodwin screamed.

In unison, the marchers responded, "ANIMAL LIBERATION!" He actually seemed to be raising the spirits of the marchers and keeping them together.

"WHEN DO WE WANT IT?" he continued.

"NOW!" the crowd responded. As the march continued on its way, news crews following en route filmed the energy and the vocal presence of the thirty-four protesters. Goodwin was unrelenting with his chants. For nearly the entire march, he strained his vocal cords, stopping only to catch his breath or to allow others to carry the chanting on. And they did. The energy level of the participants was so high, it felt as if nothing could have stopped us on our way to the center.

As the march grew closer to its goal, the chanting intensified. We must have looked like some motley crew marching into battle, especially to the multiple lines of police I could now see blocking the entire front of the complex. The cops were all dressed in riot gear, and many were beating billy clubs against their palms. My heart began racing, but I couldn't stop. I wanted to—I was scared—but I felt this was so important I had to keep on marching. So did everyone else. By now everyone was chanting together and walking with a boldness that could only have been taken as challenging to the riot cops.

Now within feet of the police lines, Goodwin continued to bark out orders.

"STICK TOGETHER! DON'T BACK DOWN! ANIMAL LIBERATION, HUMAN LIBERATION . . . ONE STRUGGLE, ONE FIGHT!"

Carrying one side of one of the first banners in the march, I was one of the first people to reach the cops. They were standing in some sort of military formation behind a chain pulled across the main driveway of the center. As I approached the chain I heard Goodwin call out, "EVERYONE OVER! GET OVER THE CHAIN! STICK TOGETHER, SOLIDARITY! EVERYONE OVER!" Out of the corner of my eye I could see others crossing the chain and walking directly into the line of riot police. In a split-second decision, I jumped over the chain and marched straight into the line. A billy club quickly pounded me in the chest, sending me flying backward. I retreated for a moment and saw that other protesters who met with the same treatment weren't backing down. With clubs swinging around me and people screaming and bouncing back and forth, I again marched forward only to be shoved back by another cop. Goodwin continued with his orders, now insulting the cops as much as he was trying to direct the crowd.

"FUCK YOU, ASSHOLES!" he shouted, sticking the megaphone in the cops' faces. "EVERYONE OVER THE CHAIN! STICK TOGETHER! DON'T BACK DOWN!"

Suddenly, all of the protesters began cheering, and as I looked across the field adjacent to the center's main building, I saw two people on top of the new Center for Comparative Medicine, which was under construction. They dropped a massive banner off the third story roof that read, "STOP UC DAVIS ANIMAL TORTURE." The police were furious and strengthened their positions.

A few more minutes into this intense and aggressive encounter, protesters began screaming for everyone to lie down. One by one, we lay down in a long line at the feet of the riot cops. Lying there on the hot cement, I couldn't help but wonder what in the hell was going to happen to us next. After a few moments, the police began pulling people up one by one, starting at the opposite end from where I was lying. Protesters screamed in pain from twisted wrists and pain compliance holds. As the police moved down the line, the cries of pain grew louder. I raised my head a bit, only to see a cop wrenching the arm of a guy a couple of people away from me in the line. He ended up being taken to the hospital in an ambulance.

When they came for me, they grabbed and painfully twisted my wrists, pulled me up, and handcuffed me. I decided to walk with them rather than go limp. Everyone was taken to a nearby bus, which the police used to hold and transport us to the county jail. The atmosphere on the bus was joyful, with everyone applauding fellow protesters as they boarded. Out of the thirty-four people who took part in the march and protest, thirty-two of these voluntarily engaged in civil disobedience and were arrested. After what seemed like a couple of hours sitting on the bus in the hot sun, we were taken to the Yolo County Detention Center for booking.

When we reached the jail, we were taken slowly off the bus, one by one, and placed in cells. I ended up in a cell with Jonathan Paul, a movement veteran I knew from the Seattle Fur Exchange action. Trying to remain calm, I sat in the cell talking to Jonathan and occasionally peering out the cell window across the hallway to see if I could locate Kattie or Leslie. Jonathan seemed unmoved by the guards' oppressive demeanor and continually screamed insults at them. I remember thinking it was kind of comical at the time—as long as it didn't get my ass kicked.

After we were photographed and our fingerprints were taken, we were all released on our own recognizance within eight or nine hours. I picked up my personal property that had been seized during the arrest and made my way to the lobby where I was amazed and quite pleased to find a crowd of people waiting with smiles, hugs, and wonderful food and beverages. By that time I was starving.

That night, we slept outdoors again. I took my place on top of the van and lay staring at the stars, thinking of the day's events. The next morning we would leave bright and early for Portland. It

was a quick trip, but one that I felt proud to have made. I closed my eyes for the night, hearing the occasional car pass on the highway next to me and the echoing sound of drunken people filing out of the bar across the parking lot.

I woke up the next morning to a chilly dawn. All nine of us invaded the strip mall grocery store one last time to stock up on food for our return trip. After we piled into the van, which now reeked as though we had all grown up living in it, I turned the key to the engine. It wouldn't start. I tried it repeatedly, to no effect. After a couple of hours of fiddling with this and that under the hood (during which time we probably made the situation worse), we set out to find help. Walking past a newsstand, I caught a glimpse of the headline on the two local papers. The top stories were all about us—the protest and our arrests. I found out later that the story had gone national, and some news media had even reported on it outside of the country.

The nine of us spent the rest of the day badgering innocent patrons of the strip mall into helping us with the van. No one seemed to know what was wrong, and none of us had any money for a mechanic. After two more days of camping in the parking lot, we finally, with the verbal assistance of an extremely helpful auto parts store salesman, changed the worn spark plugs and rebuilt the bad carburetor. We got the old van running and by some stroke of luck made it back to Portland early the next morning. Exhausted from the trip (and, by that time, each other), we went our separate ways.

We considered the trip successful, having taken part in an action that had generated impressive media coverage while placing pressure on the UC Davis primate center. All of us would later have to deal with our charges from the action (each of us faced a minimum of seven misdemeanors and one or more felonies), but the experience and contacts we had gained seemed worthwhile.

As a result of our involvement in such key regional protests and our own local campaigns, which included ongoing civil disobedience, Liberation Collective was gaining a reputation as one of the more respected animal rights groups on the West Coast (even though we continued to work against the single-issue mindset). After Davis, we resumed our local efforts against the cat research program and increased our efforts to link ourselves with other movements and campaigns, such as the boycott of Nike for its overseas labor abuses and support for political prisoners such as Mumia Abu-Jamal. Our organization continued to grow, and through the rest of the spring, we worked hard to make a difference, targeting injustices and trying to change the world—into what, I don't think any of us really knew, but it was more than enough, we felt, to just realize that things did need to change, that injustices needed to be stopped.

The ALF Makes Contact

Late that spring, the call came. "Check your mailbox," the rough-voiced caller said sternly, without identifying himself. When the phone awakened Vanessa that morning, she thought at first it was a joke, a disturbing prank. But when the caller repeated the message, she began to feel it might be serious, even urgent. Still half asleep, not knowing what to do, or even whether the call had been real, she awakened Leslie, then knocked on my bedroom door. "Craig . . . Craig," she whispered. I awakened in a daze. "Someone with a weird voice just called and told us to check our mailbox." Unable to register her words at that early hour, I rolled over and closed my eyes again. Leslie and Vanessa went down to the porch and checked the mailbox, where sure enough, a note was waiting. Shocked, they brought it upstairs and showed it to me. With the first words on the page, my heart began pounding. I could barely believe my eyes. The distorted writing stated that the Animal Liberation Front (ALF) was taking responsibility for the release of 12,000 mink from a fur farm in Mt. Angel, Oregon.

The date of the action listed on the page was May 30, 1997. The communiqué stated,

> We are simply humans who have answered a call to action with more love than fear. The animals enslaved in exploitive industries today are waiting for you. The intense joy of seeing a living creature taste freedom for the first time is truly indescribable. Animals locked in cages don't have a voice and so you may not hear their cries everyday [sic]. They still feel pain. This action took place not as an act of eco-terrorism but as an act of love. Not one of the mink imprisoned would ever have been allowed to walk more than one foot in any direction, living their short lives with an unpardonable death sentence. . . .

I read it over and over. "Holy shit!" I said.

"Do you think it's real?" Leslie asked.

"I have no idea," I admitted. "I don't know why this would be a fake message, though."

By now Casea and Josh had been awakened by the excitement and had joined us in the upstairs hallway. Neither of them could believe the message we had just received. Why did they pick us? How did they know our address and phone number? We figured that whoever had left this message and called had most likely obtained the Cleveland House address and telephone number from our promotional materials for the Against Animal Testing conference earlier in the year. Was it someone who was at the conference? I couldn't help but wonder. Maybe they even stayed in this house. We all reminded ourselves that it could have been anyone, as the conference information with our home address and phone number had reached a thousand or more people across the United States.

"What should we do?" Leslie asked.

All five of us stared at each other for a moment. At that point, I knew we were going to have to make a decision. I had read about the spokesperson work that individuals such as Robin Webb and Rod Coronado had done for the ALF, in England and the US respectively. Now we were faced with a decision that I knew would be important not only for the ALF but for all of us in the house. Either we could pretend that this note had never come to us, or we could alert the news media and try to explain the underlying rationale for the ALF mink raid.

The news stories that we might be able to stir up by releasing the message could be priceless for the ALF and the animal rights movement. The media exposure could provide a promising opportunity for publicizing the objectionable practices of the fur industry. Just as many consumers really don't want to know where their meat comes from (other than a nice cellophane package in the local grocery store), the public also avoids the truth about the fur industry—for example, that the typical mink coat contains an average of forty dead mink, and that the primary modes of killing the fur-bearing animals on the farm are gassing, neck breaking, and anal electrocution. If any or all of these facts could get into even one news story, we felt that our press release could be beneficial to the animal rights cause.

My own feeling was that if these people—whoever they might be—had in fact conducted the mink raid, the public needed to know that there are people who are sufficiently concerned about the fur industry, motivated to commit illegal actions to further their beliefs. They had a right to know that the liberation had not been a random act of lawlessness. It had a clear political and social motive, which people needed to be able to consider as they developed their own opinions on the issue. Finally, taking the communiqué to the press allowed the issue to be brought out into the open, where ideally proponents and opponents could work toward a resolution.

Since the creation of Liberation Collective early in 1996, I had been acting as one of the primary spokespeople, conducting the interviews with news media and writing and sending out the press releases for our events and actions. This was one task of many I took on, not because public relations work appealed to me, but out of a need created by the group's lack of volunteers and ever-increasing workload. The Collective sought to steer clear of hierarchical structures and simply expected everyone who joined the organization to see what needed to be done and complete those necessary tasks on his or her own. Of course, this was incredibly naïve, since most of those involved with Liberation Collective had different ideas about what the group should be, and the explanatory literature on the group and its mission was vague and open to varying interpretations. It was within this chaotic structure—or lack thereof—that I wound up acting as one of the group's spokespeople.

When the five of us in the household, and others in the organization, decided to go public with the ALF communiqué, I was expected to write the media release, send it out, and conduct the news interviews. After consulting with J.P. Goodwin—the gruff leader of the UC Davis protest—who was the founder, and at that time president, of the Tennessee-based Coalition to Abolish the Fur Trade (CAFT), I decided to schedule a press conference in downtown Portland to announce the ALF claim of responsibility and present some perspective on the reasons behind the action.

During the mid-1990s, CAFT had become a powerful and dominating force against the fur industry in the United States. By setting up chapters in multiple cities across the country, Goodwin was able to orchestrate simultaneous actions and carry out effective national campaigns. To his credit, the controversial style and strategy of his organization was the key to its effectiveness. Using an almost militaristic system, Goodwin was able to recruit many in their late teens and twenties for aggressive tactics such as ongoing civil disobedience, disruptions of businesses, and protests at the homes of executives. The group maintained a vocal and visible philosophical support of the ALF.

While I found Goodwin annoying, I also respected him. In Davis, I had noticed that there was intelligence behind his rudeness. Appearing like the commander of a small army regiment, Goodwin demanded absolute compliance from the few dozen demonstrators. And he got it; nearly all of the participants took part in the civil disobedience action and were beaten and arrested. For that particular action, I had to hand it to the guy. He took a thirty-four-person anti-vivisection protest and, with the help of other key organizers, turned it into an international news item that sparked massive national demonstrations. I had to respect his offensive organizing ability!

Goodwin and I decided it would be most logical to hold the press conference in front of the oldest fur salon in the country, Schumacher Furs. Located in downtown Portland, this small retail dealer had been the target of animal rights protests in the past and seemed like a fitting place to announce that the ALF had struck a blow to the fur industry just thirty miles away. So, with the location set, I finished and sent out the press release to print, radio, and television media in the Portland area.

Feeling certain that we had made the right decision to release the ALF communiqué, none of us in the house stopped for more than a moment to consider that the communiqué we had received could be one of the only pieces of evidence available for a future law enforcement investigation. We didn't think about the fact that we could be investigated ourselves—or, if we did, those thoughts were overshadowed by the excitement and sense of duty we felt to release the information.

Early the next morning, I gathered up the copies of the press release and communiqué and headed downtown. I had scheduled the conference to begin at 10:00 A.M. in order to get a story on the 12:00, 5:00, and 11:00 news. I really didn't know what to expect as far as the turnout was concerned. My primary experience thus far had been with Liberation Collective events and protests, where two media sources would show up if we were lucky. (Out of these two, one was usually the community radio station, KBOO—we always appreciated their consideration of our work as news.) I expected much the same this time, although J.P. had suggested to me the day before that this could be a big story.

I arrived in front of Schumacher Furs a little early and wasn't much surprised to find myself alone. For the sake of my own personal reputation and self-confidence, I hoped that someone, at least KBOO, would arrive by 10:00 A.M. It was raining, and as time ticked away, I stood under an awning, staring at the passing cars and the pedestrians huddling under their umbrellas, each thinking separate thoughts and heading to their own individual locations. How odd it was, I thought, that there I was, about to announce to the public the claim of responsibility for an illegal action, one taken in the name of animal rights. What would all these people think about it? Would they see or hear the news later that day and become aware? Would it change them at all? As my mind wandered, a question popped into my head that would return to me many times over the years: Why do some people choose to become active in social and political issues and others do not? A sudden feeling of alienation flowed through me before an interruption jarred me back into reality.

"Mr. Rosebraugh? Craig Rosebraugh?" a conservatively dressed woman asked. Her cameraman was following closely behind her.

"Yes," I replied.

"Monica Jacobsen from Channel 8 News. Do you have a copy of the statement issued by the Animal Liberation Front?"

As I handed her the copies of the release and communiqué, two more news media representatives showed up. Everyone began firing off questions.

"How did you receive this communiqué?" "Do you know who sent this to you?"

"Is this the original message from the ALF?"

Attempting to remain calm, I slowly answered each question individually while still distributing the copies. Within moments I was surrounded by reporters, all talking simultaneously, all trying to get their question in over someone else's. I couldn't believe the turnout. Never before had I dealt with this many reporters at once—it was unnerving to say the least. I felt completely hounded and slightly overwhelmed. I tried not to lose my patience, and to answer the questions to the best of my ability. Within thirty minutes, it was over, and all of the reporters had taken the sound bites they needed and moved on to their next assignments or back to their newsrooms. I stood there for a few moments in a daze, emotionally and physically drained from the excitement and concentration. Even with the press conference over, I was as nervous as before, concerned about how my statements would be portrayed. I had succeeded in handling the most reporters I had ever seen in one setting, yet I wanted to be sure that my statements were positive for the animal rights movement and didn't anger or upset the unknown parties in the ALF. I felt as if I had become, at least for this short period, the public agent of this secret group, and I wanted these anonymous people, whoever they were, to be pleased with my performance of the task I felt they had assigned me.

The news story was much larger than I had anticipated. It was reported locally in Portland throughout the rest of the day on television, and radio stations in the area also broadcast it as a featured news item. The next morning, *The Oregonian* (Oregon's largest daily newspaper) ran a sizable piece on the action, including quotes from me at the press conference. Overall, every story I saw was biased, in the sense that the writers referred to the ALF as criminals or vandals. Yet, in addition to the reporters' editorial comments, each story seemed to contain at least some information on the ALF and its motivation for the action. I felt pleased and hoped that others, including those in the ALF, would be happy with the coverage.

Following the decision to distribute and publicly support this ALF action, I came to be considered one who could be counted on for future press work. In the next several months, more anonymous communiqués from the ALF began to come my way. After this first experience, little thought went into deciding whether or not I would release subsequent communiqués from the ALF. As my philosophical support of the underground organization continued to grow, so did my willingness to support them publicly. As it turned out, however, this debut as a spokesperson for the ALF would lead me down roads I had never thought possible.

2

BRING
ON THE
ELVES

Earth Liberation Front Guidelines

- *To inflict economic damage on those profiting from the destruction and exploitation of the natural environment.*

- *To reveal and educate the public on the atrocities committed against the earth and all species that populate it.*

- *To take all necessary precautions against harming any animal, human and nonhuman.*

*A*s anonymous messages from animal liberators continued to come my way, writing the media releases, sending them out, and dealing with the interviews was becoming easier, and I felt a certain pride knowing that the ALF continued to use me as their public relations assistant. Meanwhile, I had been reading in the *Earth First! Journal* about a series of sabotage actions taken in defense of the environment that all seemed to have something in common. These actions, centered largely in Oregon, closely resembled some of the measures taken in recent years by Earth First!, at that time a loosely knit band of monkey-wrenchers committed to stopping the destruction of the environment by means of nonviolent civil disobedience and minor property sabotage. Many, in fact, simply assumed Earth First! was taking things a step further. But these acts of sabotage were clearly becoming more serious and the economic losses dramatically greater—and at each of the following sites, the letters "ELF" were found in spray paint:

- October 14, 1996: Eugene, Oregon. Locks were glued and spray-painted slogans were left at a McDonald's restaurant (Highway 99 and Garfield), and at the IZ and Pearl public relations office of Weyerhauser and Hyundai.

- October 16, 1996: Grants Pass, Oregon. Locks were glued and spray-painted slogans left at McDonald's in support of the McLibel Two (who were targeted by

McDonald's after they were caught distributing factual leaflets about the corporation's business practices).

- October 17, 1996: Exit 104 on Interstate 5, Oregon. Locks were glued and spray-painted messages left at McDonald's restaurants at exit 104 and in Cottage Grove.

- March 14, 1997: Mackenzie River Watershed, Oregon. Tree spiking at Robinson-Scott timber harvest site in the Willamette National Forest.

Two apparently related actions involved arson. On October 28, 1996, a US Forest Service pickup was torched in the parking lot of the Ranger District Headquarters in Detroit, Oregon. "EARTH LIBERATION FRONT" and other graffiti decorated the scene, and a plastic jug incendiary device that failed to ignite was found on the roof of the building. Many environmental advocates were quick to question whether the arson was perhaps carried out by law enforcement or industry to discredit the movement. Two days later, on October 30, a fire destroyed the US Forest Service Oakridge Ranger Station just south of Eugene, Oregon. Causing over $5 million in damages, this fire was immediately linked to the Detroit Ranger Station arson by authorities and the news media. As before, many environmentalists jumped to condemn this act, arguing that government provocateurs had likely started the blaze to undermine public support for the environmental cause. Few could have known that these early actions signaled that a new movement was emerging.

Early in 1997, a communiqué from unknown whereabouts was made public over the internet. Titled "Beltane," this anonymous message foretold the beginnings of a new, intensified struggle to protect the natural environment.

Beltane, 1997

Welcome to the struggle of all species to be free. We are the burning rage of this dying planet. The war of greed ravages the earth and species die out every day. ELF works to speed up the collapse of industry, to scare the rich, and to undermine the foundations of the state. We embrace social and deep ecology as a practical resistance movement. We have to show the enemy that we are serious about defending what is sacred. Together we have teeth and claws to match our dreams. Our greatest weapons are imagination and the ability to strike when least expected.

Since 1992 a series of earth nights and Halloween smashes has mushroomed around the world. 1000's of bulldozers, powerlines, computer systems, buildings and valuable equipment have been composted. Many ELF actions have been censored to prevent our bravery from inciting others to take action.

We take inspiration from Luddites, Levellers, Diggers, the Autonome squatter movement, the ALF, the Zapatistas, and the little people—those mischievous elves of lore. Authorities can't see us because they don't believe in elves. We are practically invisible. We have no command structure, no spokespersons, no office, just many small groups working separately, seeking vulnerable targets and practicing our craft.

Many elves are moving to the Pacific Northwest and other sacred areas. Some elves will leave surprises as they go. Find your family! And let's dance as we make ruins of the corporate money system. . . .

I knew little about the Beltane communiqué and the various Oregon-based actions at the time they were committed. Other than reading about them in the *Earth First! Journal*, I only knew what I had seen in the news reports on the local television networks. However, having heard the overwhelming skepticism within the environmentalist community as to the validity of these actions, I didn't spend much time thinking about them. I continued with my spokesperson work for the ALF, which was about to take the most dramatic and powerful action in its history.

A Horse Rendering Plant Fire

In late July 1997, on one of my biweekly checks of the Liberation Collective post office box, I noticed a strange-looking note. It was addressed to the organization, but the handwriting was purposely distorted. This, in addition to the absence of a return address, sparked my interest, and I decided to open the letter, right there in the post office. I tore off the top of the envelope, opened the one-page statement—and felt a familiar chill run down my spine. It was the same feeling I had experienced when Vanessa had handed me our first ALF communiqué at the Cleveland House.

Sure enough, it was another communiqué, this time claiming responsibility for burning down the Cavel West Horse Rendering Plant in Redmond, Oregon, in the southeast portion of the state. Interestingly, the communiqué was signed by a specific group apparently within the ALF, called the Equine and Zebra Liberation Network (EZLN). While I knew nothing about this group, the communiqué was clear in its description of the action and the motives behind it.

Greetings,

On Monday, July 21, 1997, under nearly a full moon, the Animal Liberation Front paid a visit to the Cavel West Horse Murdering Plant at 1607 SE Railroad Avenue in Redmond, Oregon. About 35 gallons of vegan jello was brought in with the team. Next, a number of large holes were drilled into the rear wall of the slaughterhouse office to bypass potential alarms on the doors or windows. Next, the area that housed the refrigeration units was located and again large holes were drilled through the wall at that part of the slaughterhouse. Two teams then poured the jello into the numerous holes and quickly began to assemble the three electrically-timed incendiary devices that would bring to a screeching halt what countless protests and letter writing campaigns could never stop. While these devices were being assembled some members of the team entered a storage shed/office/construction site (all part of Cavel West's operations) and left the remaining 10 gallons or so of jello for dessert. Then two gallons of muriatic acid was poured into the air conditioning vents to taint and destroy any horse flesh that may have survived the fire. Finally, the incendiary devices were set to ignite at exactly the same time. Unfortunately, as the battery was being connected to the device at the refrigeration unit, a spark started that entire area on fire! Fortunately, we had very thorough back-up plans in case anything went wrong and this ensured that our departure went quick and smooth. At least $1,000,000 of damage has been done and the entire plant is currently closed and out of operation! The media blackout of this action is intense and thorough but you know what? . . . The horses don't mind.

Animal Liberation Front—Equine & Zebra Liberation Network

Oh my fucking god, I thought as I slowly lifted my eyes from the page and scanned the post office. *Did anybody see me reading this?* There was no one around, but I didn't feel like staying there with a communiqué in my hands. I raced back to the Cleveland House; knowing the message had to be released to the media, I wanted to get a press statement written and sent out as soon as possible. Within a couple of hours news media outlets throughout Oregon knew about the action and were preparing their stories for later that night or the next morning.

Everyone at the Cleveland House was excited about the news of the most recent action. The use of fire was obviously more severe than any tactic we had previously represented, but the justification was compelling. The Cavel West Horse Rendering Plant was a horse slaughterhouse, purchased five years earlier by a Belgian company that shipped meat overseas, largely to European markets, for human consumption. Their environmental reputation was appalling; they were constantly faced with complaints regarding drainage of blood into the nearby river and a chronic odor problem. Although Cavel West had been faced with low-key picketing protests in the past, this was the first time it had been severely targeted.

The story soon went national. It turned out that the ALF had burned this horse slaughterhouse completely to the ground. As far as I was aware, this was the most extreme ALF action that had ever taken place and was definitely the most radical action I had represented to the public and press.

A few days after the Cavel West fire, the call came. "Craig . . . Craig . . . Telephone," Vanessa called out.

"I'll get it up here," I replied, jumping out of bed and trying to find the phone in the darkness. It was just after 8:00 A.M., and my attic bedroom in the Cleveland House was devoid of any light from the new day. Picking up the receiver, I wondered who would be calling me at home this early.

"Hello?" I had just woken up, and probably sounded like it. "Mr. Rosebraugh? Craig Rosebraugh?" an unknown voice inquired.

"Yes, who's calling?"

"You burned down my slaughterhouse! You son of a bitch! You burned down my slaughterhouse!" the voice yelled into the phone. My heart began racing as I tried to think who this could be. It had only been a few days since the communiqué about the Cavel West fire had gone public. Could it be someone with Cavel West? Another prank call?

At this point, especially since the Cleveland House telephone number had been printed in all the promotional literature for the Against Animal Testing conference, we were experiencing a sharp increase in the number of prank calls seeming to have some connection to the activities of the Liberation Collective. Quite often, one of us would pick up the phone to hear just silence or breathing. In recent months, some guy who claimed he was from "the militia" had been calling, threatening to assassinate us if we organized or attended any upcoming Liberation Collective protests or events. I wondered if he was a spokesperson for some militia umbrella or coalition group that represented all the militia groups globally, or if he simply had a local militia chapter. Either way, we continued with our work at Liberation Collective, always keeping an eye out for the militia assassin.

"Who is this?" I responded again into the phone.

"Why did you burn my slaughterhouse? Why did you . . ."

"Are you going to tell me who you are?" I interrupted, becoming angry. Sure enough, it was Pascal Derde, the owner of Cavel West, and he wouldn't say how he had come across my home telephone number. It took me ten minutes to make him understand that I had not burned down his business; I just spoke for those who had.

Surprisingly enough, once he calmed down and stopped accusing me of being an arsonist, we had a fairly lengthy conversation about the motives behind the ALF and the philosophy of animal rights. He asked me all about veganism and what strict vegetarians ate, and I was happy to answer, fulfilling my educational duties—so I thought. I couldn't stop thinking how weird it was that this guy, who just had his business torched by the ALF, had called my home and woken me up by yelling, "You burned down my slaughterhouse!" As he ended the conversation, he informed me that Cavel West would rebuild and be back in business in no time. As I hung up the receiver, I realized he was probably right. Nearly all of these businesses that are targeted have insurance, and so they simply rebuild after an arson attack. At least the fire generated a lot of publicity about the animal rights cause, I thought. And the insurance company would be bound to raise their rates after such a loss. There was no way in the world I could imagine that any insurance company could suffer a loss of over a million dollars—the estimated cost of the

Cavel West fire—and not raise their rates.

Within a few weeks I received the best news I had heard since the Cavel West communiqué came. It was reported in the local and state newspapers, as well as on television, that Cavel West would not be rebuilding their slaughterhouse in Oregon. It turns out that the legal codes for that particular location required Cavel West to correct all of its environmental problems before rebuilding, otherwise the permits would not be granted. The problems must have been so severe and costly that Cavel West aborted its plans to rebuild. The ALF, in one night, had put Cavel West out of business.

Buy Nothing Day

During the next few months, Liberation Collective put a lot of effort into preparing for Buy Nothing Day, an international day of protests targeting consumerism and overconsumption in society. Every year in the United States, Buy Nothing Day is held on the busiest shopping day of the year, the day after Thanksgiving. This is the traditional kickoff of the Christmas holiday shopping season, which for most businesses, particularly in the retail field, is the prime time of the year economically. The broad goal of Buy Nothing Day is simply to urge people to undertake a one-day boycott of all consumerism as a demonstration of consumer power. It is also an educational event, designed to help people to understand the dramatic waste and destruction that result from an over-consumerist lifestyle. Surely to some degree all of us on the planet consume to simply survive, but we wished to raise awareness of the fact that luxury items, either through their manufacture or use, often contribute to global human suffering or the death and destruction of species and the natural environment.

That year, Buy Nothing Day fell on November 28, and we had developed a creative plan for the day. While other more mainstream organizations in Portland were planning a march and rally at Pioneer Square (Portland's central gathering space), Liberation Collective wanted to spice up the day with some tricks of our own. At that time, a few of us, including myself, had become particularly influenced by the aggressive protest tactics recently used in various European cities, especially in the London area. I personally had been in awe of the ability of organizers there to attain tremendous turnouts for their protests. We saw that some of the European campaigns appeared to be far more successful than similar versions in the United States, especially within the animal rights movement, which in Europe was far more advanced in agricultural issues, animal experimentation, and fur.

Leslie, Josh, and I had all read accounts of protests in Europe called "street parties," where activists physically took over the streets for a particular cause. Sometimes the purpose might just be to gather people and attention, and other times the parties appeared to be specifically focused on shutting down a particular section of the city, say, a financial center. In brainstorming what we could do to liven up Portland's 1997 Buy Nothing Day, we focused on the idea of a massive street party downtown. Different scenarios filled our heads. We could shut down a few blocks, have music, even serve food. What if we rented a dump truck, filled it full of dirt and dumped it in the middle of a downtown road to plant a garden? How about getting a giant street puppet and having someone with a jackhammer inside to dig up the concrete during a march? What about dropping a large banner off one of the tall downtown buildings? While all of these ideas sounded fun, we couldn't settle on a plan at first.

After talking it over, Leslie and I decided to purchase two old beater cars, decorate them with Buy Nothing Day materials, and drive them downtown, where we would smash them together at a busy intersection. This would barricade one end of a street block, and if we did it on a one-way street we could prevent any cars from getting through, opening up the block to a party. We would definitely need help. Josh and Vanessa agreed to go down to the mainstream rally ahead of time and, as the rally ended, lead a march directly to the location where the cars would crash. Ideally, as soon as the cars hit one another, the street would instantly fill with hundreds of people. Once the cars were in place, Josh planned to start playing music on an old tape player he was going to bring. He also planned to coordinate a serving at the site with Food Not Bombs, so there would be music, food, dancing, and, hopefully, anti-consumerist fun.

After scanning the newspapers for the next few weeks, Leslie and I found two vehicles, barely running, that we decided to buy. One was a Volkswagen Rabbit that we acquired for $100, and the other was an old Datsun sedan for which we paid $150. We drove them back to the Cleveland House, parked them in the back driveway, and began the preparations for the big day. As an added visual effect, both of us decided to mount as many television sets inside and on top of both of the cars as possible. After raiding the Goodwill "As-Is" store (a thrift store selling used junk by the pound), we found enough television sets to place fifteen to twenty in or on each car. As consumerism, especially in the United States, is heavily promoted through television, we felt it was appropriate to demonstrate a strong anti-TV message in connection with Buy Nothing Day. After piling as many TVs as we could fit inside the cars, we tied the rest on the top, front, and rears.

Sitting outside examining our shitty craftsmanship, Leslie and I began talking over a proposed scenario for that day.

"So we are just going to drive these beasts downtown and smash them together?" I asked Leslie.

"Oh, yeah!" He grinned mischievously. "How fast do you think we should be going?"

"I don't know. Maybe twenty or thirty miles per hour." I really had no idea what it would take to crash the cars seriously, but not so badly that we were injured in the process.

"So after the cars hit, we are just going to join the party? Josh will have the music going, and hopefully he and Vanessa will have brought back the crowd from the square."

"Yeah," I replied. "It would be good, though, if we could do something more with the TVs. What if we smash the cars somewhat realistically, like we are really getting into an accident, then both of us emerge from the vehicles with sledgehammers and beat the shit out of the TVs on each other's cars?"

Leslie started laughing hysterically. "Yeah, that would be good. Hopefully the cops don't shoot us for having sledgehammers!"

So the plan was set. During the last few days before November 28, we finished working on the cars, fixing the television sets and covering both vehicles with spray-painted slogans. I also wrote a press release that we would fax to the news media early on the 28th. When engaging in an act of civil disobedience, it was always a bit of a game to inform the media about the event without tipping off the police. In many of the civil disobedience actions I was a part of, if the police had known ahead of time, they could have easily prevented anything from occurring. For our Buy Nothing Day action to be a success, it was crucial that the police know nothing about our plan. Of course, any cop driving past the Cleveland House would have known we were up to something after seeing the two modified cars covered in slogans and TVs. But we figured as long as the cars got smashed and into place downtown, the day would be a success.

I woke up just after 7:00 A.M. on the 28th and immediately faxed the press release to the news media. There was no doubt in my mind that the news cameras would show up. I mean, how often are people either smart or foolish enough to try to illegally blockade a downtown street by way of smashing two cars to hold a street party? The media release stated that the cars would smash at the corner of Park and Alder Streets at 12:00 P.M. By this time, the more mainstream rally would be over, and a march would be meeting us for the party. With the time set, we figured we needed to leave the Cleveland House at 11:45 A.M.

While Leslie prepared himself and finished some last-minute touches on the Volkswagen he would be driving, I slipped into the costume I had decided to wear for the event. It was a custom-made, red, white, and blue sparkling evening gown, complemented by a Statue of Liberty headdress. In my own altered patriotic way, I was going to look my best while displaying an obvious relation between overconsumption and the United States of America. At 11:45, Leslie and I climbed into our vehicles and started the engines—or at least Leslie attempted to. The Rabbit wouldn't run. *Fuck*, I thought to myself. *These stupid-ass $100 cars.* After fiddling with the carburetor, we got Leslie's vehicle to run as long as he didn't let it idle; this meant he just had to keep pushing on the gas. By this time, we were already late. It was five minutes to 12:00, and I hoped the police hadn't been tipped off already by the media or crowd of marchers who were most likely already waiting for us.

With both cars running, we took off out of the Cleveland House driveway and headed for the nearest freeway entrance. Both Leslie and I were certain that we were going to get pulled over before we even reached downtown. I mean, there were TVs tied onto the tops of our cars, some attached with only their own cords! To our surprise we made it to the freeway without seeing a cop. Crossing the Willamette River (the main waterway dividing Portland) and heading downtown, I ran the scenario through my head. About five streets above our chosen intersection, we would split off. I would go around to Park Street, which is a one-way running north. Leslie would travel straight down Alder Street, a one-way heading east. We would meet where two streets intersect and crash into one another traveling twenty to twenty-five miles an hour. Once the cars hit, Leslie would jump out with his sledgehammer and, in a fit of rage, begin smashing the TVs on my car. At the same time, I would jump onto his hood and, with a sledgehammer in hand, smash his windshield before working my way to the TVs.

As we reached the turnoff for downtown, my heart was racing. I could see Leslie in my rearview window, still with that mischievous grin on his face. I also could see that the Volkswagen he was driving now had smoke pouring out from under the hood. *Not good*, I thought. After passing a few more streets, it was time to split off from one another. I waved goodbye to him and maneuvered my way toward Park Street. Both of us apparently had forgotten that since this was the busiest shopping day of the year, the traffic downtown would be horrendous. It was now 12:15, and I could just see Park Street up ahead.

Turning onto Park, the traffic was bumper to bumper. I could see in the distance, one block down, a huge crowd, which I assumed was the march. It looked as though they were just circling one city block repeatedly, awaiting our arrival. Surely the cops must know something was going on. I slowly inched my way forward to a point half a block away from where I would smash into Leslie. Staring at the crowd of demonstrators, I suddenly noticed Leslie walk across the street to join them. "What the fuck!" I yelled. A second later, the Portland Police Bureau's Mounted Patrol Unit turned the corner onto Park Street and headed straight for me. As they reached my car, the sergeant in charge, David Pool, stopped his horse directly in front of my car.

"Stop your car!" he yelled at me. "Stop your car and turn off the ignition!"

"What?" I yelled inside the car, motioning with my hands like I couldn't hear him. For a split second, I thought of getting out with my sledgehammer and smashing my own car. Then he came a little closer.

"Turn off your ignition!" He continued to scream with a growing anger. Finally, I shut the engine off.

"Step out of the vehicle!"

"What?" I again yelled, attempting to play stupid.

"Get out of the vehicle!" By this time his face was turning interesting shades of red.

Before I could move, my car door flew open, and a police officer on foot grabbed me out of the car and slammed me down on the pavement. In the commotion, I purposely tried to throw the car keys down a street drain so the police would at least have to tow the car, thereby creating a larger nuisance. Unfortunately, I missed the damned drain and the keys ended up in the middle of the sidewalk. The crowd of demonstrators by this time had made their way to me and were circling the police. I was quickly put in handcuffs and thrown in the back of a police car, which was instantly surrounded by the angry crowd. The protesters began hitting, kicking, and rocking the police car, and one woman even yanked open the back door and motioned for me to escape. Before I could even think, it was slammed shut by another cop, and the police, in a state of panic, began backing the patrol car up to leave the area.

Because the car was surrounded, however, they were backing up into people, so the Mounted Patrol came in to clear the way. As the police car backed into the intersection where Leslie and I were originally going to crash into one another, the crowd again circled the car. My last visual memory of that location was seeing Leslie's cousin, Justin, from California, smash the Uncle Sam puppet he was wearing repeatedly into the front of the cop car.

In my dress made from American flags, I was taken to the Multnomah County Justice Center and placed into a holding cell. Within a half an hour, a detective entered the room and began asking me what my intentions were for the car.

"Where were you going to drive that car to?" he asked repeatedly. "I was merely looking for a parking spot and you people arrested me," I responded, trying to hold back my laughter.

"We received notice that you were planning on crashing into another car somewhere downtown. Is that true, Mr. Rosebraugh?"

"Of course not," I replied. "That was an art car. You know, like the ones you see in parades. I was merely looking for a parking spot to display the fine piece of art."

"And what did you have planned for the sledgehammer we found in the back of the car?"

"I have no idea." It was really difficult not to smile.

"So let me get this straight. You were driving a car with TVs and painted messages all over it, wearing an American flag dress, and you had no idea there was a sledgehammer in the back of the car?"

"That's correct, sir." I actually think he suspected I was going to smash random property downtown. Shaking his head in frustration, he left the cell and slammed the door. At this point, I had no idea what I was going to be charged with or how long I would be held. Within a half an hour, another officer entered my cell and told me to follow him. He told me that because I was already in the computer system from past arrests, they were just going to give me a citation with a date to appear in court and release me. With a slip of paper charging me with one count of disorderly conduct, they let me go out the side door of the precinct.

As the bright natural light outside hit me, I quickly noticed that the street behind the jail was closed off by riot police. I attempted to see what the commotion was all about and even asked one of the riot cops, but I couldn't get any answers. So I decided to walk around to the front of the building to see if anyone was there. Toward the front of the building, more riot police blocked all entrances to the structure. Luckily, three people from the Collective were there waiting for me and filled me in on what was happening. It turns out that after I was arrested and taken away, the police received a tip that the angry mob of protesters was heading for the jail to demand my release. The police, overresponding as usual, employed riot cops to completely shut down the "Justice Center." Interestingly enough, the only threatening crowd to show up there turned out to be Elaine Close, Kattie, and another Collective member who came to wait patiently for my release.

Later, I found out that Leslie's car had broken down in the middle of the street a few blocks from the intersection where we were supposed to stage the crash. Since he couldn't get the car started, he decided to create even more of a spectacle and nuisance by slashing all the tires before running down to meet the crowd. I also learned that the police, thinking I was a key leader of the protest, made the decision to remove me in order to calm the crowd. While my charge of disorderly conduct was eventually dropped, the police were effective, to a degree at least, in breaking up our planned party. I went to sleep that night disappointed that we had not succeeded in our deviant theatrics but at least proud that we had tried. Little did I know, in less than twenty-four hours an action would occur that would have a much bigger impact on my life.

Wild Horses and the Emergence of the ELF

In early December, I received another communiqué claiming responsibility for an action that had occurred on November 29, 1997. This was similar to the other communiqués I had previously seen, except that now, not only the ALF—but also by a group called the Earth Liberation Front—claimed credit. While I knew that the group, according to law enforcement and the news media, was somehow tied to the Forest Service incidents in 1996, I had not until now heard of any other actions actually claimed by this ELF organization.

Both the ALF and the ELF were claiming responsibility for burning down a Bureau of Land Management (BLM) horse corral near Hines, Oregon. Additionally, 488 wild horses and 51 burros held captive by the BLM had been released back into the wild. The communiqué appeared as follows:

The Bureau of Land Management (BLM) claims they are removing non-native species from public lands (aren't white Europeans also non-native) but then they turn around and subsidize the cattle industry and place thousands of non-native domestic cattle on these same lands. . . .

[This action was taken] to help halt the BLM's illegal and immoral business of rounding up wild horses from public lands and funneling them to slaughter.

This hypocrisy and genocide against the horse nation will not go unchallenged! The practice of rounding up and auctioning wild horses must be stopped. The practice of grazing cattle on public lands must be stopped. The time to take action is now.

From an investigation like the Associated Press' to writing the BLM to an action like ours, you can help stop the slaughter and save our Mother Earth.

Animal Liberation Front

Earth Liberation Front

This dramatic action taken by both groups had destroyed the office, horse pens, tack room, corrals, and chutes on the facility, causing just under $500,000 in damages. While the BLM was attempting to recover from this attack, they received notice that they would be receiving a one million dollar federal budget cut, forcing them to reduce the number of horses that they captured.

Each year in Oregon, the BLM had been rounding up between 300 and 400 of the nearly 2,000 wild horses that live freely on public lands. Their stated purpose was to regulate wild horse populations and remove all species not native to the area. These captured animals then were to be adopted out to the public. However, the Associated Press revealed in a January 5, 1997 article[15] that the wild horses taken by the BLM were winding up in slaughterhouses, destined for human consumption in foreign markets. "A multimillion-dollar federal program created to save the lives of wild horses is instead channeling them by the thousands to slaughterhouses where they are chopped into cuts of meat," the AP story stated.

BLM employees were not only aware that the horses were being sold to slaughterhouses, they were actually illegally profiting off these sales. Anyone could adopt one of these wild horses for a fee of $125, and for injured or older animals, the fee was often waived. While there is nothing in the law that prevents a public citizen from adopting a horse and then selling it for slaughter, federal law does not allow US government employees, such as those at the BLM, to use their public office for private gain. Since BLM employees were often adopting horses out to themselves and then selling them to slaughter for an average of $700 per animal, sizable profits were to be made off this practice.

---

15 "BLM's Wild Horses End Up in Slaughterhouses," *The Oregonian*, January 5, 1997.

"[G]overnment officials," the AP article continued, "offer conflicting opinions on whether it is legal or ethical for BLM officials to adopt and sell wild horses."

Coincidentally, the Cavel West Horse Rendering Plant, targeted by the ALF in July 1997, had a close relationship with this Oregon BLM facility. It turns out that many of the wild horses who supposedly had been saved and then adopted out, ended up in the cutting machines inside Cavel West. From there, the meat would be flown to Europe for human consumption. The ALF, and now the ELF as well, appeared to be working hard to disrupt this unethical chain.

As I had done with the past communiqués I received from the ALF, I wrote a press release and faxed it out to local news media.

The response was decent, especially since Cavel West had been burned in the same region just a few months prior. Stories appeared on the local television network affiliates throughout the day and in the statewide newspaper the next morning. From our Liberation Collective telephone line in the Cleveland House, I once again gave my views on, and expressed my ideological support for, the action.

The November 29, 1997 BLM action marked the first time the ELF had claimed official responsibility through a communiqué for any of its actions. While in the past they had indicated their involvement by leaving graffiti at the scenes of the 1996 Forest Service fires and other locations, the BLM fire was the first time the group had declared in writing its involvement and motives for a particular action.

Who was this ELF? While news media, environmental proponents, and law enforcement in the United States have speculated for years that the ELF originated in England, they lack the evidence to back up that assumption. The popular theory was that the ELF was formed in 1992 in Brighton, England, by members of Earth First! who felt their tactics must intensify if they were going to be successful in protecting the natural environment. After this split, the theory suggests that the ideology spread to the United States in the mid-1990s and the first ELF actions were born here in 1996.

But the environmental movement in the United States was itself debating the issue of tactics in the early 1990s. For example, Judi Bari, a leading Earth First! organizer and activist in the United States, recommended in 1994 that the organization should go mainstream. Bari felt that criminal acts, other than those pertaining to simple unlawful protests, should be left up to other direct-action organizations. Just two years later, the ELF would become active.

Wherever the ELF originated geographically, the 1997 Beltane communication gives insight into its philosophical origins: "We take inspiration from Luddites, Levellers, Diggers, the Autonome squatter movement, the ALF, the Zapatistas, and the little people—those mischievous elves of lore." Indeed, ELF tactics are quite similar to those used by many of these groups. For example, although the ALF started off as an animal rescue organization, it has used arson as a tactic. In this regard, as well as its redefinition of property and condemnation of our exploitative attitude toward the natural world, the ALF and ELF are similar. It seems that the ELF was formed to provide what some individuals considered to be a needed addition to the US environmental movement. Using elements of guerrilla warfare—limited to property destruction—the first individuals conducting ELF actions in the United States had a most definite mission: to start a movement that could not be stopped.

3

LOVE
AND
REPRESSION

*E*arly one June morning in 1997, I was sitting in the back office on the ground floor of the Cleveland House when I heard loud knocking at the front door. I waited a moment to

see if any of my roommates were going to answer it, but the knocking continued, so I got up and made my way to the front of the house. I had no idea who would be banging at the door so early in the day. *Probably a salesperson or another vulture from the church*, I thought. (Church representatives routinely came to our door attempting to convert us.)

When I opened the door, a man and woman dressed in business suits confronted me. They stared at me tensely.

"Mr. Rosebraugh?" the man asked. Without thinking, I replied, "Yes, can I help you?" Both individuals immediately informed me that they were from the Federal Bureau of Investigation (FBI). As my eyes widened in shock, both agents whipped out their badges in a style that reminded me of Scully and Mulder from the *X-Files*. In this tense and nervous moment, all I could do was laugh.

"We would like to ask you some questions. Can we come in, please, Mr. Rosebraugh?"

Now, at the time, I considered myself a devoted student of Gandhi's principles of nonviolence. I attempted to look upon all individuals with compassion and respect and told myself that even though I despised the FBI, I had to separate these individuals from the bias in my head. I didn't know them, and so I convinced myself that I had no real reason to demonstrate hostility toward them.

Furthermore, I assumed the agents had come to investigate the ALF action I had announced to the public. As I felt I had done nothing wrong, I had nothing to hide. While I certainly was not going to assist them in their investigation, I didn't see the harm in inviting them in and demonstrating a certain degree of courtesy.

"Sure, come on in," I told them. We walked into the living room and sat facing one another on the couches. "Can I offer you some tea, water, or soy milk?"

The agents stared and declined my offer. Quickly, they began their questioning.

"Mr. Rosebraugh, we've come here today to ask you about a case of burglary and vandalism that occurred at the Arritola Mink Farm on May 30 this year. Are you aware of this incident?"

"I assume you are speaking of the Animal Liberation Front action there, in which case, yes, I am familiar with it," I replied.

"Did you receive a communiqué from members of the ALF claiming responsibility for this crime?"

"You obviously know I did. Certainly you read the stories in the media where I am quoted discussing the communiqué and my support for the action. Isn't that why you are here?"

"How did you receive that communiqué, Mr. Rosebraugh?" The male agent's tone sharpened.

"I don't recall."

"What do you mean you don't recall? Didn't you tell a reporter from *The Oregonian* that a phone call came to the house that morning telling you to check your mailbox?"

Thinking back for a split second to what I had told that reporter, I was sure it wasn't that. *If they knew about the phone call, perhaps they just pulled phone records and are drawing some conclusions,* I thought. "I am sorry. I don't remember."

"Where is the original communiqué, Mr. Rosebraugh? May I remind you that it is against the law to tamper with evidence?"

"I don't know," I responded, noticing smoke beginning to come out of the male agent's ears. The female agent simply sat there without saying a word. I wondered if she was in some sort of training or if that was her role for the day.

"What do you mean you don't know? What did you do with it?"

"I don't remember," I stated.

Infuriated, the agent then began asking me about the Liberation Collective organization, our ideology, and our organizational structure. Since this information was already public—the group was registered with the federal government as a 501(c)(3) nonprofit organization—I didn't see the harm in answering these questions. Time and time again, though, the agent returned to the subject of the ALF mink raid. In addition to asking me about the communiqué, he wanted to know where I had been at the time of the raid, and I told him the truth—I was probably sleeping.

Frustrated at obtaining no real information from me, beyond perhaps a more fundamental understanding of the Liberation Collective philosophy (which I was happy to provide), both agents left after half an hour or so. On their way out the door, they handed me their business cards and mentioned that they might need to return to ask me some follow-up questions. I smiled and wished them a good day.

Later that day, when everyone at the Cleveland House came home, I told them about our morning visitors. While all of us were a bit shocked, Josh, Leslie, Vanessa, and Casea seemed to get a big kick out of my description of the agents flipping down their badges at the door. I don't think any of us really gave the visit too much thought after that.

I was not knowledgeable enough about investigations at this point to realize that this first visit would inevitably lead to more. Sure enough, during the next few weeks, more FBI visitors approached the Cleveland House. This time, however, remembering that we did not have to open the door to authorities without a warrant, no one let them in—or, in most cases, even answered the door. We considered this just a minor nuisance as we continued with our Liberation Collective volunteer activities.

Just over a month later, while working outside in the Cleveland House garden, I was approached by another agent I did not recognize. Unlike the other FBI agents, who had usually approached me with a fairly calm and polite demeanor, this man obviously was serious and got straight to the point.

"Craig Rosebraugh?" he yelled out as he approached. "Craig Rosebraugh?"

"And how can I help you?" I responded, trying to figure out just what in the hell this guy wanted.

"John Comrey. I'm an agent with the Bureau of Alcohol, Tobacco, and Firearms [BATF]. I need to ask you some questions." I just stared at him with no response.

"Where were you on the night of July 21 this year?" I continued to work in the garden, pretending not to hear him—or care, for that matter.

"Mr. Rosebraugh, I am talking to you. I asked you a question. Where were you on July 21?"

"I heard your question, and I am not going to answer you. You can ask me all the questions you want, and I am not going to help you."

This obviously didn't faze him, as he continued to shout questions at me, his anger intensifying.

"Did you receive a communiqué from the Animal Liberation Front claiming responsibility for the arson at the Cavel West company? Do you have this communiqué? Mr. Rosebraugh, where is this communiqué?"

I continued working, ignoring him as his anger continued to grow. Finally, after a few minutes of talking to himself, he stormed off down the block. Interested to see where he was headed, I followed him and watched him get into what appeared to be a government-issued sport utility vehicle. Agent Comrey had gone to the extra effort of parking a block and a half away so I would not be able to see his vehicle. *Ingenious*, I thought.

I had only been back working in the garden for ten or fifteen minutes when I noticed Comrey walking toward me again. I continued to ignore him as he approached.

"So you're not going to tell me where that communiqué is, are you?" As I looked up at him, he continued. "I just want to tell you, you are walking a very thin line, Mr. Rosebraugh, a very thin line."

"I'll keep that in mind," I replied as he walked away again in the direction of his SUV.

In early September, I responded to another knock at the front door of the Cleveland House. When I opened the door, the same FBI agents who had originally come in and questioned me handed me a subpoena to testify before a federal grand jury in Portland. I was commanded to appear at the US Courthouse in downtown Portland on September 17, 1997. Although the subpoena was basically blank, containing no information about the subject matter of the investigation, I assumed it was related to the Arritola mink release and the torching of Cavel West.

As the agents left the porch, I shut the door and read over the subpoena, feeling a sudden chill. While I knew that speaking out on behalf of the ALF would have its risks, I had simply never thought this would happen. At that point, I wasn't certain what a grand jury subpoena meant, but I knew it wasn't something positive. I had heard many stories of people involved in social and political movements being subpoenaed to grand juries only to end up in jail on contempt charges.

Not knowing exactly where to turn for assistance, I talked to a number of friends about the subpoena and was referred to an attorney in San Francisco. I was told that this lawyer, Lawrence Weiss, had experience dealing with political grand juries and was the attorney who had assisted Jonathan Paul in the early 1990s. A well-known environmental and animal rights activist, Paul had been ordered to testify in front of a grand jury as a part of the same investigation that handed down indictments on one of ALF's other spokespeople, Rod Coronado. Paul appeared in front of the grand jury but refused to supply information and was imprisoned for five months in Washington State. Unfortunately for Coronado, he ended up being sentenced to four years in a Tucson, Arizona, federal penitentiary for ALF activity.

Grand Jury 101

I called Lawrence Weiss, who was more than happy to help. While he was unable to travel to Portland to assist me—largely due to my lack of finances—he did serve as a major resource for the process. The first step Weiss told me to take was to call the US Attorney listed on the subpoena and ask for a delay so I could have time to obtain and consult an attorney. While I surely did need this extra time, I didn't think there was any way the US Attorney would agree. When I called Assistant US Attorney Frank Noonan, I was surprised to find that he instantly granted my request and pushed back my appearance date for one month.

During the next few weeks, I spoke to Weiss fairly often, trying to obtain as much information about the grand jury system as possible. I was shocked to find that if you are a witness called to testify before a federal grand jury, you do not have the right to counsel. An attorney is not allowed to go inside the room with you. Attorneys can wait outside, and you are supposed to be able to go out and converse with them at regular intervals, but they are not allowed to represent you inside the proceedings. It is important to note that you are only able to exit the grand jury room to consult with your attorney as long as this does not disrupt the grand jury process—a formula definitely open to interpretation.

While the restriction on representation bothered me, I wasn't overly concerned, as I most likely would not have an attorney anyway. What really got to me was the fact that in the grand jury process, witnesses called to testify are stripped of their right to invoke the Fifth Amendment and remain silent. Witnesses may rely upon their Fifth Amendment protection up until the time when a judge may force them to take immunity, at which point they must answer all questions under the scope of that immunity. The penalty for not answering the questions (which is pretty much the same as that for simply not showing up to the proceedings) is either civil or criminal contempt.

Civil contempt is the most common charge handed out to uncooperative witnesses. In this process a witness does not have the right to a trial, only a contempt hearing. During this public session, the prosecuting attorney (either the US or Assistant US Attorney) argues before a judge the reasons why the witness should be held in contempt. In response, the witness is then given the opportunity to provide a defense before the judge decides a verdict. For civil contempt, a witness may be held in prison for up to eighteen months or the remaining length of the grand jury (federal grand juries convene for eighteen months at a time). The up to eighteen months clause is fairly misleading, as when one federal grand jury term expires, another can simultaneously begin. It would then be lawful for a witness who has just spent eighteen months in prison to be immediately dragged before the new grand jury and, if he or she did not answer questions, to be held in contempt again.

In criminal contempt, the less common of the two types, a witness is granted a full trial and the consequences can be far more severe. In fact, there is no sentencing maximum for criminal contempt. The primary difference between civil and criminal contempt is that criminal contempt is supposed to be reserved for those witnesses who maliciously set out to disrupt the grand jury process. Even then, the prosecuting US Attorney's office is advised to pursue civil contempt before advancing to the criminal stage.

What this told me in short was that in mid-October, when I was commanded to appear in front of the federal grand jury in Portland, I could be imprisoned for up to eighteen months if I did not answer the questions. It was a bit unnerving, to say the least. In a panic, after further speaking with Weiss, I mailed off letters to the American Civil Liberties Union (ACLU) and the National Lawyers Guild (NLG) asking for assistance. Unfortunately, my letters and phone messages to these two organizations would not be answered for some time.

I also found out that grand juries deliberately operate in secrecy, behind closed doors and out of public view. Weiss had told me that public pressure is perhaps the primary method of actively opposing grand juries; hence the public is kept ignorant, to the extent possible, of its investigations and power. He said that Jonathan Paul was released after five months—instead of eighteen—due to publicity and a growing public opposition to his imprisonment. The logic made perfect sense to me, so, along with other Liberation Collective members, we planned a rally at the US Federal Courthouse in Portland on the day I was commanded to testify.

Prior to my date of appearance, I had spent a great deal of time contemplating my strategy in facing the grand jury. If I did not show up, I would most likely be quickly picked up and held in contempt. Likewise, if I entered the proceedings and refused to answer even one question, I would probably be held in contempt. Still taking my cue from Gandhi, I honestly felt as if I could walk into the proceedings and demonstrate to the grand jury that I was a compassionate and sincere person who had done nothing wrong. I was not going to offer any information that would aid in the grand jury investigation, but I really felt as if the grand jury, supposedly made up of peers from my community, would be able to determine that I was merely being harassed by the federal government due to my beliefs. I suppose I underestimated the strength of the assumption that, since I shared the beliefs of the underground groups, I was also connected to them.

The date of my appearance arrived. We had plastered the Portland area with posters advertising the rally in protest of the grand jury and sent out press releases. I really had no idea how many people would show up to the rally or how many media representatives would come to report on the day's events. Since it was a fairly high-profile grand jury investigation—involving the controversial ALF—I figured there would be a decent turnout of reporters.

The night before the big day, I was a wreck, too nervous to either eat or sleep. I was thankful to have the support of Liberation Collective and, in particular, my roommates at the Cleveland House. Furthermore, my horror at the grand jury situation was somewhat counteracted by my excitement at a growing personal relationship I was developing with Elaine Close.

I had first met Elaine back in the early 1990s when we were both volunteering for People for Animal Rights. I had broken up with Kattie Louis, my partner of two years, in early 1997, and while I had always felt a certain attraction to Elaine, she had also seemed far out of my league. Things began to change between us on my birthday that year, April 15, 1997. I was working out in the rear garden of the Cleveland House early that evening when Elaine came by and asked if I had plans for later that night. Feeling like some sort of loser who had no plans on his birthday, I admitted that I didn't, and she volunteered to take me out for a drink. While drinking strawberry margaritas at the Space Room, a trendy bar in Southeast Portland, we talked for hours and began—somewhat unknowingly on my part—to make a connection. As she dropped me off at home, she leaned over and kissed me on the cheek, a move that sent my mind and heart racing. Wanting to kiss her back, but not knowing whether I should, I patted her on the hand and went inside.

From there, slowly, we grew closer. On the night before the grand jury appearance, when I was restless and afraid, Elaine, with one sentence and one gesture, seemed to make everything all right. She had been visiting, and as I walked her outside to leave, she came up to me on the steps, hugged me, and, with tears in her eyes, told me she loved me. I couldn't have asked for a more wonderful gift.

Early the next morning, on my way to the US Courthouse, I delivered a formal letter of objection to the US Attorney's office on the grounds that I was being harassed. In the lobby of the US Attorney's office, I was met by bulletproof glass and questioning stares. After a receptionist received my letter with an astonished look (what, like they don't receive hand-delivered letters of objection every day at the US Attorney's office?), I left the building and headed up to the US Courthouse.

As 11:00 A.M. rolled around—the time I had been commanded to testify—about forty people stood outside the Courthouse holding signs with slogans against the grand jury. Much to my surprise, the only media outlet that showed up to cover the protest was KBOO community radio. At 11:00 A.M. sharp, a US Marshal came out of the building and motioned for me to come with him.

Entering the building, I had a feeling very reminiscent of one I get visiting deceased members of my family at a Portland crematorium. It was a cold, sterile atmosphere in which I was convinced

that nothing positive could ever grow. US Marshals quickly led me up to a floor reserved for grand juries and closed to the public, and into a waiting room filled with FBI, BATF, and other government agents. While I didn't interview each suit on the spot, I did recognize many of them as the agents who had been in or around the Cleveland House. As I sat down where I had been told to sit, the room went quiet and all the suits fixed their eyes upon me. While I told myself to remain calm and not to show any effects of being intimidated, inside I was shaking, and my heart felt like it was getting ready to break through my chest.

After ten or fifteen minutes of facing cold stares, I was taken across the hall to another room and led up to the front, where I was told to sit. In front of me were the twenty-three members of the grand jury. To my left was the Assistant US Attorney Stephen Peifer, and to my right were the three forepersons of the grand jury and the court reporter. As soon as I sat down, the questioning began from the Assistant US Attorney.

"State your full name," Peifer directed me.

"Craig Scott Rosebraugh," I replied.

Almost interrupting me, he demanded, "Are you a member of the Animal Liberation Front?"

"No," I responded. Peifer continued to pick up the pace of his questions.

As I examined the room more closely, I began to take some mental notes. The first observation I made was that the grand jury was entirely white, hardly an accurate representation of the Portland area. (Compared to many other US cities, Portland is an extremely white town—but definitely not to the extent represented by that jury.)

Secondly, all the jurors seemed to be over age forty, and many appeared older. While age in itself does not concern me, such a limited representation of ages on the grand jury does. Additionally, I had no knowledge of what was said about me prior to my appearance, but it was clear from the glares and the questions that came from the grand jurors that they considered me guilty of some sort of serious crime before I ever walked into that room. I would later find out that it is common for the US Attorney's office to call in the FBI and BATF, or whoever is the investigating agency, to give some background on the case and to "prep" the jury for the witness. Unsurprisingly, they didn't make me out to be any sort of Robin Hood.

After three or four questions, I began to take the Fifth Amendment and refused to answer. I was conscious at that point, at least in the back of my mind, that at any time I could be dragged into an immunity hearing and then thrown into jail. But I continued to plead the Fifth to approximately 75 percent of the questions. The questions I did choose to answer related directly to the philosophy of the animal rights movement and information about the Liberation Collective organization, both of which were already public knowledge.

Marvin E. Frankel and Gary P. Naftalis, in their book *The Grand Jury: An Institution on Trial*, comment on the atmosphere inside the grand jury room: "The opportunity to bully, to harass, to intimidate is surely present inside the grand jury room, and it has surely been exploited on too many occasions."[16] My own experience bears this out. After nearly an hour of questioning, Peifer turned the proceedings over to the grand jurors. The grand jury members seemed far more interested in arguing with me over the ethics of animal rights issues than in the task at hand, investigating the two ALF actions that had occurred. One of the forepersons of the jury, who admitted he owned a fur farm, argued with me endlessly over the morality of fur farming. I was frequently cut off when trying to answer ideological questions and often snickered at when offering my viewpoint on a given issue. It became extremely frustrating, especially when I noticed two jurors sleeping in the back row. It added to my agitation to know that US tax dollars were being spent to have these individuals sleep during this oppressive proceeding.

After an hour and a half of questioning, I was led outside the room and told to wait in the hall while Peifer spoke with

16 Marvin E. Frankel and Gary P. Naftalis, *The Grand Jury: An Institution on Trial* (New York: Hill and Wang, 1977).

the grand jury to determine if they wanted to ask any more questions. I was soon taken back inside, where I sat through another fifteen minutes of questions, again exercising my Fifth Amendment right.

At this point, I was told that I was done for the day, and Peifer reminded me that I could be called back at any given time to face more questions. A US Marshal then escorted me down the elevator and out of the building. I had not expected to be released that day, or perhaps for a long time, figuring my Fifth Amendment protection would be challenged and I would be held in contempt. As I walked out the doors of the Courthouse, I felt completely dazed. I was reeling from the psychological stress invoked in that hostile atmosphere—and from the fact that the stress had been created by people who were supposed to be caring for society and upholding the law.

I was greeted with cheers from the patient demonstrators who had waited to see the outcome of the grand jury. I hugged my friends and hurried home, still mentally a wreck. Once inside the closed door of my bedroom in the Cleveland House, the tears streamed from my eyes; I couldn't hold them back. I told myself that I would never again put myself through that psychological hell. *How foolish I was*, I thought to myself, *to think I could have any positive influence over the grand jury. Why did I even go in?*

During the next couple of months, the surveillance on the Cleveland House intensified. It became a regular occurrence to look out the window and see a forest-green, American-made sedan or SUV parked across the street. The primary agent we repeatedly noticed monitoring the house was Daniel Feucht of the FBI. He and BATF agent John Comrey, as it turned out, would target me for years to come. In late October, tiring of the continual surveillance, Leslie, Josh, and I charged one of the cars sitting on the street near the back of the house. While Josh took pictures of the agent and his car, Leslie and I screamed obscenities until the agent fled. That was one of the last occasions we *noticed* agents watching the Cleveland House.

Meanwhile, Elaine and I continued to become closer. In early November, after she had come over to watch a PBS documentary on the Irish Republican Army, we ended up talking and then hugging for most of the night. It was one of those rare moments in which you find someone with whom you can sit for hours in comfort without saying a word. This magical night was the beginning of a partnership that would last for nearly five years.

Early in December, just days after I had been arrested at the Buy Nothing Day protest in Portland, I was rushed to the emergency room of the nearest hospital with severe chest pains. In the middle of the night, I had awakened to a dull but painful feeling around my heart. My breathing was also impaired and getting worse. While I was trying to make some tea in the kitchen, the pain and breathing trouble became so bad that I went over to the couch where Josh—for whatever reason—was sleeping. I literally shook him awake and demanded that he drive me to the hospital. In a half-comatose state, with some kind of hippie makeup on his face from a party earlier that night, Josh took my keys and drove me the ten or so blocks to Emmanuel Hospital.

When I arrived, the doctors immediately shot me full of anti-inflammatory drugs to relieve whatever swelling might be occurring. After repeated tests failed to find the problem, one of the doctors came back and listened to my chest again. Instantly, she diagnosed me with pericarditis, a dangerous swelling of the lining around the heart. This lining, the pericardium, expands, thereby making the heart virtually beat against a wall. In my case, the pericarditis had no doubt been made more severe by the heavy stress load of the recent grand jury investigation and Liberation Collective activities.

I stayed in the emergency room for most of the remainder of the night, thankful that Josh was there by my side. At one point, he returned from the bathroom, angry that I had not told him that he still had makeup all over his face. Even though I was in pain, I still found it comical that he had been wondering all night why the hospital staff was treating us like a couple. Upon my release, I was given medication and told to go home, where I would need to rest for a couple of weeks.

Back then, I was still in the habit of answering the door when I heard someone knocking and continually paid the consequences. On December 12, 1997, I again made the mistake of going to the door and, as a result, received two more grand jury subpoenas. One of the subpoenas called me to testify again before the same grand jury in Portland, led by Stephen Peifer. The second commanded me to produce any materials and/or objects belonging to me or the Liberation Collective organization that related in any way to the three incidents listed on the subpoena, which together had caused over $1.5 million in damages: "(1) The November 29-30, 1997, trespass, burglary, and fire at the US Bureau of Land Management Wild Horse Corral in Harney County, Oregon; (2) The July 21, 1997, trespass, burglary, and fire at the Cavel West, Inc., facility in Redmond, Deschutes County, Oregon; and (3) The May 30, 1997, trespass, burglary, and 'mink release' at the Arritola Mink Farm, in Mt. Angel, Marion County, Oregon." The subpoenas demanded my appearance in court on a date that was less than a week away.

I called Assistant US Attorney Peifer to once again ask for the court date to be delayed, again on the grounds that I needed time to obtain and consult an attorney. My request was immediately denied. On the advice of Weiss, whom I had again contacted as soon as I received the subpoenas, I faxed a copy of my delay request in writing to the US Attorney's office. Unfortunately, this too was denied.

Meanwhile, as the appearance date approached, Weiss mentioned to me that it might be a good idea to file a couple of motions in federal court to try to fight the subpoena. He told me that the court should have to inform me whether or not illegal electronic surveillance had been used to gather the information that led to my subpoenas being signed. If this was the case, my subpoenas would be void. So, after Weiss faxed me samples of motions to disclose illegal electronic surveillance and to quash the subpoena, I spent the next few days typing my own motions in some semblance of legal format. On December 16, one day before I was commanded to testify, I put forth my motions in federal court. I couldn't help but think the clerks there who received my motion requests thought I was an idiot. Early the next morning, the Court Clerk called and told me my motions had been denied and I was still required to appear.

Later that morning, another demonstration was held outside the US Courthouse in Portland. I had made up my mind that I would not even go into the Courthouse but would protest the continued harassment I felt from the federal government. At 11:00 A.M., BATF agent Comrey emerged from the building and asked me if I was planning on going up to testify.

"It's 11:00 A.M., Mr. Rosebraugh. Do you plan on going up to testify?" he asked.

"No," I replied, standing on the sidewalk near the road with an "ABOLISH GRAND JURIES" sign.

Comrey went back into the Courthouse only to reappear ten minutes later.

"Mr. Rosebraugh, Assistant US Attorney Stephen Peifer is commanding you to appear in the grand jury room to testify. Now are you going to come and testify?"

"As I told you before, no." I could see the anger building inside of him.

Once again, Comrey went back inside the building but returned immediately, accompanied by a US Marshal. They came directly over to me, handcuffed me, and told me and the crowd of demonstrators that I was going to be held in contempt. At that point, they walked me into the Courthouse and frisked me in the lobby. *That's it*, I thought, *it's over*. I was pleased that I had been able to hug Elaine at the start of the protest—who knew when I would see her again?

Once inside the building, still handcuffed, I was transported to the second floor in the prisoner elevator and taken into a courtroom. Inside, Assistant US Attorney Peifer, US Marshals, BATF agent Comrey, and a court reporter were all present. I did not realize at the time that this must have been the equivalent of my contempt hearing, a process that is supposed to be open to the public. Soon a judge entered the room and, still in handcuffs, I was told to sit down at a table near Peifer. The judge immediately asked me why I was refusing to testify.

"I have three reasons why I am refusing to testify," I told him. "The first is that I was only given three business days—from the time the subpoenas were delivered until the time I was commanded to appear—to obtain and consult with an attorney. That is not enough time. My understanding of the law is that I am required to have at least five business days. Secondly, I put forth motions yesterday in this Courthouse requesting disclosure of illegal electronic surveillance, and I feel I have a right to an answer before the proceedings begin. The judge who considered the motions dismissed them without providing any answer to the question of whether illegal electronic surveillance was used to obtain information for my subpoenas. I feel this matter should be resolved. The last reason I am refusing to testify is that I was recently hospitalized with pericarditis and am in no condition to sit through a grand jury inquisition."

Needless to say, the judge did not find any of these reasons valid enough to excuse me from testifying. He immediately ordered the US Marshals to take me down to the grand jury room, where I would be forced to sit through more questioning. After traveling back down in the prisoner elevator, I was led into the grand jury room and seated in a chair at the front. The US Marshals then took off my handcuffs and waited outside in the hall with the other BATF and FBI agents.

This was a brand new Federal Courthouse, and I found the atmosphere even worse than before. Not only was I back in front of this group of people who had been led to dislike me, but the lighting in the room was unbelievably oppressive. I was in what felt like a spotlight with Peifer, while the light elsewhere in the room was so dim that I had a difficult time making out the faces of the jury. This was a spectator sport—one in which I had not chosen to participate. What made matters even worse was a long, buffet-style table positioned by the wall behind Peifer, to my right. It was completely full of holiday cookies, cakes, and other treats for the grand jury to consume during the proceedings—no doubt paid for once again by taxpayers. All through the session, jurors were busily stuffing their faces as I was put under the grill.

As soon as I sat down and the room was cleared of the US Marshals, Peifer began the questions. This time, except for maybe two questions (I answered my name and gave them a definition of the term *vegan*), I consistently took the Fifth Amendment. I figured I was already going to be held in contempt, so why should I respond at all?

After an hour of questioning, Peifer asked me for the materials I had been ordered to bring. I told him that the only items either I or Liberation Collective had were copies of the press releases concerning the two ALF actions and one ELF action. I hadn't brought them, I told Peifer, because I knew he already had copies of them. I had noticed them sitting on his table as he was showing me copies of my sent and received email correspondence.

Peifer then reminded me that I had been commanded to bring all copies of any relevant materials. He said that if I was willing to go and get the copies and be back in a couple of hours, I would then be free to leave and would not be held in contempt. Aside from going along with the process of the grand jury proceeding, I didn't see the harm in producing items that were already public and in the hands of the authorities. It was obvious that any items would be scanned for fingerprints and other clues, but I was 100 percent certain that the copies were clean. So I agreed and was released to retrieve the items.

Upon my return just over an hour later, I was led back into the grand jury room, where I sat through another fifteen minutes of questioning to which I again pleaded the Fifth. To my disbelief, Peifer then excused me for the day, informing me that I might be called back yet again. As I walked out the front doors of the Courthouse, I was met by a support group that was shocked and thrilled to see me.

As if all of the grand jury pressure thus far hadn't been enough, in January 1998, I received a fourth grand jury subpoena delivered by an FBI agent. This time, the subpoena commanded me to submit to fingerprinting by the FBI on or before January 28. After talking with Weiss, I immediately began working on a motion to quash this subpoena based on my belief that giving my fingerprints would be a violation of my Fifth Amendment protection against self-incrimination. On January 26, I submitted this motion in federal court. The next day, I received notice that my motion had been denied and I was still commanded to give my fingerprints or be subject to contempt charges.

Many states already had my fingerprints on file for past civil disobedience arrests, and I figured if I was arrested for contempt the FBI would instantly obtain a new full set anyway. So I reluctantly consented to the fingerprinting. At 9:00 A.M. on January 28, I was fingerprinted by Special Agent Daniel Feucht of the FBI in the US Marshal's office in the Federal Courthouse. An hour later, I walked out of the Courthouse hoping that would be the end of the grand jury pressure—and it was, at least for a short while.

FIRE ON THE MOUNTAIN

"For whatever reason, Vail won this one. They went through the process, jumped the hurdles and won. That's that. You play the game, and if you lose, you have to accept it. I guess all we can do is hope that the skiing will be good."

—Kevin Knappmiller, local Sierra Club representative, Frisco, Colorado[17]

hroughout 1997, Liberation Collective experienced a surge of interest from the local community. People were drawn to our multi-issue approach to social and political justice, our attempts to demonstrate the common bond between justice pursuits. As a result, the group continued to grow in size and at least a few of us, including myself, realized that it might be wise to move our base of operations from a private house into the public arena. I knew early on that attempting to run an organization out of a residential house was exclusionary and would limit the number of people who could become directly involved. An office in someone's home just doesn't sound as professional as one open to the public in a commercial setting, and those hesitant to come to an unfamiliar home for a meeting might feel a bit more at ease in a traditional office. An office would also serve as a more efficient lending library than the one we'd been maintaining at the Cleveland House for Collective volunteers who might happen to come over. And after the owner of the Cavel West horse slaughterhouse had called me at home, accusing me of burning down his building, the organization also just seemed a bit too close to my personal life. Despite our lack of finances, for the health of the organization and the sanity of all of us living at the Cleveland house, I became increasingly motivated to figure out how we could obtain an office. Late in the year, on my way to downtown Portland, I noticed a "for lease" sign in a window in Old Town. It was at street level, across from an alternative clothing and record store and a historic local music venue. The storefront was directly on Northwest Burnside Street, the busy dividing mark between the north and south

---

17 Robert S. Boynton, "Powder Burn," *Outside Magazine*, January 1999.

side of town. This block also had a radical history that included Wobbly activity and, in the early 1990s, an anarchist riot.

Could there be a better location in town?

The available space was approximately 1,200 square feet and was going for $750 a month. While I knew that Liberation Collective on its own could not have afforded this rate, $750 per month was incredibly cheap for a street-level storefront in downtown Portland. After talking it over with a few of the Collective members, I quickly began contacting other local organizations to see if they would be interested in sharing the office. As luck would have it, two other organizations were searching for office space as well.

After discussion of the joint venture, both Cascadia Forest Alliance and the Oregon Wildlife Federation Collective agreed to share the office with Liberation Collective. In theory, it seemed like this relationship would not only be mutually beneficial in providing office space for all three groups but also could serve to create a well-rounded activist space that was open and accessible to the public. All three organizations focused on issues that, different though they were, fit in some way under the "justice pursuit" umbrella.

Cascadia Forest Alliance (CFA) was Portland's premiere grassroots forest defense organization. At the time, CFA was working on a campaign to stop the Eagle Creek Timber Sale on Mt. Hood, in an area near Estacada, Oregon. Their expertise on forest and timber issues would be an asset to any diverse activist space in the Pacific Northwest. The Oregon Wildlife Federation Collective (OWFC) was a canvassing group that went door to door throughout the Portland area raising money for both the Oregon Wildlife Federation parent group and the Collective's own activities. OWFC focused primarily on wildlife issues, which complemented the work of CFA and brought an added importance to the new office. It seemed that both organizations would only add to the strength of Liberation Collective.

Although the Liberation Collective had dabbled in human rights and environmental issues, we had devoted most of our time and energy to animal rights causes. Our new relationship with these two other groups would provide a central location where the public could go to acquire information on or become involved with forest, wildlife, and/or animal issues. The move was also expected to further demonstrate the motto of Liberation Collective—"linking social justice movements to end all oppression." Our new combined office space would enable us to really walk the walk.

All three groups moved into the new space in January and February 1998. For the first six months, the mood was energetic, as many of us sought ways—from decorating the space with Che Guevera, Zapatista, and Earth First! shirts and other merchandise to hanging an enormous street sign on the exterior of the building to filling the shelves with magazines and free literature—to make the office accessible, educational, and inspiring not only for the members of all three groups, but for visitors as well. Liberation Collective volunteers, including myself, also attempted to turn the new office into a community organizing space for all Portland activists. Feeling tired and frustrated at the lack of communication and cooperation between various organizations, we attempted to make the new office a resource for event coordination as well as a clearinghouse for local campaign information. We even went as far as to donate the back wall of the office for a giant community calendar. When planning events, groups could call the office or stop in and check the calendar to see what else was scheduled during or around the same time.

The public, likewise, could stop in or call and receive information on Portland area meetings, protests, and other justice-related activities. Although we made a sincere attempt at bringing together various facets of the community, our efforts were not hugely successful, since we failed to convince other organizations of the necessity of our community calendar. Indymedia, to a certain extent, would serve as a much more effective organizing tool in years to come.[18]

While the relationship between the three organizations inside the office was never as close as I would have liked, there

18 Indymedia (www.indymedia.org) is a primarily web-based global network of non-hierarchical cooperatively run independent news resources.

were honest attempts made by all three groups to work together. This was not always an easy task since, despite our shared politics, we differed from one another on questions of strategy. At first, my public defense of the ALF and ELF, with the backing of Liberation Collective, was not an issue in our office relations, perhaps because of the break in activity during the first part of 1998. As the year progressed, ideological differences regarding strategy quickly sparked hostile relations, creating friction in the office.

Vail Is Burning

In the early morning hours of June 21, 1998, the ELF and the ALF together destroyed two Animal Damage Control buildings in Olympia, Washington. The fires cost an estimated $1.5 million in lost research along with $400,000 in structural damage. Just one week after the Olympia fires, the ELF claimed another action on the opposite shore of the continent. At the Mexican Consulate in Boston, the ELF painted blood-red handprints on the walls, spilled pools of red paint on the ground, and painted "VIVA EZLN" (Zapatista Army of National Liberation) on the entrance to the building. The communiqué stated that the ELF had targeted the consulate in response to the Mexican government's war against the people of Chiapas.

On July 4, 1998, the ELF once again joined the ALF for a daylight raid at United Vaccines Laboratories and Research Farms in Middleton, Wisconsin, cutting holes in the fence to release 310 ferrets and mink. Equipment and windows were smashed, and "INDEPENDENCE DAY FOR FUR FARM PRISONERS" was painted at the scene. The ELF/ALF communiqué claiming responsibility for the action stated that United Vaccines's primary purpose was to research ways to decrease losses from fur farms.

Three months later, on October 28, 1998, five thousand animals were freed from their cages by the ELF at the Upper Peninsula Pipkorn Mink Farm in Menominee County, Michigan. "This act was not done in front of us, in daylight hours, but rather during one of the darkest, foggiest nights of the year," owner Carol Pipkorn stated in a letter printed after the action in local newspapers.[19] "These criminals had stealthily cased our property using airplanes and scouting techniques."

While the ELF was definitely increasing its momentum and expanding its geographical reach, one action taken by the group that year still stands out as the most remarkable to date. It would quickly gain the ELF international attention and exposure in the news media and further amplify the debate within the environmental movement over tactics.

At that time, the Cleveland House had broken up and all of us had gone our separate ways as far as living quarters were concerned. While Leslie and Vanessa moved into a shared house in Southeast Portland, I found a cheap one-bedroom apartment in a polluted and semi-industrial area of town. Even though I had enjoyed living in a cooperative household, I couldn't help but feel thrilled to be on my own. Yet one aspect of this new experience was unwelcome, to say the least: I began to notice some of my belongings disappearing from the apartment. The first item to disappear was my personal phone and address book, which I always kept in the same location. Suddenly, it was gone, and as I looked around for signs of intrusion I found nothing. I thought carefully and only became more certain that I had left the address book in its usual spot the day before. Nothing else in the apartment had been touched or taken.

Now that I was living alone, and in a state of heightened awareness and slight paranoia thanks to my experience with the FBI and BATF, the one thing I always made sure to do before I left the apartment was to check that all the doors were locked. Yet on two occasions I arrived home to find the back door either unlocked or completely open. On these occasions I could not detect any items missing from the apartment, so whoever the intruder was did not fit the profile of a common thief. My only hypothesis for all of these events involved law enforcement or even the possibility of industry-backed detectives. Perhaps they believed they would find the gold mine of ALF and ELF membership lists inside the address book. Perhaps they wanted

---

19 Tom and Carol Pipkorn, "ELF Terrorism in Michigan," National Animal Interest Alliance website, www.naiaonline.org/body/articles/archives/pipkorn.htm.

to mess with my head and trick me into panicking and making a mistake that would reveal the entire global network of direct-action participants. Or perhaps they were clueless and grasping at extremely small straws. Whatever the case, these intrusions were unnerving, to say the least.

My paranoia reached new heights when I checked my email from home on October 21. After scanning a few of the messages, my eyes fixated on one in particular. When I opened it, my jaw dropped.

On behalf of the lynx, five buildings and four ski lifts at Vail were reduced to ashes on the night of Sunday, October 18th. Vail, Inc. is already the largest ski operation in North America and now wants to expand even further. The 12 miles of roads and 885 acres of clearcuts will ruin the last, best lynx habitat in the state. Putting profits ahead of Colorado's wildlife will not be tolerated. This action is just a warning. We will be back if this greedy corporation continues to trespass into wild and unroaded areas. For your safety and convenience, we strongly advise skiers to choose other destinations until Vail cancels its inexcusable plans for expansion.

Earth Liberation Front (ELF)

Holy shit! I muttered to myself over and over as I stared at the message, my heart racing. I had heard the news about Vail burning a couple of days before, but I couldn't have been more surprised at this communiqué. I instantly knew it was the largest act that the ELF, or the ALF, for that matter, had ever been involved with. Without any further hesitation, I began writing a press release and prepared to send out the message across the United States. Though I had no way of knowing it at this point, the statement had also been sent to a few other locations.

Before I even finished faxing the news releases to media outlets, the calls from reporters began piling up. I quickly learned this was going to be the largest news story I had ever helped to publicize and would provoke interest from media internationally.

Before I started dealing with the media circus, I attempted to find out all I could, as quickly as possible, about Vail and the motives behind this sizable arson attack.

It turns out Vail was no stranger to controversy; its proposed expansion had already turned local Colorado communities against the corporation. Vail was seen by many—from local merchants to environmentalists to residents tired of watching the pristine landscape continually disappear—as an aggressor, plotting its imperial expansion only to add to its already ridiculously high revenues. The battle to stop the expansion had been going on for years.

In August 1996, the US Forest Service had approved an expansion of Vail into a location known as CAT (Category) III, south of the existing ski area. The proposed development was to include construction of four new lifts, 885 acres of ski runs, 12.2 miles of service roads, and a new restaurant. A large portion of this expansion was to be built on land that made up the Two Elk Roadless area, the only roadless location in the vicinity. While the surrounding area was already heavily developed, including the I-70 freeway, the Shrine Pass area, the towns of Vail and Miniturn, and the Vail ski area, the Two Elk Roadless Area was the last place available for wildlife and even human solitude.

In October 1996, a coalition of Colorado environmental groups announced that they had appealed the Forest Service's approval of the expansion. The coalition included the Colorado Environmental Coalition (CEC), the Rocky Mountain Chapter of the Sierra Club, the Southern Rockies Ecosystem Project, the Biodiversity Legal Foundation, the Colorado Wildlife Federation, and Ancient Forest Rescue. The coalition submitted an official request that the Rocky Mountain Regional Forester, Elizabeth Estill, overturn the White River National Forest Supervisor's decision to approve the expansion.

The CAT III area contained a diverse mix of species, including marten, golden-crowned kinglet, boreal owl, olive-sided flycatcher, and many others. Altogether, CAT III was home to an estimated seventy-two species of mammals, 202 species of birds, and five amphibian species—but the real controversy concerned the Canadian lynx.

Arguing that the Forest Service had not adequately addressed the possible impact of the proposed expansion on the lynx habitat, representatives from the coalition maintained that Vail's plans could destroy the last of the Canadian lynx. Even Dr. Gary Koehler, considered by the Forest Service to be one of the leading lynx experts nationwide, believed that Vail's expansion could destroy lynx in Colorado and would at least "hamper lynx recovery efforts" in the area.[20] He said that the expansion would likely destroy some of the best habitat for lynx in the state, noting that most of the sightings in Colorado have been in the area around Vail.

Proponents of Vail's expansion responded to these arguments with the assertion that there was not sufficient evidence that any lynx were in the area or had been in the vicinity for quite some time. Even government agencies insisted that the lynx had not been seen in the Vail area since 1973. Yet documents obtained through the Freedom of Information Act (FOIA) revealed that the Canadian lynx had been observed in the CAT III area as recently as 1992. Furthermore, DNA samples that were taken from hair collected in the area tested positive for lynx.

The environmental groups fighting Vail weren't the only ones opposed to the expansion. Although Vail would have liked to believe the public was behind them in their development, this couldn't have been farther from the truth. Citizen comments received by the US Forest Service in 1997 ran eighty to one in opposition to the expansion.[21]

Vail Resorts, Inc., was not primarily concerned with their encroachment on the Two Elk Roadless Area or the devastation that would come as an inevitable result. Rather, Vail was concerned with increasing its revenues and further driving up real estate prices in the surrounding area. Jeff Berman of Ancient Forest Rescue argued in March 1998 that the expansion "has nothing to

20 "Opponents of Vail Ski Expansion Label Project a 'Cat Killer,'" Colorado Environmental Coalition press release, October 8, 1996.
21 Gretchen Biggs, "Arson isn't all that's wrong on Vail Mountain," *Colorado Central Magazine*, December 1998.

do with skiing. This is about increasing the value of nearby real estate so they can sell it."[22] Representatives of Vail never disputed this fact; even their annual report noted that improvements made in ski facilities would raise the value of its real estate.

During the second week of October 1998, a federal court in Colorado ruled in favor of Vail Resorts, giving the corporation the green light to proceed with the expansion. Legal tactics had failed, and some environmentalists felt all they could do was shake hands with Vail and admit defeat. Kevin Knappmiller, a local Sierra Club representative in Frisco, Colorado, told *Outside Magazine*,

> I guess I am a fundamentally legalistic kind of person who believes in the country and the laws it is based on. For whatever reason, Vail won this one. They went through the process, jumped the hurdles and won. That's that. You play the game, and if you lose, you have to accept it. I guess all we can do is hope that the skiing will be good.[23]

I wonder just how much of Sierra Club's massive donor base realizes the group likens environmental protection to playing a game. Probably as few as realize that, near the end of 2002, the environmental group publicly supported the use of US force in Iraq.

When the legal efforts to stop Vail's expansion were finally defeated, the local grassroots contingency prepared for a battle in the forest. Members of Ancient Forest Rescue made plans to interfere with and disrupt Vail's work crews, hoping to prevent them from logging the site. The activists began camping out in the expansion area, monitoring Vail's preparations and planning their resistance. They were set to move in and block access roads as soon as the work crews attempted to bring logging and construction equipment up the mountain. Fifteen or so activists, camping in and monitoring the Vail area, were playing a waiting game after which they hoped their efforts would prove more successful than the court battles. On the night of October 18,

22 Dustin Solberg, "Locals Protest Vail Expansion," *High Country News*, March 30, 1998.
23 Boynton, "Powder Burn."

AFR members were camped on the mountain, with a scout down below, waiting to see if Vail would begin work the following day.

On their scanners the next morning, the AFR crew heard bits and pieces about a fire on the mountain and emergency crews on the scene. Soon they, and the rest of the nation, would learn that Vail had been targeted for an arson attack. Seven fires set over a one-mile distance along a ridgeline had destroyed three buildings and damaged two more in addition to four ski lifts. The targeted structures included Vail's Two Elk Lodge and Patrol Headquarters. Feeling vulnerable, Ancient Forest Rescue sent out a press release within hours, clarifying the organization's position. The statement appeared as follows on Monday, October 19, 1998:

Ancient Forest Rescue Activists Adhere to Strict Nonviolence Code, Including Repudiation of Damage to Persons, Property, or Wildlife

Vail, Colorado. Ancient Forest Rescue (AFR) has been active in opposing Vail Resort's "CAT III" expansion over the last year, as it would destroy the Two Elk Roadless Area. AFR activists and local opponents have been monitoring Vail Resort's expansion for violations of their permit granted by the US Forest Service.

We have heard from media reports that today's fire atop the ski mountain may have been caused by arson. AFR strictly adheres to a code of nonviolence, including repudiation of damage to persons, property, or wildlife. If the fire atop Vail Mountain was indeed arson, such an act is completely against AFR's code of nonviolence.

AFR opposes the Vail CAT III expansion; we have and will continue to do so in an exclusively nonviolent manner. AFR's nonviolent code includes repudiation of physical, verbal, or other assaults; preclusion of contributing to escalation of violence by police, workers, management, or bystanders; and preclusion of property damage. This code also includes absolute opposition to any activity that has even the slightest potential for harm to human beings, their property, or wildlife.

AFR is not opposed to reliance on the skiing of Vail Mountain for the community's economic health and recreation for the public. AFR is committed to the communities of the Vail Valley, and will remain so through these difficult times.

Obviously, AFR members felt the need to immediately distance themselves from the fires. Some of them had been on the mountain that night, and all of them had comprised the most radical opposition facing Vail prior to October 19. AFR certainly knew they would be the first group pressured in the ensuing arson investigation.

As rapidly as the flames had engulfed Vail, federal agents swarmed over the area. Dozens of FBI and BATF agents converged on the crime scene, a motley crew that included investigators who had worked the Oklahoma City and 1993 World Trade Center crime scenes. With this considerable law enforcement presence on location at Vail, one would have expected any evidence to have been collected and indictments quickly returned. Yet it seems the first move investigators made was to place pressure on the local environmentalists.

On October 20, just one day after the fires, the FBI telephoned the family of an AFR activist to ask where he had been on the night of October 18. Thus began a months-long period of ongoing harassment of local students and AFR activists. AFR member Ben Doon wrote about the intense and hostile atmosphere faced by local environmentalists shortly after the Vail arson.

FBI agents approached two women who work for a University environmental group. When they refused to cooperate, their supervisor was questioned. He was asked by the feds why the girls wouldn't cooperate. He replied, "because they fear COINTELPRO, the FBI's policy used against radicals. When the meeting ended, the feds stated, "You can tell those girls we are not going away."

A few weeks later, the FBI began snooping around another corner of the state and probed into the lives of other university students. One woman became the target of serious intimidation and isolation. Agents approached her friends; her boss was questioned for three hours, and her professors were visited. Her environmental ethics professor was asked to produce all the papers the woman handed in during the semester. The feds insinuated she was a terrorist and wanted to know about her lifestyle. After all that, they finally knocked on her door."[24]

After three months of this badgering, federal agents began issuing grand jury subpoenas to local environmentalists in January 1999. Since I had received a copy of the communiqué and had represented the ELF in numerous news articles, I wasn't pleased to hear of a grand jury investigation in Colorado. I began to expect the dreaded subpoena.

Local Activists Stand in the Way

The grand jury subpoenas called on specific activists to testify on January 28, 1999. One of these activists, who had actually received the first subpoena, was served in Boston while visiting her parents for the holidays. Doon writes, "They (FBI) followed her while she dropped her mom off at work and approached her while she was taking garbage to the dump, wearing only pajamas and an overcoat." Several subpoenaed young activists agreed to cooperate with the grand jury during this time. Thankfully, for the sake of the those who set Vail on fire, these few activists must not have had any pertinent information to share.

Through the spring and summer that year, federal agents continued to harass local environmentalists. AFR even began to declare publicly that the organization believed the Vail arson investigation was politically motivated and geared toward disrupting the lives of activists. But AFR and other grassroots environmentalists didn't let the pressure stop them from continuing their work against Vail.

Vail had scheduled the cutting for the expansion to commence on July 1, 1999. Knowing this, activists planned to use every tool they could think of in their nonviolence toolbox to prevent the development. Just before sunrise they erected a thirty-foot tripod

---

24 Ben Doon, "Vail Arson: Colorado Activists Face Grand Jury," *Earth First! Journal*, Brigid 1999.

over an access road where one activist, referred to as "Bobcat," hung from the top.

In response, the US Forest Service and Vail called in a cherry picker to get Bobcat down so they could dismantle the tripod. But when the cherry picker reached the site, a man known as "Mookie" locked himself to the axle with a U-lock. After Mookie was cut and taken away, another activist, Emily Wolf, stepped in and locked herself to the cherry picker's basket with a lockbox.

For five days this display of nonviolent action tied up the access road as other activists took turns with the blockades. Unfortunately, there was more than one access road, and Vail, in the meantime, was successful in bringing most of its required equipment up through this alternative route. In response, the activists positioned what they called a "batmobile" on the back access road.

On July 6, Earth First! activist "Opie" locked himself to the upside-down van that served as a roadblock. With both access roads blocked, law enforcement quickly moved in. Thirty-eight Forest Service and law enforcement officers, dressed in full camouflage, raided the blockades early the next morning. The police placed a closure on the area and arrested seven people. Within a few short hours, all the activists who were locked to the cherry picker and the van, and suspended from the tripod, were cut free and taken into custody. Vail once again had come out victorious.

But on July 21, the activists returned, erecting a tree-sit at eleven thousand feet. While "Moonshadow" occupied the tree-sit, the Forest Service responded with floodlights, generators, and heavy machinery to force her out of the tree. After being taken from the tree, arrested, and later released, Moonshadow related her experience.

> My removal from eighty feet up in the spruce tree was one of the scariest moments of my life. Trees fell within five feet of my platform. After the feller-buncher downed all the trees
>
> close to me, the operator cut trees further away and dropped them right next to me. I begged law enforcement

to intervene, but they ignored my pleas, stating that I was perfectly safe and that the feller-buncher was highly accurate.

Logging was again halted two days later, but this time not because of environmentalists. On July 23, the Army Corps of Engineers stopped any further logging after discovering that Vail had constructed a road illegally through a rare forested wetland. The Environmental Protection Agency (EPA) considered this a clear violation of the Clean Water Act.

This antagonistic atmosphere likely contributed to further local repression by the Feds. In September 1999, more subpoenas were issued to AFR activists. But this time around, the prosecuting attorney would not have as much luck with cooperating witnesses. AFR activist Kirsten Atkins stonewalled the grand jury by refusing to provide any names at the US Attorney's Office's request. Witnessing Atkins's resolve to stand up to the grand jury system, other subpoenaed activists followed in her footsteps.

In response, the US Attorney's Office moved for contempt charges to be filed against four AFR members. All four were facing contempt hearings during the week of November 15. During the same week, five more AFR activists had been subpoenaed to testify. As the local environmental and civil rights community in Colorado prepared for what appeared to be inevitable jail support, Assistant US Attorney Kenneth Buck made a surprising move. On November 17, he informed the four activists that he did not intend to pursue contempt charges against them. The contempt pursuit was called off, as Buck believed that the four activists had no relevant information to aid in the investigation.

The seven fires set by the ELF on the night of Sunday, October 18 caused at least $12 million in damages. Yet, sources from the grand jury investigation suggested that the damages were more than twice what was reported to the news media. In either case, at the time, this was the costliest act of eco-sabotage in the history of the country.

As is unfortunately common after extreme acts such as property destruction, some local and even national environmentalists were quick to condemn the arson as the work of those attempting to discredit "the movement." Many, including Daniel Glick in his 2001 book, *Powder Burn*, argue that the fires could have been set by a variety of interests with varying motives. *Powder Burn*, which focuses specifically on the mystery surrounding the Vail controversy, even makes a strong case for Vail itself. The corporation's expansion plans were extremely unpopular, and what better way to rally public support than by becoming a target of radical, "extremist" tactics? Indeed, after the fires, a great number of those opposed to the expansion rallied in support of the corporation.

Additionally, Vail would have millions of dollars in insurance money to rebuild their structures—including Two Elk Lodge—bigger and better than before. And, indeed, in just over a year, on Christmas Eve 1999, Vail completed and opened the new, larger, $10 million Two Elk Lodge.

What benefits, then, did the ELF arson strike on Vail have? What did it accomplish? Critics of the ELF were quick to point the finger at direct action supporters after Vail not only continued with its expansion but rebuilt the torched structures even larger. In analyzing this particular case, it is necessary to keep in mind that years of work, sizable amounts of money, and other resources were poured into the legal opposition to Vail's expansion. These efforts also ultimately failed on their own to stop Vail. In addition, as AFR proved again in 1999, the grassroots civil disobedience actions also failed to create enough pressure to stop Vail. The sheer size and power of the Vail corporation seemed to render every method ineffectual; a "by any means necessary" approach appeared to be the last option.

Since Vail was expanding for one reason, financial gain, the ELF recognized that only by targeting the corporation's finances would the effort to stop the expansion stand any chance of success. While the seven fires did not ultimately prove to be enough to convince Vail to stop the project, the action is not to blame as much as the lack of additional radical acts and support for direct action.

While it is true that Vail's insurance protected it from suffering the bulk of the monetary losses, I would be surprised to find any insurance company in the world that could suffer a loss of over $12 million and not raise its premium rates. In theory, if additional acts of property destruction were committed against the same corporation, or even a corporation in a similar industry, insurance firms would have an increasingly difficult time supplying coverage. By far, the most effective outcome of the Vail arson attack was the public education that came as a result. Prior to the fires, the effort to stop the expansion was extremely localized in the Colorado area. Few people besides the local residents and the groups involved knew of the intense battle being waged for the CAT III and the Two Elk Roadless Area. After the 1998 blaze, people across the country and even outside the US had heard of the controversy surrounding Vail and the issue of expansion or over-development into natural habitat.

Jasper Carlton, himself a part of the legal resistance since the beginning, argued one month after the arson, "We don't know what the motives were. But what did it accomplish? It elevated the industrial-recreation issue from a local issue to a national issue. People are talking about it all over the country. Now it's going to be pursued."[25]

Fortunately or not, repercussions from the Vail arson were felt in activist communities across the United States. The sheer size of the action was so controversial that the Vail fires were cited for the following decade in arguments over whether property destruction is morally and strategically acceptable. Back in Portland, the fires at Vail, and my role in helping to promote the ELF's statement of responsibility, immediately created tension in the office shared by Liberation Collective, Oregon Wildlife Federation Collective, and Cascadia Forest Alliance. While the subject was rarely discussed between the different organizations, the frequent rumors and "he said, she said," and a growing hostility in the atmosphere, slowly led to a restructuring of the entire space. It became apparent that, as in Colorado, environmental groups in Portland disapproved of

25 Ron Baird, "Vail fires shed light on controversy," *Boulder Planet*, November 18–24, 1998.

the Vail action. Before long, both CFA and OWFC had moved out, and in early 1999, Liberation Collective took over the entire office. We quickly created a new twenty-foot-wide sign and nailed it to the front of the building. It read, "LIBERATION COLLECTIVE—CENTER FOR REVOLUTION."

5

TIMBER
IN THE
NORTHWEST

"To celebrate the holidays we decided on a bonfire. Unfortunately for US Forest Industries it was at their corporate headquarters office.

On the foggy night after Christmas when everyone was digesting their turkey and pie, Santa's ELFs dropped two five-gallon buckets of diesel/unleaded mix and a gallon jug with cigarette delays; which proved to be more than enough to get this party started.

This was in retribution for all the wild forests and animals lost to feed the wallets of greedy fucks like Jerry Bramwell, USFI president. This action is payback and it is a warning to all others responsible, we do not sleep and we won't quit."

—Communiqué released by the ELF taking responsibility for burning the US Forest Industries office in Medford, Oregon, on December 27, 1998

*A*fter dealing with the enormous media response from the Vail arson, I felt more than ready for at least a short break. My prayers were unexpectedly answered by Elaine's brother, Glen, who asked us if we wanted to come and visit him just after Christmas in San Francisco. He would be there attending a convention and would have extra room in his hotel suite if we wanted to make the trip south for a few days. Elaine and I were delighted to accept the offer.

On December 26, 1998, Elaine and I set out in my truck for San Francisco. While my trips to San Francisco—and even to Los Angeles—usually averaged about a day's drive, this was supposed to be at least a mini-vacation, so we gladly took a bit more time. We stopped for the night in Ashland, the quaint, artsy southern Oregon town that many consider the halfway point between Portland and the Bay Area. The scene couldn't have been more romantic. A fresh snowfall lined the few downtown streets, and the community came out at night and enjoyed the festive and decorative atmosphere. Ironically, as Elaine and I were relaxing and breathing in the fresh mountain air, just twelve miles away in the city of Medford, persons unknown were lighting up the winter sky.

Elaine and I woke up early and continued our trip south, unaware of the sizable law enforcement presence that would converge on Medford later that morning. In the early evening, we arrived in the Union Square area of San Francisco and checked into the ritzy hotel where Glen was staying. Though I felt completely out of place in that setting, I appreciated the opportunity to simply relax, however briefly.

Upon arriving back in Portland the next week, I was shocked to read the news stories about a timber company office being burned to the ground in Medford the very same night Elaine and I had stayed nearby in Ashland. Confirming many people's suspicions, including my own, I received a communiqué from the ELF on January 16, 1999, claiming responsibility for torching the corporate headquarters of a timber company called US Forest Industries in Medford, Oregon. I knew by that time that the arson had destroyed at least $200,000 worth of property and caused an additional estimated $300,000 in structural damage to the building.

I was vaguely aware that US Forest Industries offices in Colorado had been targeted in the past by protesters, but I was not fully up to date on the specifics. In preparing the media release for the action, I learned exactly why this nearly unheard-of timber company had become so controversial. After sending out the release to various news agencies, I once again took on the role of the defender, explaining the motives and rationale behind this radical act.

The Culebra Range of the Sangre de Cristo Mountains, known locally as La Sierra, lies just outside San Luis, Colorado. A 77,500-acre ranch, then owned by North Carolina resident Zachary Taylor, dominates the Culebra Range and is home to the largest logging operation in the state. Early in 1998, Taylor released documents that indicated plans to log 210 million board feet from his land in the coming years. He estimated the profits from this massive operation would be over $73,000,000. The area designated for logging included a mixture of conifer, ponderosa, and pinion forests, some of which contain old growth trees.[26] US Forests Industries—the target of this latest ELF attack—held a timber contract with Taylor to log a portion of his land.

Residents of San Luis, including rancher Joe Gallegos, argued that Taylor's logging was devastating the mountain ecosystem with unsustainable forestry practices and unregulated road construction. After witnessing the landslides coming from the eroding hillsides caused by the logging operation, Gallegos declared, "The acequias [traditional irrigation ditches] are like the arteries of this community. When they become full with sediment from the logging, like cholesterol in our human arteries, they will cause a heart attack and kill this community."[27]

Many locals in San Luis were well aware that this was not the first time the Taylor family had angered the people of Mexican, Indigenous, and Spanish descent who lived in the valley before them. In San Luis, Chicano/a farmers practice a way of life that has sustained them for seven generations. Prior to the Taylors' arrival, the mountain region, including the Taylor Ranch property, was used as common land, which the locals relied on for fishing, hunting, firewood, and spiritual necessities. Then Jack Taylor came into the picture in the 1960s, purchasing the land and making it completely inaccessible to the people who had shared it for ages as a matter of survival.

In the late 1990s, a coalition of environmentalists, locals from San Luis, and Chicano activists joined together to stop the industrial logging of La Sierra. By engaging in a fierce grassroots organizing campaign, this group was slowly gaining support. Using a variety of nonviolent means, including outreach to the public, political pressure, litigation, and even nonviolent civil disobedience, the members of this coalition dedicated themselves to stopping the destruction of La Sierra.

One of the most confrontational points of this campaign came on January 12, 1998, when six coalition representatives attempted to shut down the US Forest Industries/South Forks Saw Mill. One person was locked to the arm of each of the

26 "Old growth" is defined as over 250 years old.
27 "Destruction at Taylor Ranch La Sierra: A Homeland in Peril," San Luis Ancient Forest Rescue Action Alert.

mill's two loaders, preventing them from being operated without risking the activists' lives. Additionally, one man locked his neck to a machine sixty feet above the ground, while another woman locked her arms to a separate machine just twenty feet below. After the fire department cut through the locks with a torch, six people were taken into custody and charged with trespassing.

Ancient Forest Rescue (AFR) also became involved with the coalition, and the grassroots battle on La Sierra continued on through 1998. Unfortunately, the coalition's hard work and devotion was proving insufficient to fight the multitude of corporations they faced, including US Forest Industries, Inner Mountain, Rio Grand Forest Products, and Southwest Mountain Resources.

Then, just before 1:00 A.M. on December 28, 1998, firefighters arrived at a blaze at the US Forest Industries corporate headquarters, located at 2611 Whittle Avenue in Medford, Oregon. Thanks to the efforts of some fifty firefighters, the fire was reportedly contained within ninety minutes; however, the mop-up operations continued into the morning. In a preliminary comment to the *Mail Tribune*, Jerry Bramwell, president of USFI, appeared calm, claiming that most of the company's key files were stored in other locations. He later admitted, "There are a tremendous amount of records that are ashes."[28]

Within hours of the fire, investigators were called to the scene from the FBI, BATF, Oregon State Police, and Medford Fire and Police Departments. Later that morning, as employees were arriving to work, Bramwell sent them to the company's White City mill office. While there had been an environmental protest at the USFI building earlier that year in May, Bramwell claimed he could not even begin to imagine why someone might torch his business. He stated, "We are not aware of a reason to take that kind of action. . . . To the best of our knowledge, things have settled down."[29]

This latest action only added to the ELF's growing reputation in the Pacific Northwest, perhaps the most prominent environmental hot spot in the nation, with a long history of public

28 David Preszler, "Arson Evidence Found," *Mail Tribune*, December 29, 1998.
29 Preszler, "Arson Evidence Found."

consciousness and action aimed at saving the land. To anyone who has lived or visited the area, the reasons for this concern are obvious. The land is beautiful and contains some of the last remaining unmanaged wilderness area in the country. For many years, much of the focus of the environmental movement has been centered here, an area that in the recent past has hosted such notables as the *Earth First! Journal*, the largest annual environmental law conference in the country (ELAW),[30] a host of local and national environmental protection organizations, and some of the most dramatic and active campaigns in the United States.

The Pacific Northwest is also home to some of the last remaining old growth forests in the country. The World Resources Institute has estimated that prior to the arrival of European Americans, between 6 and 7.6 million hectares of old growth spread throughout Oregon and Washington.[31] In the mid-1980s, the estimate dropped to between 1.3 and 1.8 million for the two states, and the amount continues to shrink.

The only question on the minds of many environmentalists is what action to take—what will stop the destruction of the land they rely on for food, water, clean air, and beauty? In response to this question, the members of the ELF had obviously made a conscious choice to step up the battle.

The Liberation Collective Goes on Tour

With the news of the US Forest Industries fire, I rode into 1999 on a wave of excitement and uncertainty about what the new year would bring. It was obvious to me that with the recent Vail action, and now USFI, the ELF was definitely gaining momentum. As I waited to see what would come next, and the media attention surrounding the latest arson slowly died down, I settled into my daily routine of working at the Liberation Collective office.

This was going to be a big year for Liberation Collective as we prepared to launch our most intense campaign yet, a summer-

---

30 Held annually at the University of Oregon and organized by Land, Air, Water, the student environmental law society there.
31 *Old-Growth Forest in the United States Pacific Northwest.* World Resources Institute, 1994.

long protest tour of the primate research centers in the United States. Based on our experiences from a 1997 tour of regional primate research centers, Rick Bogle and I came up with the idea to organize a caravan to travel around the country, ending with protests at the National Institutes of Health in Bethesda, Maryland, and at the Capitol in Washington, DC. Where the tour in 1997 had consisted of Rick merely sitting alone (or with me or another Liberation Collective volunteer) in front of each of the seven regional primate centers, this new plan would, we hoped, have hundreds of people at each stop, gaining media exposure and placing pressure on the entire animal research industry to end its fraudulent practices.

Liberation Collective had taken on the role of the primary organizing group for the tour, a workload that far surpassed our available workforce. But, after many long hours spent sending out national mailings, fundraising, and organizing the nearly thirty stops, we felt we would be ready for the kickoff, scheduled for June 1 in Seattle. As the days before the tour flew by, however, I noticed that my expectations for the campaign were far from being met. For one thing, the response, both from the general public and from the animal rights movement, was frustrating. Not only did very few people reply to our enormous mailings and national advertisements, but an even smaller number actually expressed an interest in taking part in the tour. Furthermore, of those who did express an interest in going along, most could only commit to a few stops. This reality was a far cry from my dream of a group of hundreds starting the tour in Seattle and growing city by city. I had envisioned thousands of people converging on the Capitol in DC and forcing the NIH (the main governmental funding agency for animal research in the US) to stop its primate experimentation.

Funding was also a major concern, as a campaign of this caliber would require sizable sums. After borrowing $5,000, I purchased what would become the main vehicle for the tour, a 1983 articulated bus in excellent running condition that had been part of the public transportation service in Portland. When I picked up this sixty-foot-long beast of a machine, I learned that the price had been so low because of the bus's size. With the original seats intact, the bus could hold seventy-two passengers, which I figured would be plenty of room for the tour. When we had ripped out most of the seats and built storage racks and sleeping lofts in their place, the bus was almost ready for action. As a last-ditch funding effort, Rick came up with the idea of selling advertising space on the sides of the bus to animal rights groups. Fortunately, this worked and became one of our main sources of finances.

Feeling as prepared as we were going to be, a few of us from Liberation Collective boarded the bus on June 1 and headed for the kickoff in Seattle. When we arrived, we found out that our intended camping location had fallen through, so I drove the bus into the city and parked in an industrial area near the University District. We set up camp on the side of the road, hoping that the police wouldn't mess with us and we would be able to keep out of sight. The latter, at least, was wishful thinking, as the long white bus with the huge "1999 PRIMATE FREEDOM TOUR" slogan on both sides stuck out ridiculously.

Later that day, at the opening ceremony inside a community building in the U-District, I was further disappointed. The one-hundred-plus people I had envisioned embarking on this tour turned out to be a mere thirty—or so it seemed when I first arrived. Then I discovered that most of those in attendance were local activists who would not be traveling with the group once the bus left the city. Nevertheless, through the opening sessions we went, detailing the itinerary and strategy for the tour.

By no means did we actually expect to stop primate experimentation in the United States by merely traveling around the country. Instead, we decided that there should be a primary goal of public education—both the scientific and moral arguments against the use of primates in experimentation. We felt this could be accomplished through a variety of means, including protesting, community meetings, leafleting, civil disobedience, and direct media exposure.

Part of our strategic approach with the media was to challenge each individual research facility to explain in detail what benefits their work had yielded that were applicable to human health. I knew that none of the facilities we would be visiting would be able to honestly claim any advancement directly useful to humans that they had produced through primate testing. The usual line of defense was something like "We engage in research, which is a process. We may conduct research that is then built upon by other scientists at other facilities until an advancement is made."

While it is an interesting argument I have repeatedly heard from these different institutions, there surely must be a final facility that comes forward with the end result, the breakthrough. This strategic line of questioning was successful in at least beginning to expose the myths associated with animal research.

The second media tactic we decided upon at the beginning of the tour was to challenge each facility to a public forum where members of the local community could come to hear both sides of the debate on animal experimentation to make an informed decision on their beliefs. I also knew full well that this was a win-win situation for us. If we continued to sincerely ask for a forum with each facility and were repeatedly denied, the animal research industry would begin to appear as if it had something to hide. However, if any institution accepted our offer, the public education such a debate could provide would be priceless. In my many years of dealing with the issue of animal experimentation I have only known of a few, very irregular occasions when researchers and facilities have actually engaged in public debates with the opposing side. In most of these episodes, the research industry failed to convince the public of the necessity of nonhuman animal-based testing and lost a great deal of credibility.

Our first stop on the tour, after the opening ceremonies, was the University of Washington, home of the Washington Regional Primate Research Center. As one of the eight main regional centers in the country (since the 1997 tour, the Southwest Foundation for Biomedical Research in San Antonio, Texas had been added to the list), this was a primary stop on the tour, and we spent four days targeting the facility with vigils, protests, press conferences, and demonstrations at the homes of researchers.

A highlight of the stop came when a dozen of us took over the dean's office on campus for twenty-four hours after he refused to accept our offer for a public forum. As daylight came, the group decided to leave the premises rather than be arrested, in order to continue our direct pressure on the dean. So, straight from the dean's office, we headed to his home, where we were met by news media and interested neighbors. Fearful of not living up to his "open door" policy at the university, the dean emerged from his house and was struck by a series of educated and directed questions—all in front of the television crews. He declined to answer them, and could not or would not tell the protesters and the press what benefits had ever come from primate research at the University of Washington.

Everyone present at this first stop was pleased with the progress and energy level of all involved, and I began to have a bit more hope for what might come during the tour in the next few months. As we continued on our way south, through Portland, Davis, and San Francisco, it became clear to me that while we (and I, personally) had worked hard organizing the necessities of the tour—where people would sleep, what we would eat, making sure we had enough money, etc.—major areas of preparation had been neglected. One item of crucial importance was personal dynamics. Out of pure ignorance, I had assumed that everyone on the tour would be motivated by a sincere and honest desire to do whatever it took, in a nonviolent sense, to progress the movement. While I had expected that some participants would have more activist experience or education on animal issues than others, I had not considered the possibility that not everyone would feel equal devotion to the cause. Many of the participants had honestly come to make a difference, but there also was a strong contingent of "free riders" who either wanted to travel purely for adventure and to party or wanted a free lift across the country. How to effectively deal with these distractions should have been a number one concern in the planning stages.

In retrospect, I believe that the lack of preparation in this and similar areas was one reason the tour did not achieve what we had hoped. Wanting to operate on as much of a consensus and cooperative basis as possible, those of us organizing the tour put very little thought and even less action into creating rules and guidelines, scheduling daily activities, and creating a general overview of what would be expected of each participant. While this sort of regulated approach may not have been popular with everyone, I found that it was needed to actually make the effort useful. The problem was, I realized this only after the tour had been underway for some time. After San Francisco, I hitched a ride back to Portland while the tour continued south and east into Phoenix, Arizona. It was tough leaving the group even for one stop, as I felt responsible for them, but I had to return to Oregon for my graduation from Marylhurst University. Immediately after the ceremony, I jumped into a friend's van and drove two and a half days to Alamogordo, New Mexico, the home of White Sands Missile Range, Holloman Air Force Base, the Coulston Foundation, and the next stop after Phoenix on the tour.

Upon my arrival in the desert, it became clear to me that in order to be effective and accomplish the goals of the tour, we would need much stronger discipline and a set routine of daily activities. I had no idea how difficult it would be to convince the other participants of this, and how much resistance I would face in trying to implement these changes. Throughout the southern stops on the tour (Texas, Louisiana, Mississippi, Georgia, South Carolina) I tried my hardest to empower and energize the participants to remain (or, in some cases, become) committed.

In Madison, Wisconsin, some two months into the journey, I noticed a renewed sense of energy on the tour. For me, the reason could have been that Elaine had finally joined us. For the first two-thirds of the trip, she had been unable to leave her job but had helped with the campaign from home, taking care of mail orders for shirts and literature. I was extremely happy to see her and to have her with us for the remaining month of the journey. For most of the participants, however, the intensified interest could have been at least partially due to the location of the center in Madison. While nearly all of the primate centers across the country are hidden from public view, the University of Wisconsin displays its Wisconsin Regional Primate Research Center in plain sight on the main campus in Madison. For probably the first time on the tour, participants could actually touch the buildings that housed thousands of primates. Perhaps this reality brought a final charge to the campaign.

In addition to the regular vigils, protests, and other ongoing events we would have at each stop, a civil disobedience action, which I hoped would energize the other participants, was planned for Madison. With a rented U-Haul truck parked to block access to the primate center, a Liberation Collective volunteer, Michael Brassell, locked his neck to the axle underneath the vehicle so that it could not be moved. The media response was decent (how many times do you get to see someone locked by his neck to the bottom of a U-Haul to save the monkeys?) and, for at least a brief period, this action seemed to spark an interest in even the free riders of the tour. It was a busy day for me, as I attempted to relay media interviews about the civil disobedience to our chosen spokesperson of the day (we routinely changed spokespersons to give everyone an opportunity to fill the position) while simultaneously giving an entirely different set of interviews regarding a mink release claimed by the ALF in the area on the same day.

So when the FBI and Madison State Police pulled the bus over as we were leaving Madison, I wasn't surprised. I had driven a hundred miles or so ahead in my truck, and as soon as I received the call on my cell phone about the stop, I pulled off the highway to wait and see if I needed to head back. (By this time on the tour, we had realized that we needed more vehicles than just the bus, which was very long and difficult to navigate, for errands and to scout ahead to make sure the bus wouldn't get stuck). As the bus was registered in my name, and I was the only one technically insured to drive it, I assumed there would be trouble. The Feds told the activists they had been pulled over because one of the bus tires was wearing thin. This was a wonderful educational experience for me, as I had been unaware until then that the FBI pulls over vehicles for having worn tires. After half an hour of questioning, the Feds and state police, remarkably, left, and the bus continued on its way toward Ann Arbor, Michigan.

Just over a month later, the caravan pulled into Washington, DC for the final four days of the exhausting campaign. Here, where I had originally hoped to see thousands of people gathering to protest animal experimentation, I was again let down and somewhat depressed. By this time, it seemed that most of the participants had given up trying or even hoping to make a difference with the tour. For myself, I had decided that just getting through the tour, just finishing this three-month-long mission, would be a test of my own discipline, patience, and tolerance. I knew full well that the tour had been far less successful than originally anticipated. I also accepted most of the responsibility for this failure because I had not insisted on doing the unpopular—coming up with a firm set of guidelines and rules before we left Seattle.

The last few events of the DC stop included a march on the Capitol and then a rally at the base of the Washington Monument. On many occasions, I had watched television footage or seen photographs of massive demonstrations in Washington for this or that cause, and I had imagined a similar scene for our march. I quickly learned that in DC, a group of a thousand or even ten thousand people can easily go unnoticed, not only on Capitol Hill but in all of the area media.

To me, the two hundred or so people who participated in our march looked more like a sightseeing group than a protest movement. As the march reached the steps of the Capitol, Leslie and I, and a few other people, continued walking up toward the building. Little did we know, the rest of the crowd had stopped about a hundred yards behind us—that now it was just the few of us and dozens of police. Within a few moments, we were down to four people, who were promptly taken into custody and arrested on disorderly conduct charges. It seemed very odd, since tourists continued to walk by the four of us up the stairs to the Capitol building, where we had been denied access for voicing political concerns. After a day in the DC Central Cell Block (by far the worst holding cells I have ever been in), we were all released.

Next came the rally that would officially end the tour. While the two hundred people in attendance displayed a warm show of support and appreciation for our efforts of the previous three months, it seemed almost embarrassing to me that this was the end, the place where all roads were supposed to lead, where thousands of people were to meet and celebrate success, and there were hardly more people than there had been in Seattle at the start. By far, the most interesting highlight of the day came when Leslie, Michael Brassell, and John Bachelor scaled the Washington Monument (at that time being renovated and surrounded by scaffolding) and dropped a banner against primate experimentation. After a tense standoff with Capitol police, the three were escorted down the monument, taken into custody, and housed at Central Cell Block for a couple of days.

When the tour was over, I tried to honestly critique its effectiveness. For all practical purposes, other than a few select news stories in the various cities we visited, I am skeptical at best that the lengthy mission was worthwhile (though I personally learned many valuable lessons about organizing and being prepared). One of the key problems, I believe, was our single-issue focus, our failure to demonstrate a sincere overall concern for all of society's injustices. It felt distasteful, regrettable, and simply wrong to drive into poverty-stricken areas of the country, where residents were fighting just for decent housing, health care, and food, and attempt to persuade locals to care about primate experimentation. Often, the participants seemed angry and incredulous at the dearth of activists from marginalized communities involved in the struggle to free the monkeys. However, there we were, this privileged group of overwhelmingly white young men and women, attempting to convert people to the cause of anti-vivisection—without taking on the entire political and social system that underlies not only vivisection, but also poverty and severe classism. It was a classic example of a privileged group of people arguing that "my morals or concerns are more important than yours," all the while remaining ignorant of why less privileged people are not rushing to agree with them.

Tensions Rise at Home

Back in Portland at Liberation Collective, we were facing similar difficulties, and my frustration from the tour transferred itself to the organization. Any social or political movement or organization must constantly evaluate and re-examine its strategies and tactics to ensure effectiveness and progress toward success, and, even before the tour, I asked myself daily how I could assist in creating a more organized and, therefore, more effective, social change organization. Now, as the group appeared to be quickly heading downhill, I pondered the question again.

I had to admit that our new public space had consumed the organization. Rather than assisting the group with its workload and public accessibility potential, the office had taken on a life of its own. Staffing and maintaining the HQ (as we often referred to it) began to play a dominant role, leaving community campaigns in a secondary position.

Additionally, personality conflicts were increasingly rearing their heads—a potential problem within any organization, but perhaps most severe with lefty "progressive" groups attempting to live out each member's individual utopian dream simultaneously. During the year before the tour, I had begun to face criticism from within the organization pertaining to my dominant position in the group. This sector, mostly made up of newer and inexperienced members of the group, argued—rarely to my face—that my growing power within the organization conflicted with the group's "collective" ideology. As a result of this belief, and from a perception of disenfranchisement within the group, many of the younger members formed an offshoot known as the KIDS group. Meeting in the Liberation Collective office, the KIDS group held as a core belief the opposition to any authority, hierarchy, or appearance thereof. As I had been identified by them as a power figure within the group—largely because I worked my ass off organizing campaigns, taking care of the bills, and acting as a spokesperson for both Liberation Collective and the ALF/ELF (all activities for which no one else would assume much responsibility)—I was a perfect target.

Returning to the Liberation Collective office in Portland after the tour only amplified the frustration I had built up during the previous three months on the road. It dawned on me that perhaps I had become so angry on the tour because, despite my hopes, the experience had only been a continuation of the ineffective political atmosphere I faced back at home. Walking into the HQ that first day back in Portland, I saw all of the problems within Liberation Collective as if through a magnifying glass. I realized I was facing the same problems as on the tour, only in larger proportions. The organization had declined to the point where it would be next to impossible to reform it into a serious and effective force. By the time I returned from the tour, the office had become more of a punk rock hangout—with "crusties" passed out on the couches—than the headquarters for an effective political organization. As on the tour, the most crucial element of any political effort—a clear mission and guidelines—had not been properly decided before the birth of Liberation Collective. To instill them at this point seemed impossible.

But I vowed to myself that I would not give up. I had helped to create this out-of-control monster back in 1996, and it just pissed me off to no end to think that all the work we had put into building the organization might have been wasted. For me to be happy with and in the group, I knew things had to change. So, with our thinking caps on, Leslie, Elaine, a few other members, and I struggled to find the means of improvement.

Leslie and I got right to work in creating a new initiation program for volunteers just becoming involved with Liberation Collective. Until that point, those expressing an interest in the group had been expected to just show up for meetings and, on their own initiative, become involved. This practice was an ongoing source of problems, as most people would immediately lose interest—or lose themselves in vague ideological pursuits. In an attempt to remedy this situation, Leslie and I began a more thorough orientation program in which new volunteers would be walked through a series of mini-courses on the group's ideology, mission, and activities in an inspiring and proactive manner. Unfortunately, for many of the younger KIDS hanging out at the Collective, the new rules and organizational guidelines represented a further incursion of the hierarchical system they opposed.

As the tension grew within Liberation Collective, we prepared for two major actions toward the end of the year—the international week of protests in support of Mumia Abu-Jamal and the World Trade Organization protests in Seattle. During the latter part of October, many cities around the globe would be hosting demonstrations at US federal buildings or embassies in support of Mumia, an outspoken African-American journalist who was convicted of killing a cop and sentenced to death in 1982. Since his trial, an exceptional amount of evidence has surfaced proving his innocence, and an international movement emerged demanding his freedom. In 2001, Mumia's death sentence was overturned, and he is currently serving a life sentence without parole. About a month after the action for Mumia, we would join with thousands of other activists to protest the actions of the WTO at its conference of world leaders in Seattle.

On the day of the Portland protest in support of Mumia, I was feeling a bit under the weather and took the passive role of holding a banner I had made. Outside the US federal building, the crowd listened to various speakers, all demanding Mumia's release. When the crowd began moving off on a march through the downtown streets, Elaine and I decided to stay in front of the federal building holding our "FREEDOM FOR MUMIA ABU-JAMAL" banner. We knew the marchers would be returning to end the protest back where it had started, so we just waited, talking to passersby, making plans for dinner later than evening, and shivering in the chilly air.

As the march ended back at the federal building, a long line of riot police faced off with the protesters across the street. After another round of megaphoned statements, the protest concluded and people began leaving. Within seconds, I noticed the Mounted Patrol Unit of the Portland Police Bureau charging after a friend of mine, Chad Hapshe, across the street in a city park. Elaine and I quickly rolled up our banner and, with Leslie and a few others, ran over to see what was happening. As I reached Chad, I could see he was being taken into custody and handcuffed. Looking up, I saw Sgt. David Pool, a cop who had hassled me many times before, sitting on his horse.

"Why are you arresting him?" I asked, in a manner I considered fairly calm.

"Craig, stay back," Pool replied.

"Why are you arresting him?" I repeated. "What did he do?" I continued to demand an answer from Pool, knowing full well the history of the Portland Police Bureau in arresting protesters on false or made-up charges.

"He threw a stick down on the ground," Pool finally answered.

"What? You can't arrest someone for throwing a stick on the ground in a park. How is that illegal?" I asked.

"We arrested him for offensive littering," Pool replied.

"You can't arrest him for offensive littering. He was on his way home, and you guys just picked him off for no reason."

"Your friend had quite an attitude, and he littered," Pool stated.

"That's bullshit," I said. "You cannot arrest someone for throwing a stick in a park. Where is the stick supposed to go?"

"Craig, don't get involved in this," Pool warned. I noticed that after Chad had been taken away, the Mounted Patrol began to concentrate on me, circling me with their horses. As I continued questioning Pool, he moved toward me again.

"The demonstration was over," I stated. "Why did you guys have to go and instigate . . ."

"Craig, Craig, you've made yourself a martyr," Pool interrupted.

"There would have been no problem here if you guys hadn't caused one," I continued.

"Craig, Craig, don't get shitty with me," Pool yelled as he reached down from his horse and grabbed my shoulder. As a reflex, I pulled away, fearing I would be hit by his out-of-control horse. Still holding the banner rolled up on a wooden pole, I regained my balance, only to have another Mounted Patrol officer lunge for me. Off balance, he missed me but struck the banner pole, sending it flying into the back of Pool's horse. Before I could catch my breath, I was forcefully grabbed from behind by a riot cop who attempted to place me in an arm bar. As Lieutenant Scott Winnegar slammed me to the ground, I felt my left arm snap and give way to a surge of mind-numbing pain. I smacked the ground face down, only to have one of the out-of-control Mounted Patrol horses land on my left leg.

"Aaaaaaaahhhh!" I screamed. "You broke my arm, asshole! I need an ambulance! AAAAAAAAAAAAHHHHHH!" As Winnegar tried to handcuff me, my nerve repeatedly rubbed back and forth against the broken portion of the bone. Each time it rubbed, I seemed to lose all feeling in my left hand, but the pain in my arm would not let up.

"I need a fucking ambulance! My arm is broken!" I screamed. I could hear both Leslie and Elaine screaming at the cops around me. Winnegar lifted me by the handcuffs on my wrists, pulling the break in my left arm further apart. He then proceeded to drag me by the handcuffs a block and a half to the jail. Elaine, frantic and angry, tried to follow me there, yelling at the cops to stop hurting me. For her efforts, the Portland Police shoved her down off the sidewalk into the street, where she fell, barely missing being hit by the oncoming traffic. She was then taken into custody and walked to the "Justice Center." In addition to Chad, Elaine, and myself, a few other protesters were arrested at the end of the event—when all of us were simply attempting to go home.

Inside the jail, I was thrown into a holding cell, where laughing police officers tormented me, pretending to not believe my arm was broken. They poked and prodded my arm, finally calling an ambulance at least half an hour later. Upon releasing me to the ambulance, they handed me citations to appear in court on charges of disorderly conduct and tampering with a police animal. At the hospital, where I was immediately pumped full of morphine, X-rays showed that I had suffered a spiral fracture to my left humerus. I chose not to have surgery and was then told I would be in a cast for about five months. After a number of hours, my arm was wrapped and I headed out to the lobby to find Leslie, Vanessa, Elaine, Alan (a protester and a nurse, who had generously ridden in the ambulance with me and persuaded the attending hospital staff to slow down my morphine injections), and Walidah, a then-local activist whom I had always admired for her responsible, revolutionary, and hardworking ethics. The majority of the protesters, I found out, had chosen to go to a party rather than stand by to support those who had been arrested or hospitalized. *Another classic situation*, I thought.

In response to my arm being broken, Leslie quickly organized a march against police brutality in Portland. While I could not attend, as I was stuck in bed, I was pleased to see the news reports of some four hundred people marching through town in defiance of the Portland Police Bureau's strong-arm tactics. In my opinion, the march was not enough retribution—the police deserve a far greater opposition—but it was a marvelous start.

During the next month, from my bed, I watched Seattle explode into the kind of war zone that had been unknown in the United States since the antiwar protests of the 1960s. I wanted so badly to be there, where the action was, taking my aggressions out on the cops and the world leaders. Stupidly, I made plans to go despite my broken arm, but thankfully, Leslie was there to talk some sense into me. So I watched on TV as the police fought the protesters, the protesters fought each other, and the WTO meetings were severely disrupted.

During that period of forced inactivity, I was able to do some thinking and personal reflection on my own beliefs regarding strategies and tactics of social and political change. Up to this point in my so-called "career" as a political activist, I had lived, breathed, and preached nonviolence as the only tool to achieve lasting and positive social change. Having gained a sound education on nonviolence philosophy from Thoreau, King, Gandhi, Gene Sharp, the War Resisters League, and others, I not only practiced the belief but had also taught it in workshops and classes in Portland and across the country. The only area in which I broke with the Gandhian nonviolence doctrine was politically motivated property destruction, which I supported as nonviolent action. Violence against living beings, however, I believed would only lead to more violence.

At this time, however, I began noticing myself questioning the logic on which I had based my entire political life. The first reason I had to re-evaluate my own nonviolent philosophies was Ward Churchill's essay "Pacifism as Pathology." In this early work, Churchill effectively argues against strict adherence to nonviolence principles, using the case of the Jewish response to the Nazi Holocaust as his most compelling study. According to Churchill, the overwhelmingly pacifist approach of Jews in attempting to resist the Holocaust did little to prevent the extermination of an estimated six million Jews. After reading Churchill's short but challenging essay, I could not help but begin to see some profound logic to his arguments.

I was also prompted to question my philosophical principles by a meeting I had had with Ramona and Sue Africa of the MOVE organization in 1998. Like Ramona and Sue, I had been invited to participate in a small conference in Boca Raton, Florida, called Total Resistance. The main purpose of the gathering was an attempt to network various single-issue movements together to build a unified force against injustice in the United States. After driving nonstop from Portland for four days with some friends (a trip that ended with an FBI raid on our van when we reached Boca Raton), I was thrilled to meet Ramona and Sue.

Ramona had lived through the first attack by the police on the MOVE headquarters in Philadelphia on August 8, 1978, and had been the sole adult survivor of the May 13, 1985, police firebombing of MOVE's Philadelphia townhouse. (In the May 13 attack, the police actually used a helicopter to drop firebombs onto the MOVE house, burning an entire city block and killing eleven MOVE members.) I was immediately amazed by Ramona's presence. This was a woman who had been to hell and back, at least a few different times, who had several family members in prison—and she still seemed stronger and more dedicated to abolishing the corrupt US system than ever. What I didn't hear Sue or Ramona talk about in our conversations was nonviolence. Instead, they talked about the need for self-defense. This really began to hit home with me as I started to wonder if perhaps the nonviolent movement in the United States was actually promoting violence by encouraging adherents not to fight back if attacked. Furthermore, I considered the possibility that the nonviolent advocates were allowing a greater degree of violence to occur by not vigorously and—yes, violently—attacking the system. Was it possible that the lack of any serious resistance to US policies was creating a greater degree of US-sponsored violence, both domestically and abroad? I began to seriously consider these ideas.

Now, after having been arrested and brutalized for merely questioning an officer of the law, I again questioned the logic of only adhering to state-sanctioned legal and nonviolent strategies. Here was a case in which a completely peaceful protest in support of a political prisoner had become out-of-control and violent due to aggressive acts not by any of the demonstrators but instead by the police force—the ones who are supposed to uphold the law and protect all citizens. Even more frustrating was the fact that this was not a rarity but an everyday occurrence. While the particular incident involving me gained a considerable amount of positive media attention—because I am white and fairly privileged—we are now painfully aware that police crimes like this and others far more severe happen on a daily basis in this country, largely to people from marginalized communities. Of course, no attention is paid to most of these crimes; the victim is made out to be the villain and winds up locked away in a cell, and any violence and brutality at the hand of the police is rarely punished.

As I watched the WTO protests, I was excited about the numbers of people at the protests and the militant nature of some of the demonstrators. Yet, I couldn't help but feel sickened after watching many of the so-called nonviolent protesters going out of their way to verbally and physically attack others who were engaging in property destruction against many of the companies who helped sponsor the WTO. It began to seem to me that a primary problem preventing real societal and political change in the United States is not only the so-called right wing or conservatives but also the leftists, the liberals, and the often self-identified progressives. Often members self-identifying in this leftist political spectrum seek to control entire movements and actions within them and believe their methodologies are the only ones possible. As a result, those who don't adhere to this control are marginalized and often fought against.

Bedridden with my arm in a cast, facing major problems in the Liberation Collective, my year came to a close . . . or so I thought. I had almost forgotten about those creatures of the night, the unknown ELF activists who had been planning their next move.

The ELF Takes On Boise Cascade

"I have seen a lot of logging up there, but there was never an operation like Boise. We didn't know the name of the company back then, but whoever was behind it, [they] were taking everything: old trees, new trees, dead trees, live trees. If they had a permit

for 6,000 cubic meters, they'd take 10,000 and no one would say anything."

—Rodolfo Montiel, Mexican farmer and ecologist, sentenced to six years in jail on false charges after organizing a campaign to halt Boise Cascade and other logging companies in the Mexican state of Guerrero

In the Willamette Valley area of Oregon, some sixty miles south of Portland, lies the city of Monmouth. Located near the state capital in Salem, Monmouth is a small agricultural town that houses a few local businesses, Western Oregon University, and the Northwest Headquarters for the Boise Cascade corporation. Aside from the busy highway dividing the community, Monmouth is normally a quiet city where serious crime and controversy are nearly nonexistent. However, a Christmas 1999 visit by some elves would change that.

It had been just over a year since the ELF had struck in the United States, and I was beginning to wonder if the group had faded from the scene—and why they might have backed off. Certainly neither the ELF nor the rest of the environmental movement had succeeded in gaining protection for our air, water, and soil. Maybe they were burnt out, I thought, or tired of running the exceptional risk of being caught. Whatever the reasons were for the scarcity of actions since US Forest Industries, I wasn't pleased.

While I did enjoy a break from the pressures of publicly representing the group, I knew that more actions were desperately needed. The year-long break from public visibility ended for the ELF on December 25, 1999. Early that morning, representatives from Boise Cascade arrived at their Northwest headquarters in Monmouth to find their eight-thousand-square-foot building reduced to a pile of ashes. A few days later, I received the following communiqué from the ELF:

Boise Cascade has been very naughty. After ravaging the forests of the Pacific Northwest, Boise Cascade now looks toward the virgin forests of Chile. Early Christmas morning, elves left coal in Boise Cascade's stocking. Four buckets of diesel and gas with kitchen timer delay destroyed their regional headquarters in Monmouth, Oregon.

Let this be a lesson to all greedy multinational corporations who don't respect their ecosystems.

The elves are watching.

Earth Liberation Front

While the action at the nearly unheard-of US Forest Industries a year before had taken me by surprise, the ELF's new choice of targets didn't astonish me in the least. In fact, my initial thought was, *What took them so long?*

As the largest logger on federal public lands in the United States, Boise Cascade is no stranger to controversy.[32] Boise was the number one buyer of timber from public lands in the US from 1994 through 1998, a period in which the corporation purchased at least 538 million board feet. Boise is also the second-largest buyer of timber from national forests, specifically in ancient forest regions. More than 90 percent of the timber the corporation purchased from public lands between 1994 and 1998 came from national forests in the Southwest and Pacific Northwest.

Despite appeals and protests against the practice, Boise Cascade continues to be one of the primary loggers of old growth timber in the country. In the mid-1990s, the Sugarloaf Timber Sale, located in the Siskiyou National Forest in southern Oregon, was awarded to Boise. Originally designated as a protected area by the Clinton Forest Plan, this old growth forest was to be set aside as an Ancient Forest Reserve. Instead, Boise Cascade managed to buy it and thoroughly logged the entire area. In 1995, over two hundred people were arrested for protesting this particular crime against nature.

---

32 Rainforest Action Network newsletter, 2002.

Boise has also attacked the old growth areas inside the Umpqua National Forest outside of Eugene, Oregon. Under the 1995 Salvage Logging Rider (thanks to which environmental laws and citizen appeals were suspended), Boise was able to get away with massive clear-cutting in the Mt. Bailey Roadless Area.

As if this weren't enough, Boise Cascade was also the primary player involved in reducing the old growth habitat in the Payette National Forest to less than one percent. Located on Cuddy Mountain in Idaho, this old growth area was once called "the best undeveloped wildlife habitat in southwest Idaho" by the Idaho Department of Fish and Game. Of course, the landscape changed drastically with Boise's clear-cutting in 2000 through 2001.

While I had known a few very basic details of Boise Cascade's horrendous business practices at home, I was largely unaware that their crimes had spread internationally. The fourth-largest logging company in the United States, Boise sells lumber, paper products, building materials, and office supplies not only within the country but also throughout Western Europe, New Zealand, and Australia. Boise's logging and manufacturing practices had also begun to spread outside the United States into Mexico, Canada, Brazil, China, and, most recently, Chile.

The communiqué sent by the ELF for the Boise Cascade action mentioned that the corporation was now looking "toward the virgin forests of Chile." In 1997, Boise had entered into a joint business venture with Maderas Condor to pursue a project called Cascada Chile (and later renamed Company Industrial Puerto Montt, or CIPM). Together the companies planned to build a $180 million wood chipping and oriented strand board (OSB) facility in Bahia Ilque, Chile. Cascada Chile had expected this new plant to be able to produce over four hundred million square feet of OSB annually, doubling Boise's OSB capacity.

Numerous lawsuits were filed against Boise Cascade's planned extraction of massive acres of Chilean forests. The lawsuits seemed to come from all directions, including the local salmon industry and adjacent property owners. One lawsuit argued that the Chilean Congress had improperly approved the plan. Another lawsuit was filed on behalf of small farmers, NGOs, scientists, and local residents who argued that Boise Cascade's plan would violate their Constitutional right to a clean environment. As two of the only legal measures taken against Boise Cascade in this project, the Chilean Court of Appeals fined Cascada Chile $825,000 in May 1999 for destroying a five-thousand-year-old archaeological site. This was to be added to another fine for illegally cutting trees.

Clearly, this new merger with Maderas Condor had provoked the Christmas Day ELF attack in Monmouth. But Boise's track record in Mexico added fuel to the ELF's fire. In 1995, Boise moved some of its milling equipment from a closed plant in Council, Idaho, to Papanoa, Guerrero, Mexico, to set up another mill with its subsidiary Costa Grande Forest Products. Boise's plan was to cut twenty million board feet of old growth pine over five years, which would be exported to the United States. They also planned to open a second mill in nearby Tecpan.

On June 28, 1995, just two months after the governor of Guerrero signed the Boise contract, local police murdered seventeen members of the Organization of Campesinos of the Southern Sierra (OCSS). This group of local farmers was headed to a protest against logging, and some of those killed had warrants for their arrest dated the day after Boise's contract was signed.[33]

Governor Figueroa of Guerrero was later forced to resign his office after unsuccessfully attempting to cover up the massacre. Six days after the seventeen farmers were killed, Boise signed another logging contract in Guerrero. For the next three years, from 1995 through June 1998, Boise logged and exported wood back to the United States. Citing an "inconsistent wood supply" and "bad weather," Boise then closed its mills in Guerrero.

Just under a year later, on May 2, 1999, Rodolfo Montiel and Teodoro Cabrera, two local farmers who had been protesting Boise Cascade's logging, were arrested and severely beaten.[34] After being tortured with electric shock, the two were forced to

33 "Globalizing Destruction: A Human Rights Disaster in Mexico," Rainforest Action Network leaflet, 2002.
34 "Globalizing Destruction," Rainforest Action Network leaflet.

sign confessions and were then given six- and ten-year prison sentences. Both stayed in jail, listed as political prisoners by groups such as Amnesty International, until their sudden release on November 8, 2001. What direct relation the imprisonment of Montiel and Cabrera had to Boise Cascade is uncertain. However, it is clear that corporations that value profits over life and the health of the natural environment, such as Boise Cascade, will choose to set up business in locations where either the government suppresses all dissent and resistance, or protests aren't likely.

Perhaps that was why the Chilean project had stalled. In Chile, Boise Cascade had been met with ongoing protests at every step of the way since 1997. Opponents of the Cascada joint venture began to see some light at the end of the tunnel when on December 15, 1999, the project was postponed indefinitely. At the time, Boise Cascade declared that, since "international plywood prices are on a downward trend," they would be forced to postpone the ground-breaking of the Cascada Chile project.[35]

But they did not permanently call off the plan. Perhaps Boise Cascade was merely waiting until the political climate in Chile and the United States eased a bit (or, more officially, until the "international plywood prices" began on an upward trend!). In any case, the December 25 ELF action definitely stepped up the pressure on the corporation to cancel its Chilean plans. On February 23, 2001, the good news came that Boise Cascade had finally canceled its

$160 million OSB project in Chile.[36] Once again, the corporation cited "changes in the OSB market" as the reason for the cancellation. Environmental activists, however, above ground and below, knew they had succeeded. Boise Cascade had retreated, at least for the time being.

---

35 "Environment Chile—Massive Cascada Logging Project Called Off," Interpress Service, December 15, 1999.
36 "Boise Cascade Cancels $160 Million Chile Forest Project," Reuters Limited, February 23, 2001.

DOES GE BRING GOOD THINGS TO LIFE?

> *"I lost basically my entire professional life. I've lost every paper I ever wrote that analyzed the benefits and risks of this technology."*
>
> —Catherine Ives, genetic engineering researcher at MSU, commenting after being targeted with a $900,000 fire by the ELF on December 31, 1999[37]

As the year came to a close, I was pleased and excited that the ELF, which had lain dormant for a year, was again speaking up in defense of the Earth. While Americans across the United States collected their bottled water and food rations in preparation for Y2K (and jammed to Prince's "1999" on the radio), I did my best once again to represent the underground saboteurs to the national media. Owing to the sheer size of the Boise Cascade corporation, the story instantly went nationwide, and I was busy as hell.

I began to wonder at this point if the end-of-year holiday season would continue to be the most active time for the ELF. In November 1997, the group had attacked the BLM Horse Corral; on December 27, 1998, US Forest Industries had been targeted. Now, for the third year in a row, the group had struck at year's end, on Christmas day, in the Pacific Northwest.

Then, on New Year's Eve, while eyes and ears around the globe awaited the imagined havoc of Y2K, the ELF was busy in the Midwest. At 8:15 P.M., a member of the faculty working in the Agricultural Hall at Michigan State University (MSU) reported a fire. As fire crews responded to the scene, they were faced with a blaze threatening the entire building.

Investigators on the scene at MSU quickly found evidence of accelerants used to help spread the fire and declared that arson had taken place. They discovered that the fire had started in Room 324, the offices of Catherine Ives, Associate Professor with MSU's International Institute of Agriculture. It didn't take investigators or the news media long to realize that the growing movement against genetic engineering (GE) had just dramatically increased the severity of its tactics.

---

37 "Green Terror," *Eye on America*, CBS Evening News.

Nearly three weeks later, I received the following communiqué:

The ELF takes credit for a strike on the offices of Catherine Ives, Rm. 324 Agriculture Hall at Michigan State University on Dec. 31, 1999. The offices were doused with gasoline and set afire. This was done in response to the work being done to force developing nations in Asia, Latin America and Africa to switch from natural crop plants to genetically engineered sweet potatoes, corn, bananas and pineapples. Monsanto and USAID are major funders of the research and promotional work being done through Michigan State University. According to local newspapers, the fire cost some $400,000 in damage.

Cremate Monsanto, Long live the ELF. On to the next G.E. target!

The ELF already had a growing reputation nationally, and the MSU fire only added to the interest from both the news media and the general public. Not only was the damage quite significant (from their original estimate of $100,000, investigators later raised the amount to $400,000 and finally $900,000), but this was the first time arson had been used to further the cause against genetic engineering in the United States. Furthermore, it was the first time the ELF had taken credit for any GE-related action.

It's now widely known that genetic engineering involves altering the traits of living organisms by adding genetic material that has undergone some manipulation outside of cells. This artificial mode of gene transferring steps far outside natural boundaries and is exclusive to new genetic engineering technology. While biotech industry representatives, trusting in public ignorance, suggest that genetic engineering is really no different from conventional breeding practices, the contrast is enormous. In conventional breeding, genes are selected from traits that already exist within a species gene pool to create a variety. This historic process of creating diversity does not splice genes together from completely foreign entities to produce a new organism unknown to humankind and the planet.

The term "genetic engineering" was first used in 1941 by Danish microbiologist A. Jost during a lecture on sexual reproduction in yeast at the Technical Institute in Lwow, Poland. From there the technology slowly developed within the global research community. In 1973, Stanley Cohen and Herbert Boyer were deemed to have perfected techniques that allowed scientists to cut and paste DNA and reproduce the new DNA in bacteria. Then, in 1977, Genetech was founded in San Francisco as the world's first genetic engineering company. Using the new recombinant DNA methods, Genetech worked to create some of the first genetically engineered medical drugs.

In 1980, the US Supreme Court, in Diamond v. Chakrabarty, approved the principle of patenting genetically engineered life forms—a landmark decision with possible ramifications for the entire planet. This immediately allowed the Exxon oil company to patent an oil-eating microorganism. That same year, the US patent for gene cloning was awarded to Cohen and Boyer.

Over the next twenty years, genetic engineering technology would find its way into the fields, forests, waterways, grocery stores, and homes of people around the world. In 1981, scientists at Ohio State University announced that they had produced the first transgenic animals by transferring genes from other animals into mice. The same year in China, scientists cloned the first fish, a golden carp. In 1985, genetically engineered plants resistant to insects, viruses, and bacteria were field tested for the first time.

In 1986, the US Environmental Protection Agency (EPA) approved the release of gene-altered tobacco plants, the first genetically engineered crop. Two years later, Harvard scientists were awarded the first US patent for a genetically altered animal after creating a transgenic mouse. The year 1988 also marked the launch of the Human Genome Project. With the goal of determining the entire sequence of DNA composing human chromosomes, the project intensified many people's concerns about the artificial production and management of life. It would take ten years before a rough draft of the human genome map was produced, a map that showed the locations of more than thirty thousand genes.

With the year 1990 came the first product of recombinant DNA technology successfully introduced into the US food supply. ChyMax was introduced as an artificially produced form of chymosin, an enzyme for cheese making. The first transgenic dairy cow was also created with the ability to produce human milk proteins for infant formula—good news for the commercial dairy industry, since the more kids who can suck the udder earlier in life, the greater the industry's financial gain.

Just three years later, the US Food and Drug Administration (FDA) declared that genetically engineered foods are "not inherently" dangerous and do not require special regulation. This was an especially interesting announcement, since scientists both for and against genetic engineering have repeatedly commented that the precise danger to the health of humans and the environment is unclear. With this announcement by the FDA came the FLAVRSAVR tomato. This product, genetically engineered for a longer shelf life, marked the first genetically engineered whole food on the market approved by the FDA.

Scottish scientists made global news in 1997 after reporting that they had successfully cloned a sheep, named Dolly, using DNA from adult sheep cells. The United States was not far behind, as researchers at the Oregon Regional Primate Research Center claimed, in an announcement that same year, to have cloned two rhesus monkeys. The following year, the cloning announcements continued—first at the University of Hawaii, where scientists cloned three generations of mice from nuclei of adult ovarian cumulus cells, and then at Japan's Kinki University, where eight identical calves were cloned using cells taken from a single adult cow.

According to the US Department of Agriculture, over 90 percent of corn, upland cotton, and soybeans are currently produced in the US using genetic engineering.[38] It is a lucrative industry valued in 2023 at $22.29 billion (USD) and growing. Historically, the major player in the genetic engineering game was Monsanto, acquired by Bayer in 2018. Monsanto started

---

38 "Recent Trends in GE Adoption," USDA Research Service. ers.usda.gov/data-products/adoption-of-genetically-engineered-crops-in-the-u-s/recent-trends-in-ge-adoption

out as a chemical company featuring such products as dioxins, Agent Orange, polychlorinated biphenyls (PCBs), agricultural chemicals (perhaps most famously the herbicide Roundup), and DDT, and went on to become a main player in a global genetic engineering industry.

Even though genetic engineering proponents argue that the technology is safe and needed to preserve forests and feed the world, the general public has been skeptical at best. This skepticism led to the USDA passing a regulation in 2022 requiring all genetically modified foods to be labeled with either "bioengineered" or "derived from bioengineering."[39] However, there appears to have been little consumer impact from this labeling, evidenced by the fact that the annual growth rate for genetically engineered goods is averaging 5.8 percent.[40]

Taking on Monsanto and Genetic Engineering
"I can't think of a worse target for them than this project. We're trying to help the environment."

—Catherine Ives[41]

When the ELF communiqué went public, announcing that the group had officially claimed responsibility for the MSU arson, the national news media was in a frenzy to get the story. While, prior to the ELF attack, the anti-GE efforts in the US had consisted largely of lobbying, public education, protests, and nonviolent crop-pulls, this was definitely uncharted territory for the relatively new movement. But for the ELF, while the issue may have been new, the strategy of arson and property

---

39 "GMO food labeling has been required in the U.S. for a year. Have consumers noticed?" Nebraska Public Media. nebraskapublicmedia.org/en/news/news-articles/gmo-food-labeling-has-been-required-in-the-us-for-a-year-have-consumers-noticed/
40 "Genetically Modfdied Crops: Global Market Report 2023," ReportLinker, February, 2023. finance.yahoo.com/news/genetically-modified-crops-global-market-184300907.html?guccounter=1&guce_re ferrer=aHR0cHM6Ly93d3cuZ29vZ2xlLmNvbS8&guce_referrer_sig=AQAAANiE8ZL9nRxNP0--GgECHZA-i9RK1k3wmuKkgQ2R13obU_g7VyF5_vLwg2tOHjBQ20QRPdhH8P9d7bv-IFS1HsdVGy9bpLFE SinxE47kKgSyS7jTxrNw1OFBACh0OVT-VE6M3KuLtjp5CkNbA_WPaC36fdpulG3Dpxfq8PFrR74M
41 "Harvest of Fear," *Frontline/Nova*, PBS, originally aired April 23, 2001.

destruction was business as usual—more than that, it was the group's calling card.

The specific project targeted by the ELF was headed by MSU researcher Catherine Ives and funded jointly by Monsanto and the United States Agency for International Development (USAID). Ives was conducting research to further develop genetically engineered crops, and lobbying developing countries to abandon traditional farming practices and rely on genetically engineered crops. These, of course, would be conveniently supplied by US chemical corporations such as Monsanto.

Catherine Ives immediately defended her work as crucial to helping feed starving people in various African, Latin American, and Asian countries. Furthermore, she reiterated the industry's standard line that her work would mean a great reduction in the amount of chemicals needed for crop growing. Referring specifically to various African nations facing a massive starvation crisis, Ives stated on PBS's "Harvest of Fear" program,

> People understand that if they can produce more food, they can feed their families and keep their children healthier. They understand that if they can make their land more productive, maybe they can send their children to school, as opposed to have them out in the field all day.[42]

On the *CBS Evening News* and *60 Minutes* segments covering the ELF and the MSU attack, Ives was made out to be an ethical and caring individual who honestly believed she had been wrongly targeted. She came across as a woman genuinely concerned with protecting the environment and alleviating hunger through her work. The ELF, on the other hand, were the villains, criminals who just hadn't done their homework on the issue.

PBS's "Harvest of Fear" program, which aired on April 23, 2001, also featured an interview with Florence Wambugu, a Kenyan scientist. Wambugu was portrayed by PBS as an independent voice, concerned for the welfare of her country. Her words of support helped Monsanto and the biotech industry

---

42 Michael Dynes, "Africa Torn Between GM Aid and Starvation," *London Times*, August 6, 2002.

to maintain and even attempt to build their public credibility in relation to genetic engineering. Wambugu stated,

> May I say that organic farming has not worked in Africa, and it is not going to work. It is not the answer . . . What farmers need is technology that is packaged in the seed, the seed that actually is resistant to the pests and diseases, and plant it the way they have always planted. That to me is sustainable. The GM technology is appealing, and to me, I say it's user friendly. It does not demand the farmer go out to be educated on how to use it.

Indeed, Monsanto, Novartis, and the other leading genetic engineering companies undoubtedly prefer that farmers educate themselves as little as possible regarding the possible dangers of their products, including the danger of economic reliance on these corporations.

Though the program doesn't mention it, from 1992 through 1994, Wambugu worked at Monsanto's headquarters in St. Louis as a post-doctoral research associate in plant science. Now, with a position in the International Service for the Acquisition of AgriBiotech Applications, African Regional Office, Wambugu works with companies such as Monsanto to introduce and open up the genetic engineering marketplace in Africa.

Ives, Wambugu, and many others promote the idea that genetic engineering can stop the food shortage in Africa and, furthermore, that people in those countries desire genetic engineering technology and aid. However, there is a startling amount of evidence to the contrary.

As the UN World Food Program attempted to raise money to buy 1.2 million tons of food to prevent 13 million people from starving in Africa, the United States donated nearly 300,000 tons of food aid, much of it containing genetically modified ingredients.[43] In response to a growing concern over possible health and economic problems associated with genetically engineered foods coming into southern Africa, President Mwanawasa of Zambia publicly stated that he would rather let his people die than feed them hazardous food.[44] After rejecting a

---

43 Dynes, "Africa Torn."
44 Dynes, "Africa Torn."

shipment of maize from the United States that was genetically engineered, Mwanawasa asserted, "If it is safe, then we will give it to our people. But if not, then we would rather starve than get something toxic."[45] Zimbabwe, where the hunger was greatest (with an estimated six million facing starvation), also refused to accept imports of GM maize for six months. Additionally, Mozambique demanded that all World Food Program shipments carrying food aid into the country be sealed with plastic to minimize the threat of genetic engineering contamination.

In many Latin American, African, and Asian countries, there was a growing concern that the United States was attempting to force in its genetic engineering technology and products. In 1998, Monsanto's PR company advised them to avoid the controversial issues associated with genetic engineering (environmental, health, economic effects), to demonize Western environmentalists for opposing the biotech attempts to feed the world, and to shift their campaign strategy to focus on supposed benefits for the poor.[46] So the corporation sent an appeal to all of Africa's heads of state entitled "Let the Harvest Begin," that called on them to endorse genetically engineered crops.

The response to the appeal was not at all what Monsanto had hoped. The Food and Agriculture representative of every African nation—excluding South Africa—signed a joint proclamation entitled "Let Nature's Harvest Continue," condemning Monsanto's unethical attempts. The response sent to Monsanto from these various countries stated,

> [We] strongly object that the image of the poor and hungry from our countries is being used by giant multinational corporations to push a technology that is neither safe, environmentally friendly, nor economically beneficial to us. . . . We think it will destroy the diversity, the local knowledge and the sustainable agricultural systems that our farmers have developed for millennia,

45 Robert Vint, "The US Is Force-Feeding Developing Countries with GE Foods and Crops," Genetic Food Alert, August 26, 2002.
46 "Why African Countries Maintain Tight Restrictions on Genetically Modified Food," *World Politics Review*, May 28, 2019. worldpoliticsreview.com/why-african-countries-maintain-tight-restrictions-on-genetically-modified-food/

and that it will thus undermine our capacity to feed ourselves.[47]

Since that statement was issued to Monsanto over two decades ago, only four of 47 African nations allow the planting of any genetically modified crops.[48] Unfortunately, US efforts to push genetic engineering internationally involve far more than the many African nations. On May 1, 2000, Sri Lanka's Health Ministry banned genetically engineered imports for a year due to the lack of safety testing on GE food. The governmental agency renewed this ban a year later, in May 2001, after discovering that chocolates, soups, and oils containing genetically modified organisms had been imported into the country.[49] The US immediately stepped in and threatened sanctions against Sri Lanka if they did not agree to lift the ban on GE imports. After four months of protests by Sri Lankan groups, the Sri Lankan government gave in to the United States and lifted the ban on September 3, 2001.[50]

Mexico fell under diplomatic pressure from the United States regarding the labeling of genetically engineered food. The Mexican Senate approved GE food labeling in November 2000 and instantly became threatened with NAFTA (North American Free Trade Agreement) sanctions as a result.[51]

In May 2001, China introduced genetically engineered food labels and documentation requirements for genetically modified imports. Within five months, US Secretary of Agriculture Ann Veneman—a previous director of a Monsanto subsidiary—began pressuring China to abolish its new import inspection standards, particularly those for US genetically engineered soybeans. In March 2002, China gave in to a "temporary" abandonment of its inspections and began allowing unregulated imports of US genetically engineered soybeans.[52]

---

47 Andrew Simms, "Selling Suicide: farming, false promises and genetic engineering in developing countries," *Christian Aid* report, May 1999.
48 Vint, "The US Is Force-Feeding Developing Countries."
49 Ibid.
50 "Asian Groups Strongly Protest US Threat of WTO Retaliation on Sri Lankan GMO Ban," Pesticide Action Network Asia and the Pacific (PANAP) press release, August 14, 2001.
51 "Industry Mobilizes to Modify Mexico's Labeling Measures," Cropchoice News, February 12, 2001.
52 Vint, "The US Is Force-Feeding Developing Countries"

Thailand has been faced with the same pressure from the US government. In July 2001, the Secretary General of the Thai Food and Drug Administration publicly stated that a US trade delegation had threatened to impose trade sanctions on Thailand if the proposals to label genetically engineered food were approved.[53] Sanctions have also been threatened by the United States government against Canada,[54] Argentina,[55] and the entire European Union for their regulation of genetically engineered crops and labeling of GE foods.

While Monsanto pretends that their motives are truly humanitarian, some scientists have been skeptical and even offended. Jane Rissler, a representative of the Union of Concerned Scientists, stated the following on the "Harvest of Fear" program:

> I think it's a ploy. It's playing on the guilt of relatively well-off people that . . . if they don't approve of this technology by agreeing to buy the products, that somehow the result will be people dying of starvation in the developing world.[56]

Commenting specifically on the joint venture between Catherine Ives, Monsanto, and USAID, Rob Horsch of Monsanto pushed the recommended line about helping to feed the poor of the world:

> Projects like the sweet potato for Africa we will never make any money from, have no expectation to. The reason to do it is several-fold. To my mind, the most important one is because we can. And it doesn't cost us that much to do it. In the longer term, as poorer farmers do better, they become richer farmers. And at some point, those richer farmers can start buying our other products.[57]

---

53 "US Threatened Trade Sanctions to Block GM Labels, Says Thai FDA," *Just Food*, July 19, 2001, just-food.com/news/usa-thailand-us-threatened-trade-sanctions-to-block-gm-labels-says-thai-fda/.
54 In response to plans to introduce labeling, March 2002; see Vint, "The US Is Force-Feeding Developing Countries."
55 "Monsanto Warns Argentina to Loosen GE Crop Restrictions," April 2002; see Vint, "The US Is Force-Feeding Developing Countries"
56 "Harvest of Fear," *Frontline/Nova*.
57 Ibid.

Indeed, the company worked to build a market for their genetically engineered products, to phase in the use of genetically engineered seeds, crops, and other goods. Since many countries refuse to accept the technology, every country that does is a victory for them. And, by attempting to convince the individual farmer that genetic engineering is needed to feed a starving planet, Monsanto—now Bayer—aims to make the farmer and local farming industries within each country reliant on their patented technology for their mere survival. In these terms, Monsanto's efforts were far from philanthropic.

Are genetically engineered foods needed to save the hungry of the world? No. It has been argued for many years, even well before the famous Band Aid rock concerts to raise money for famine victims, that people are starving not because of a lack of food but instead due to a lack of distribution and an enormous, unhealthy gap between the rich and poor.

Tewolde Egziabher, Ethiopia's Food and Agriculture spokesperson, stated,

> This notion that genetically engineered crops will save developing countries misses the real point. The world has never grown as much food per capita as it is doing now, yet the world also has never had as many hungry. The problem is not the amount of food produced, but how it is both produced and distributed. For example, farmers in developing countries who buy genetically engineered seeds that cannot reproduce—and so can't be saved and used for next year's crop—become tied to transnational companies like Monsanto/Bayer.[58]

Some of this excess food can be found in India, where its vast surplus stocks of rice could supply an estimated sixty-five times what Africa would need to end the current hunger disaster. But when countries in dire need seek international assistance, organizations such as the World Food Program and various wealthy countries willingly offer financial assistance only if certain requirements are met.

---

58 Vint, "The US Is Force-Feeding Developing Countries"

Take for instance the recent case of the United States offering a virtual "GE or death" ultimatum to Mozambique, Zimbabwe, and Zambia. The United States offered Zambia $50 million if they would adhere to strict conditions that the money only be used to buy genetically engineered maize from the United States.[59] Even though India's rice would be available at half the cost of the US maize, the conditions imposed by the US aid forbid Zambia to purchase the rice. The Zambian national newspaper, *The Post*, rightfully asserted, "If the US insists on imposing this genetically modified maize on our people, we will be justified in questioning their motive."[60]

For the ELF, the threats to life on the planet posed by genetic engineering technology certainly warranted the group's involvement in the issue. Catherine Ives's project at MSU was an excellent choice for a first action targeting genetic engineering. With the international coverage of the action, the debate over genetic engineering widened and the major player in the GE game, Monsanto, suffered a major public relations blow. But for the ELF, this would only be another beginning.

59 "Dignity in Hunger," *The Post* (Zambia), July 30, 2002.
60 Ibid.

NAELFPO
AND
URBAN SPRAWL

*F*rom November 1997 through 1999, I had received communiqués from the ELF and distributed them to news media, sometimes representing only myself and sometimes representing the Liberation Collective. For the Liberation Collective, this had its drawbacks, as the group was often seen as taking on a media role for the ELF. The organization had not chosen this position; I had imposed it upon the group through my role as ELF spokesperson and my use of the office for activities related to that role (faxing out news advisories, conducting interviews in person or via telephone, etc.). When the *New York Times Magazine* decided to run a lengthy profile of me entitled "The Face of Ecoterrorism," with full color photographs of the inside of the Collective headquarters, things had clearly gone too far. While there had been no vocal opposition to my dual activities as a Liberation Collective organizer and ELF spokesperson, the group, like it or not, had suffered as a result.

By far, the most dramatic example of the effect on the Liberation Collective was an increase in pressure from all levels of government against our activities. Immediately after my fingerprints were taken by the FBI early in 1998, the Internal Revenue Service began a full investigation into the Liberation Collective, which at the time was two years into a five-year 501(c)(3) nonprofit probationary period. Even though the Collective had lost money over the first two years and, therefore, had not had to file full tax forms (just a declaration letter), I received a notice from the IRS stating that they were planning a full audit of the group.

Now, at that time, I really had no idea that the IRS had any direct connection to other branches of government, particularly the US Justice Department. I didn't realize their historic link with the various federal law enforcement agencies in battling groups such as the American Indian Movement and Black Panther Party. Yet I did find it odd, to say the least, that a new 501(c)(3) organization was being subjected to a full audit, especially when it had lost money each year. My suspicions grew when I found out that there are just a few agents assigned to Oregon and normally 501(c)(3) organizations aren't pressured at all by the IRS until the five-year probationary period is coming to an end. Of course, with the audit notice coming directly after I had received four grand jury subpoenas in six months, I knew something was strange.

According to the IRS, the stated purpose of the investigation was to determine if the Liberation Collective had strayed outside the guidelines for a 501(c)(3) group by supporting and taking part in illegal activity. The group had spoken out in support of both the ALF and the ELF—which all of us felt was legal based on our right to freedom of speech—since its formation back in 1996. However, the IRS argued that this behavior, and our vocal support, teaching, and practice of nonviolent civil disobedience, violated 501(c)(3) regulations. True, it was obvious, even to the most casual observer, that as an organization we advocated breaking unjust laws for the greater good of society.

Additionally, in the short time period the group had been in existence, the number of volunteers who had been arrested at protests sponsored by Liberation Collective— some twelve to fifteen—was sizable. This, the IRS was arguing, constituted grounds for revoking our nonprofit status. Of course, Liberation Collective was far from being the only nonprofit organization in the United States that openly took part in nonviolent civil disobedience, but most other organizations were not speaking out in support of growing "domestic terrorist" groups such as the ALF and ELF.

I couldn't help but laugh when the two IRS agents appeared at the Liberation Collective offices early one spring morning in 1998. They immediately demanded to see all of our records, receipts, tax forms, bank statements, and even copies of our literature. Now, in our ragtag grassroots organization, certain aspects of the operation did not receive as much attention as others. For example, our entire record-keeping system was so haphazard that when the agents opened up the filing cabinet drawers in the office, there was virtually nothing there—nothing of importance, anyway. The files that were there were so out of order and incomplete that the agents just began grabbing handfuls of paper and stacking it into piles on the desks, then told me they were going to copy and return them. Halfway into this audit session, which had been scheduled to take most of the day, I left in frustration, leaving the agents there alone with other volunteers.

It didn't surprise me much when we received a letter from the IRS a few weeks later, stating that the agency was going to revoke Liberation Collective's nonprofit status. Apparently the IRS had located all the evidence it needed within our "records" and literature to demonstrate that we supported, advocated, and took part in illegal activities. Throughout 1998 and 1999, federal agents, primarily from the FBI and BATF, frequently came into the downtown office and attempted to question me regarding one ELF incident or another. Occasionally, Leslie and I would have fun locking the doors when we were fortunate enough to see them coming. Often they would just stand there in front of the windows, banging with their fists as we continued to work inside directly in front of them.

This increasing pressure from the outside, combined with problems within the organization itself, was leading to animosity between the group's members. With the start of the new year, some members, especially Leslie and I, undertook new efforts to reform the Liberation Collective. We had already implemented our new orientation program and felt we were making positive steps toward creating an effective organization when we hit a stone wall. When the HQ first opened in January 1998, and the Collective shared office space with Cascadia Forest Alliance and the Oregon Wildlife Federation Collective, the rent was cheap enough for the Collective that we either paid out of our pockets or through a few irregular donations each month. A few months later, we agreed to begin distributing political merchandise (T-shirts, stickers, magazines, buttons, punk music, etc.) to assist us in paying rent and raising finances for the group's other activities. Thanks to Neil—a new volunteer who had recently moved to town—the office quickly became full of radical propaganda that we hoped would enhance the organization's ultimate productivity by providing some much needed funds.

Over a two-year period, Neil's distribution did indeed assist the group in paying rent and raising money for other purposes. The only drawback as I saw it was that in exchange for this income, nearly half of the office was devoted to punk rock music and paraphernalia. As a result, the office became a hangout for punks shopping for the latest band's CD, patch, T-shirt, sticker, or button. Additionally, many of the Collective's new volunteers had obviously only become involved to be a part of the punk rock scene that the office had become. While many members, including myself, labored endlessly to create an environment that was open and inviting to all of the public, many of the newer scenesters appeared content with passing out on the couches, cranking punk tunes endlessly on the stereo inside the office, and sneering at those who entered the space without the black clothing and patches that were de rigueur in their eyes.

I recalled that when the distribution items were first brought into the space, we had agreed that the items that weren't directly political, such as the punk rock merchandise, could be phased out once the Liberation Collective was more self-sufficient. After returning from the Primate Freedom Tour in September 1999, Leslie and I agreed to work on fundraising (once again by default, as no one else would) with the overall goal of attempting to get the non-applicable merchandise out of the store, thereby decreasing the scenester atmosphere. So, for the rest of 1999, we worked to bring in all different sorts of political merchandise— from a full line of Earth First! gear to "SUPPORT ELF" hats and shirts and new magazines.

In early January 2000, it appeared as though we were ready to start getting rid of the items that didn't directly support the ideology of Liberation Collective. Even though the two other organizations had moved out during the course of the previous year, we had enough applicable merchandise in the store to begin paying for the rent entirely. I had no inkling of the enormous eruption that would occur once I mentioned to Neil that I felt the punk materials should be phased out.

Within a day I was called everything from sexist to a dictator, from fascist to even racist and homophobic. I also learned from others that I had a massive ego problem. A divide sprung up between longtime members and those who had more recently become involved. The overwhelming majority of the KIDS group immediately rallied behind Neil and together voiced fierce opposition to the removal of the punk materials.

An impressive array of rumors began to spread around the entire Portland activist community—mostly relating to the names I was being called by some Liberation Collective members. Unfortunately, as the federal government knows, rumors are extremely powerful and can tear apart relationships and organizations. In a state of utter disgust, feeling like I had just wasted four years of my life, I announced that I would be leaving the organization. Shortly after I left, the entire board of directors and many other volunteers also severed ties with the group.

I then had to decide whether or not to allow Liberation Collective to continue operating at all. While I would not be involved, I certainly did not want to see the organization continue to go downhill, especially after so many of us had spent so many long hours on its creation. But I was forced to make a decision, as my name was the primary one attached to all of the legal forms—the IRS documents, state and local forms, insurance, bank and internet accounts, etc. In an attempt to reduce the growing atmosphere of hostility, I chose to simply sign over all of the legal forms and accounts to new people so the organization could continue.

Still in a cast and in pain from my broken arm, I was also dealing with a dramatic increase in media attention regarding the ELF and their actions. Initially, all I could feel was anger and resentment toward the people I felt were destroying the Collective—yet, before long, I also discovered a sense of relief. No longer did I have to keep myself up at night worrying about how to make the organization effective. A sizable load had just been lifted from my shoulders.

While part of me mourned what felt like the loss of four years of labor, I was now free to continue following my own path. After pondering just what work I felt was the most productive for me at that time, it was only a matter of days before I made a decision. Along with Leslie, who had been a supporter of the ELF and ALF for years, I decided to form the first ever North American Earth Liberation Front Press Office, or NAELFPO.

Prior to this time, I had felt that the lack of an official headquarters, a stable location where news media could contact me, made me vulnerable to constant challenges to my credibility from reporters and prevented me from doing the best job possible in representing the underground saboteurs. Furthermore, I was aware that press offices for the ALF—in the United States, England, and elsewhere—had done an excellent job of increasing the accessibility of information about the group. Leslie and I both felt that being freed up from the Collective to work full-time at the NAELFPO would allow us to spend more time and resources disseminating the group's ideology—a necessary step if the organization was to continue to grow.

With our own funds, Leslie and I acquired a post office box and telephone message service and rummaged around for used office equipment. We located and leased a run-down office suite in a soon-to-be-leveled downtown high rise. It was from here that the NAELFPO would carry the ELF ideology to news media and the public, distribute ELF communiqués, conduct interviews, and produce informational literature for mail distribution.

Immediately after the decision to form the NAELFPO came the announcement from anonymous individuals that a website, earthliberationfront.com, had just been launched to support the ELF. This new educational resource, from the beginning, proved to be an excellent tool in providing news of ELF actions, ideology, and history to news media and the public internationally. Additionally, downloadable recipe booklets began to appear on the website that instructed the reader on everything from building incendiaries to security measures.

These new forms of support for the ELF received widespread media coverage, especially in the US. The NAELFPO and the new website were recognized as important for the growth of the ELF because the primary manner in which an organization such as the ELF can grow is through the spread of its ideology. Since the group is made up of individual, anonymous cells, there really is no way a new person can get involved in an already existing cell. New cells can be created only if the ideology reaches and appeals to more people. The new press office and the website surely would assist in the distribution of this ideology.

The creation of the NAELFPO and the launching of the website also gave the ELF a new aura of legitimacy. Now the group, at least in North America, had an official office—above ground— speaking on its behalf. Furthermore, with a website also listed in the group's name, any internet user conducting a search under the ELF name would be sure to pull the page up. Both the website and the NAELFPO gave the ELF at least the appearance of being a more organized, growing—and, therefore, threatening—force.

The press releases announcing the NAELFPO and website only added to the media interest kindled by the recent Boise Cascade and MSU actions. I was happy that Leslie had agreed to work in the office and share the growing workload, as it was becoming increasingly time-consuming and often mentally draining. (Try defending a group that openly uses arson to hostile news reporters on a daily basis!) But along with the larger workload came a certain satisfaction in knowing that the ELF was growing.

Tackling Urban Sprawl

Before Leslie and I even had time to move into the new office space, I received notice that another ELF action had been taken. This act, again in the form of arson, was not specifically against deforestation, genetic engineering, or the fur farm industry, but rather another new target: urban sprawl.

The communiqué appeared as follows:

Greetings from Bloomington, IN:

The Earth Liberation Front would like to take credit for a late night visit to the Sterling Woods development on the evening of January 23rd.

During our visit, we torched one house that was under construction. It was completely destroyed. The walls had caved in by the time the fire department arrived. Damage has been assessed at

$200,000. When finished the house was to be worth $700,000. "NO SPRAWL, ELF" was painted on the developer's sign.

The house was targeted because the sprawling development it is located in is in the Lake Monroe Watershed. This is the drinking water supply for the town of Bloomington, Indiana, and the surrounding area. It is already being jeopardized by existing development and roads.

Once again the rich of the world are destroying what little we have left in terms of natural areas and collective holdings (the water). Hopefully they will get the message that we will not take it anymore.

Vince Scott never suspected that his soon-to-be-finished dream home would be targeted by radical environmentalists. He even believed he was following environmentally sound building practices. But on January 23, 2000, the ELF surprised Scott and the nation with its first-ever action against what the group referred to as urban sprawl.

On January 31, 2000, I went live on the national cable show *Court TV* to debate Scott and defend the ELF action taken against his home. Located in the Sterling Woods development just outside of Bloomington, Indiana, Scott's home was one of many that had come under intense criticism from locals angry over a threatened watershed. Defending the construction of his home as being environmentally sound, Scott stated on *Court TV*,

I know the developer personally. . . . I know that he spent many years trying to develop this property the right way. . . . He took all the concerns that you have as far as the environmental issues of keeping the trees and minimizing the damaging of the water that you guys claim is happening in this particular development. He did everything he possibly could. . . . He spent thousands and thousands of dollars. . . . He went over and above the law.

On the program, my one response to Scott's reasoning was that the developer had used all the legal possibilities except for one: he could have chosen not to develop that natural land, thereby not threatening that water supply.

Travel through Los Angeles, Chicago, Phoenix, or nearly any major urban center, and you'll find endless miles of strip malls, suburban tract housing, and Wal-Marts. Reid Ewing, an associate professor in the College of Engineering and Design at Florida International University in Miami, has described sprawl as "random development characterized by poor accessibility of related land uses such as housing, jobs, and services like schools and hospitals."[61] Sprawl can be more simply defined as development pushing urban areas further out into previously undeveloped areas, at the expense of human health and environmental quality.

The dramatic growth in suburban areas has been accompanied by a massive increase in automobile use. According to data in Traffic Volume Trends —a report published by the Federal Highway Administration—the total vehicle miles of travel (VMT) in the United States increased from 1 trillion to 3.25 trillion between 1971 and 2022. This significant rise in automobile use has been directly linked to increasing commuter and trip distances resulting from a greater gap between homes and employment.[62]

According to the AAA Foundation for Traffic Safety, the average American driver spends approximately 293 hours annually behind the wheel.[63] This striking increase in automobile use, resulting from sprawl, produces devastating effects.

61 Charles Schmidt, "The Specter of Sprawl," *Environmental Health Perspectives* 106, no. 6 (June 1998).
62 "Annual Vehicle Miles Traveled in the United States," Alternative Fuels Data Center. afdc.energy.gov/data/search?q=VMT+1971++2022.
63 "Americans Spend 293 Hours Driving Each Year," Automotive Fleet. automotive-fleet.com/136735/americans-spend-an-average-of-17-600-minutes-driving-annually.

A 1995 report, "Health Effects of Motor Vehicle Air Pollution," published by Mark Delucchi of the Institute of Transportation Standards at the University of California at Davis, demonstrated just how dangerous this growth in auto use is to human health. Delucchi showed that air pollutants from vehicles are responsible for 20,000 to 40,000 cases of chronic respiratory illness annually in the United States. Vehicle air pollution causes respiratory-restricted activity days for an estimated 50 to 70 million people per year.[64]

Urban sprawl has also been linked to deteriorating water quality in previously rural locations. The EPA's 1994 report—National Water Quality Inventory—indicated that 12 to 50 percent of all surface water pollution originates with urban runoff, particularly from sprawling communities. This pollution from new development commonly includes oils, nutrients, road salts, and sediments, in addition to solid and hazardous waste. This particular problem was one of the ELF's concerns in targeting Vince Scott's home.

Another threat to water quality posed by sprawl is the rapid destruction of wetlands across the country. Wetlands possess a unique ability to remove up to 90 percent of pollutants in water, so their decline doesn't bode well for reducing pollution. Unfortunately, an estimated 80,000 acres of wetlands are destroyed annually in the United States, due largely to sprawl.[65]

As sprawling developments push further out into rural areas, habitat depletion also becomes a major concern. In the Pacific Northwest, steelhead trout and salmon are severely threatened with extinction due to loss of tree cover and polluted runoff—all sprawl-related. Results of a 2000 study published in *Bioscience* suggest that urbanization endangers more species listed under the US Endangered Species Act than any other cause.[66] The National Wildlife Federation further proclaims that sprawl has been responsible for the loss of habitat for the red-cockaded woodpecker, panther, and black bear in Florida, and the desert

64 Schmidt, "The Specter of Sprawl."
65 Infographic: Value of Coastal Wetland Habitat. fisheries.noaa.gov/infographic/infographic-value-coastal-wetland-habitat
66 Brian Czech et al., "Economic Associations among Causes of Species Endangerment in the United States," *BioScience* 50, no. 7 (July 2000): 593–601.

tortoise in southern California—to name just a few examples. The group also states that "the Puget Sound area has lost 37 percent of its tree cover from 1974 to 1998, resulting in increased runoff, sedimentation, and air pollution destroying forest habitat and degrading aquatic habitats."[67]

While Vince Scott may have believed that his developer followed all the rules and environmental regulations, the problem lies with the fact that developers rarely get turned down in proposing new projects. New developments mean money coming into and supporting local economies, a goal for which city governments strive. Don Steuter, an air-conditioner repairman and anti-sprawl activist in Phoenix, Arizona, has stated, "Nobody in this town has ever said no to a developer. We spend tax dollars to encourage sprawl, and then it comes back to us as air pollution."[68]

Among other assistance the government gives to encourage sprawl, subsidies directly finance consumer use of the automobile. Without this form of transit, sprawling communities could never exist. In its 1995 report "The Technological Reshaping of Metropolitan America," the now-defunct White House Office of Technology Assistance (OTA) discovered that automobile drivers only paid an estimated 73 to 88 percent of the actual monetary costs of auto use. Once non-monetary costs, such as air pollution, were figured in, the cost paid by drivers dropped to 53–69 percent. Another report, included in a 2006 hearing entitled "The Hidden Cost of Oil" before the US Senate Committee on Foreign Relations stated that if the indirect costs of air pollution, parking, and congestion were included, the actual price of gasoline would be over ten dollars per gallon.[69]

The most obvious solution to many of the problems associated with sprawl is not to build. Of course, to the developer whose livelihood is primarily based on increasing sprawl, this option is rarely acknowledged and arguably never considered. Much of urban sprawl derives from the common desire to live

---

67 "Evidence of Habitat Loss Due to Sprawl," National Wildlife Federation.
68 Sierra Club fact sheet, www.sierraclub.org/sprawl.factsheet.asp#Traffic.
69 "The Hidden Cost of Oil" Hearing before the Committee on Foreign Relations US Senate. govinfo.gov/content/pkg/CHRG-109shrg34739/html/CHRG-109shrg34739.htm

out the classic version of the American Dream—a huge house in the suburbs, complete with large green lawn, white picket fence, 2.3 kids, and the new BMW in the driveway—paired with economic power. The developments that are often created serve the wealthy, while the poor increasingly are left in more urban areas with degraded schools and housing.

Vince Scott's home, for instance, was a mansion that would be valued at over one million dollars after its completion in the year 2000. While Scott felt he should have the right to build his dream house, the people of Bloomington and outlying areas also have a right to clean drinking water. As the developer obviously received no serious resistance from the local government, the ELF felt there was little else that could be done other than to send a strong and clear message to Scott and developers across the country: "We will not take it anymore."

While this was the first action the ELF had taken against urban sprawl, it also marked the first time that an individual, rather than a company, was targeted. The news that radical environmentalists had burned a new home under construction in Bloomington sent shock waves across the country. Vince Scott wasn't directly tied to any large corporation or government organization, which had been the previous commonality among ELF victims. Rather, Scott was a private citizen attempting to build his dream home. Suddenly, news reporters, and thus the general public in middle-and-upper-class America, began to realize that they too could become potential targets, as the issue of sprawl is widespread.

Two months later, the ELF struck against highway construction in Minnesota. The following communiqué was received by the NAELFPO:

Over the weekend of March 24, maintenance work was done to vehicles belonging to CS McCrossan construction, and were [sic] being used for the construction of the highway 55 reroute in Minneapolis. 4 machines had wires and hoses cut, dirt and sand poured into gas tanks, oil tubes, and exhaust pipes, [and] engine parts smashed, removed and destroyed, which has happened several times before and gone unreported. This site is only a quarter mile from Coldwater Springs, a sacred site to the Dakota people, and the last source of fresh spring water in the twin cities. After cutting hundreds of old trees and decimating a once wild area, the road now threatens to cut off Coldwater's underground source, which has already happened to other springs in the city because of road construction.

Also on 3 separate occasions, large amounts of rock and table salt was mixed into the sand piles being used for cement. The piles are not gone and it is assumed that they were used in the cement building the land tunnel. This is being told because salt will weaken the integrity of the cement.

The road is not nearly done and neither are we.

Earth Liberation Front

The rerouting of Highway 55 in Minneapolis was threatening to destroy the ten-thousand-year-old Clearwater Spring, in addition to sizable quantities of parkland and prairies. Local activists, including Native Americans, anarchists, and environmentalists, had been working to fight the reroute since its beginning on August 10, 1998.

Prior to the ELF attacks on construction property, opponents of the reroute had tried a variety of tactics, from spiritual ceremonies to nonviolent civil disobedience. By far the most extreme act was an urban occupation of activists called the Minnehaha Free State. This inner-city base camp was set up to slow and ultimately stop all construction on the reroute using various means of civil disobedience. In what would become another example of classic tactical escalation, the ELF action only came after local activists had attempted and exhausted other, less severe methods.

In the most intense display of activity ever in the Midwest by the ELF, the group conducted another action on April 30 in Bloomington, Indiana. In this second strike in the area against overdevelopment and sprawl, the ELF targeted Crider and Crider Construction—the same developer responsible for the Sterling Woods subdivision that contained Vince Scott's home. Even before a communiqué appeared, authorities in Bloomington suspected that the ELF was to blame. The messages "ELF," "GO DEVELOP IN HELL," and "THIS MACHINE IS EVIL" were left spray painted on the scene.

Just a few days later, Leslie and I received the following communiqué from the ELF:

Greetings,

Early Sunday, April 30th, the Earth Liberation Front struck again in Bloomington, IN. We entered the site of a massive clearcut on the west side of town, and poured sand into the engines and cut hoses of 6 large earth destroying machines. We then set fire to a trailer full of wood chips destined to become paper trash.

According to the local paper, the damages caused by our midnight soiree were in the vicinity of $500,000. Not bad for one night's work, though certainly no Vail. The reason this site was targeted was the ongoing development of the wooded areas around Bloomington have turned what was once forested land into parking lots, luxury houses for rich scum and expanded roads. The government and developers are mad with greed and there will be no limit to what they destroy until we take away the profit from their schemes. The local paper was right when they wrote that we take direct action when we don't get what we want through the usual bureaucratic channels.

We dedicate this action to Craig Rosebraugh and other Earth Warriors that are being persecuted for their beliefs. For the Wild and an End to Sprawl!

ELF

Honestly, it felt good. I had never knowingly been in contact with any members of the ELF; this made it difficult to obtain any sort of feedback as to the role I was performing as the spokesperson. While the eyes and ears of the news media around the United States focused on me and relied upon my words to explain the ELF, I had little way of knowing whether my public relations work was actually supported by those performing the actions. The only indication I had that those underground were satisfied with my work was the fact that I continued to receive communiqués. I told myself that if the underground activists were unhappy with my work, they would stop sending me messages. As this had yet to happen, I simply assumed I was valued to some degree. This latest communiqué confirmed my assumptions.

The equipment destroyed on site was being used to create new roadways in the Bloomington area, particularly a new terrain stretch of Ind. 46 to connect South Pike to Ind. 37.

This second strike in Bloomington made the area, which had seen no ELF activity before January 2000, one of the hotbeds of action for the group. Additionally, this latest attack had contributed to one of the most crucial implied goals of the organization: creating an atmosphere where no one who profits from the destruction of the natural environment is safe.

This surge of activity in the Bloomington area prompted local activist Lisa Spector to organize a public forum to discuss the recent ELF activities there. The forum, entitled "Direct Action: Violence or Self-Defense," was held in June 2000 and consisted of me, retired FBI agent Tim Pitchford, and Indiana University professor Jim Hart. While I had a personal policy of accepting virtually all speaking invitations as long as my basic expenses were covered, I was especially excited to take part in this engagement because it was geared toward community discussion. It was also one of the first opportunities I had had to visit a community where the ELF had made a visible impact in prompting people to discuss and debate the issues of sprawl, environmentalism, and property destruction.

Upon my arrival in Bloomington, I received a communiqué from the ELF claiming responsibility for another action in the area. The timing couldn't have been better. Already, the impending forum had caused quite a stir in Bloomington, becoming so controversial that the Mayor of Bloomington, John Fernandez, publicly denounced the event and encouraged the community not to participate. "I strongly encourage the community and media not to give the eco-terrorists and their supporters the attention they seek to fuel their violent crimes and the terrorizing of innocent victims," he declared.[70] Of course, the Mayor's statement swelled not only the controversy surrounding the event but also the attendance.

When I received the communiqué announcing the ELF's claim of responsibility for this new action, I knew that, if it was released before the forum, it would boost attendance and generate more publicity for the group. It stated,

The Earth Liberation Front would like to make public that we have placed hundreds of spikes in trees in the timber sales that are about to be cut on Crooked Creek Road in Brown County and Buskirk Road in Monroe County. These spikes have been placed both high and low in the trees to prevent the cutting of the trees. The trees are now worthless at the mill and dangerous to cut down.

We ask that this action be widely publicized in order to prevent injury to any timber workers who might be working in the area. It is not our intention to cause any harm to anyone. We also hope that this action will discourage companies from buying timber sales in the State Forests. This is a warning to all those who want to turn the beings of the earth into cash. We are committed to protecting every last square inch of our forests that remain. Too much has been lost, let the corporations beware, the ELF is everywhere.

Sure enough, with this statement released on top of all the other controversy, local citizens and news reporters filled the Unitarian church for the event.

When I was seated at the panelists' table at the front of the church, a woman approached me with a slip of paper in her

---

70 Marda Johnson, "Fernandez Critical of Forum on Protest," *Bloomington Herald-Times*, June 27, 2000.

hand. I had seen that image so many times before that I knew it could only be another grand jury subpoena. *Fuck!* I thought as she moved closer to the table. While I had requested security for the event, this move caught them off guard and the woman was allowed to approach me freely.

"Mr. Rosebraugh," she said, handing me the paper, "You have been served."

I placed the folded paper on the table without even peeking at its contents. I didn't want to give her the satisfaction of thinking she had disrupted my presentation. As the forum began seconds later, I put the paper out of my mind—at least until the event had finished.

Much to my surprise, when I did open the letter at the end of the night, it wasn't a grand jury subpoena at all but a notice of intent to sue. The paper stated that on behalf of the ELF Family Lore a lawsuit was being filed against the ELF and myself as the organization's representative. This ELF Family Lore—whoever the hell they were—claimed that the ELF had defamed them by using their name. *This has to be a joke*, I thought as I studied the document.

The situation only grew more bizarre when I consulted with some of the local activists, who informed me that the ELF Family Lore were a "bunch of pothead hippies who get drunk and dance around naked on their wooded property." Upon returning to Portland, I ended up having to hire an attorney in Bloomington to make an appearance for me to get the charges dropped. Thankfully, it was a fairly simple maneuver, as I could not be sued for a group to which I had no direct connection. As it turned out, however, my perceived association with the ELF was about to cause much more serious repercussions in my life.

8

WITH
GUNS
DRAWN

"**K**NOCK, KNOCK, KNOCK!" The ferocious pounding woke me from what felt like a deep slumber. It seemed like only seconds had passed since Elaine had kissed my cheek on her way out the door to her temp job in the suburbs. The banging resumed, and I stumbled out of bed and into some clothes so I could see who it was threatening to break down the door at 7:00 A.M.

"FBI, SEARCH WARRANT, OPEN UP!" a stern voice yelled from the front porch. The knocking continued, and just as I made my way out of the bedroom Elaine and I were renting from two of her college friends, Carrie and Jim, the front door flew open.

"FBI, GET YOUR HANDS UP! GET DOWN ON THE GROUND!" the six agents screamed almost in unison. Storming in with guns drawn, the agents forced Carrie, Jim, and me to the ground within seconds. After searching the three of us, our faces pressed to the icy linoleum, the agents led us into the front living room and gave us two choices. We could leave the house or stay through the duration of the raid. If we left the premises, we would not be allowed back inside the house until the search and seizure was completed. If we chose to stay inside, we would be confined to the living room—from which, I soon realized, it was impossible to see what was going on in the rest of the house. Within an hour, both Carrie and Jim had left for work and I was alone, a prisoner inside my house, attempting to listen to the federal agents as they ransacked both floors.

The timing of this raid couldn't have been much worse. It was February 2, 2000, just under two weeks after the disastrous split within Liberation Collective. In this atmosphere of rumors and a low point in local support (or so I felt), the federal government had conveniently—perhaps deliberately—picked this vulnerable time to step up its pressure against me. Additionally, Leslie and I had yet to move our office equipment and supplies to the new press office, and the bulk of our materials were stored in my basement.

At the time of the raid, I was living on Couch Street in the northeast section of Portland. Upon returning from the Primate Freedom Tour the previous summer, Elaine and I had made the decision to try living together for the first time. So instead of both of us moving, we opted to live in her room in a tasteful house shared by Carrie and Jim. As a precautionary measure before I actually moved in, the four of us sat down and had a discussion to ensure that everyone in the house knew about my political work and its associated risks. While we'd discussed the possibility of agents coming to the door to question me and even possibly raiding the house, it had been hypothetical.

Neither Carrie nor Jim had been directly involved in activist politics, a reality I had been respectful of in agreeing to co-rent Elaine's room in the house. Carrie, a massage therapist and writer, and Jim, a painter and waiter, had likewise been respectful of Elaine and me, and of our drive toward social and political change. Up until this day, the relationship had worked fairly well, but as the raid began, I wondered if this might change.

At the beginning of the search, government agents presented me with a copy of the official warrant authorizing them to search the entire house, my vehicle, and another location. It appeared that a simultaneous search was being conducted at the Liberation Collective office downtown. The warrant authorized the agents to seize a wide variety of items—anything and everything that might possibly contain information about the ELF and ALF. It went on to cite the following actions as those under investigation by a current federal grand jury:

The December 31, 1999, fire at the Agricultural Hall of Michigan State University;

The December 25, 1999, fire at the Northwest headquarters of Boise Cascade in Monmouth, Oregon;

The December 27, 1998, fire at US Forest Industries in Medford, Oregon;

The October 18, 1998, fire at Vail Resorts, Inc. in Colorado;

The November 29, 1997, fire and horse release at the Bureau of Land Management Horse Corral in Burns, Oregon;

The July 21, 1997, fire at the Cavel West Horse Slaughterhouse in Redmond, Oregon; and

The May 30, 1997, release of some 12,000 mink from a fur farm in Mt. Angel, Oregon.

This lengthy list of incidents under investigation brought more than just agents from the FBI and BATF to my house on that winter morning. I soon learned that US Forest Service agents and two Michigan State University police officers were also present at the raid that day. I counted a total of twelve agents inside the house when the raid began.

As eleven agents disappeared and began rummaging through every nook and cranny of the house, a twelfth agent was assigned to watch me, most likely ensuring that I would not interfere or observe. As the seconds slowly ticked by, I sat on the couch wondering what to do. I did not want to leave the house, as I felt someone should be there to observe the agents. Yet, I also felt it would be important to immediately contact an attorney and some friends or supporters who could advise me and also come to the house. The feeling of being alone in my house with twelve government agents executing a raid was eerie. Furthermore, I was quite uncomfortable with the fact that other than Carrie and Jim, no one (other than the federal government) knew what was transpiring that morning on Northeast Couch Street.

Paranoia kicked in, and I began thinking about how easy it would be for the agents to realistically do anything they wanted to me—and get away with it. Thoughts of Fred Hampton ran through my mind.

A member of the Black Panther Party in the 1960s, Hampton was murdered by police in his Chicago apartment. *The government gets away with murder daily*, I thought. How simple it would be for them to physically injure or kill me and then claim I had attacked them. They could also easily plant drugs in the house, I realized, trying not to let my fears distract me from the sounds of ransacking coming from the other rooms and the basement.

Within a short time, the FBI agent assigned to monitor me began questioning me about various ELF actions. It seemed the Boise Cascade fire was of particular interest to him, and he threw questions at me relentlessly, attempting to make me talk. I didn't, except to say repeatedly, "I am not going to answer your questions." After I had stated this a few times in a row, the agent would usually give up for a few minutes, then start again. I quickly picked up a book and pretended to read. Of course, with my nerves tense and my concentration focused on the other agents in the house, I would have been just as successful in reading that book if it had been flipped upside down. At least it gave me something to focus my eyes on instead of the yellow letters "FBI" on the agent's blue jacket.

About an hour into the raid, I suddenly remembered that I had a truckload of sandwiches, cookies, and muffins out in my Toyota waiting to be delivered to local stores. (At the time, I was working at a small organic, vegan wholesale food company that I had started in 1999.) As it was nearing 9:00 A.M., I was already late for my deliveries, so I asked the agent in the room if I could call someone to drive my truck. The agent had to leave the room and consult with the others before "granting" me the opportunity to make one and only one phone call from my house. I called Leslie, figuring that he could make the deliveries and then, I hoped, stick around, alert more people, and provide support for me during the raid. When Leslie answered the phone, I calmly asked him to come make deliveries for me. He naturally asked why, and, with the federal agent staring at me, I told him the truth—my house was being raided and I could not leave. Shortly after I hung up the phone, an agent came from the back of the house and asked for my keys. This was one of the few agents I recognized that day—Special Agent Daniel Feucht, who had harassed me so many times before. Now he took my keys, went outside, and proceeded to search my truck.

Within a half an hour, Leslie arrived outside and came up to the front porch, only to be stopped by FBI agents. He wasn't able to come in, so through the doorway I handed him my keys, trying desperately to communicate without words my wishes for support. I didn't want to let the Feds know I was trying to get people there, since they might have taken it as a sign of fear and weakness. As Leslie left in my truck, I felt a little better knowing that at least someone outside knew what was happening.

As the morning slowly crept by, it became apparent to me that I was little more than a prisoner in my own home. Not only was I confined to one room with a guard monitoring my every move, but I couldn't even go to the bathroom without an escort. In fact, when I did have to go, the agent assigned to watch me had to yell to the rest of the crew in the house that I was coming through. He then proceeded to stand in the open doorway of the bathroom as I went. Comforting.

Nearly three hours into the search, another government-issued vehicle arrived at the house, filled with more federal agents. They entered my house carrying briefcases and immediately headed to the other rooms, out of sight. What in the world could they be doing? I wondered. Just over an hour later, the same agents, with briefcases in hand, left with no explanation. To this day, I do not know why they came or what they did. My only hypothesis was that they might have brought in listening devices to be implanted in the house.

Shortly after they left, Leslie returned in my truck and I was again thrilled to see a supportive face—even if it was through the house window. After handing me back my keys, he walked back toward his car, only to be chased down by Feucht. When Feucht reached Leslie, instead of even attempting to question him about any of the actions under investigation, he chose to play psychological mind games. He asked Leslie about the various health problems he had experienced over the years. Through the house window, I watched Leslie shake his head at Feucht, get in his car and drive off. While it might have served no purpose other than to calm my nerves a bit, I wished he had stayed.

After Leslie left, I continued attempting to read until I was approached by a different FBI agent carrying a white document. He handed me the sheet of paper and told me I was being served with another subpoena to testify before a federal grand jury. While I would later find out that this was a new grand jury, the investigation into the ELF and the ALF was essentially the same—except for including a number of additional actions that had occurred since 1997. The date I was commanded to appear in the Federal Courthouse in Portland was February 29, 2000.

When the raid had reached the six-hour mark, the agents began bringing full, closed moving boxes out into the living room and stacking them by the front door. As the boxes piled up, an agent presented me with an inventory list allegedly accounting for all the items in the boxes that were being seized. Interestingly, I was not allowed to compare the inventory list with the actual property that was already sealed in boxes. Once the inventory list was in my hands, the twelve agents quickly loaded up all the boxes into their government SUVs and sped off without another word.

Speechless and feeling violated, I walked around the house to survey the damage. Two rooms in particular, it appeared, had been purposely trashed. One was the basement, which had contained a sizable number of files, computer equipment, and other items destined for the new press office. The other room was the bedroom that Elaine and I shared and also used as a temporary home office. It looked like a typical burglary scene from a Hollywood movie—everything torn off the walls, furniture turned over and belongings thrown about. It appeared that the agents had made a special effort to ensure that I felt their impact. Left on top of a pile of belongings was a freshly torn painting made by Elaine and a crumpled announcement of the funeral of my recently deceased grandfather.

In utter disbelief, I went back into the living room and began reading the inventory list so graciously supplied by the agents: three computers, videos, magazines, books, address books, media directories, mailing lists, photographs, receipts, and much more. Hundreds of items were listed, and it appeared the agents had cleared the house of nearly all of the records, equipment, and office supplies that had any link whatsoever to Liberation Collective or the ELF and ALF. Unfortunately for my roommates, the items seized in the raid didn't just belong to me or Elaine, but also to Carrie and Jim.

When Elaine, Carrie, and Jim returned from work that evening, we all rummaged through the destroyed interior of the house, attempting to determine what exactly was lost. Jim got off the easiest, with little or nothing taken, but Carrie lost her computer system—her main writing tool. It would take weeks before Elaine and I actually had any real idea of just how much personal and political property we had lost.

None of us had actually thought a raid would happen. It wasn't as if I was totally unprepared, but when federal agents burst through your door and hold you at gunpoint, it can catch you a bit off guard. Elaine was taken aback by the incident, but it appeared to make her, like me, only more determined to stand up for justice. Carrie and Jim, on the other hand, didn't take too well to the federal government's invasion of their lives. It was only a short time later, within the next month, that Elaine and I were told they did not want to live with us anymore.

This latest housing problem added to the already enormous pressure on both Elaine and me. A broken arm, a messy breakup with Liberation Collective, a raid, and now having to search for a new home all within six months led me to wonder what model of Mack truck had just struck me. If all this wasn't enough, Feucht again came knocking on our front door.

It was February 15, two weeks since the raid, when Feucht showed up on our front porch. Since I had already had one subpoena served to me during the raid, I answered the door, interested to see what else this demon planned to lay upon me. It was a letter to me from the US Department of Justice, stating that I was considered an official target of this grand jury investigation. This meant that no longer was I just considered a "witness," as had been the case with the 1997 and 1998 grand jury subpoenas. Now, still lacking any captured ELF members to prosecute, it seemed the US Attorney's office was going to see what charges could be brought against me, the messenger. Before Feucht left my porch, he informed me that he didn't like being referred to as "Agent Bastard," a remark obviously intended to demonstrate that the federal government was reading my email.

According to the US Attorney's office, the charges that were being looked into regarding my work as a spokesperson for the ALF and ELF included,

18 USC. Section 844 (1), Use of fire or explosive to damage property used in interstate commerce; 18 USC. Section (f)(1), Use of fire or explosive to destroy United

States property; 18 USC. Section 1951, Interference with commerce by threats of violence (Hobbs Act); 18 USC. Section 43, Animal Enterprise Terrorism; 18 USC. Section 371, Conspiracy to commit (such) offense; and, 18 USC. Section 2, Aiding and abetting.

This letter declaring me a target of the grand jury was just the latest sign that the government was attempting to pick up the pressure against the ELF in the United States.

As with the 1997 grand jury subpoenas, shortly after I received this new summons on February 2, I began working to organize a national day of action against state repression for the date I was required to appear, February 29. Elaine, Leslie, and I created posters and advertisements for the day of action and mailed them around the country and even internationally to encourage people to hold protests on the 29th against the repressive measures continually taken by the US government. The day was also intended as a demonstration to the federal government of broad-based support for the ELF and its spokesperson. The advertisements asked people living in the US to organize demonstrations against US federal buildings, and other activists to target US embassies.

Thanks to a great deal of hard work and cooperation from people across the United States, when February 29 came, protests were held in eleven cities in the US and in front of one US Embassy in England. When I arrived with my attorney at the Federal Courthouse in Portland shortly before 11:30 A.M. (the time I had been commanded to appear), I was pleasantly surprised to find over 150 people demonstrating outside. It felt reassuring to know that whatever the federal government decided to do to me that day, there would be supporters outside rallying in my defense.

When 11:30 arrived, I entered the Courthouse with my attorney and rode the elevator up to the grand jury room. As I entered, the familiar oppressive atmosphere hit me. The tension, hostility, and chill inside the room were just as I remembered them from my last appearance there in December 1997. As soon as I sat down, the questioning began from Assistant US Attorney

Stephen Peifer, who also didn't seem to have changed much in the couple of years since I had last seen him.

Many of the questions were very similar to those asked in 1997—Did I have any previous knowledge of specific actions? Did I know who had committed these actions? How did I receive communications about these actions? etc. The main difference by far, though, was related to the numerous questions asked about specific individuals and about property that had been seized from my house during the raid.

"Why were you in possession of aerial photographs of mink farms on the Oregon Coast?" Peifer asked. "Why were they taken?" To all of the questions excluding my name I simply took the Fifth Amendment. Frustrated as usual with my lack of cooperation, Peifer continued, "Regarding an email from you stating that you wanted to close the Oregon Primate Center, what are your intentions? What is the purpose of having aerial photographs of the Oregon Primate Center? Where did you get these? Why were you in possession of vendor lists from the Oregon Primate Center? What was the source of these? Why were you in possession of videos of lab raids? Regarding an email from you stating you want to disrupt the Americans for Medical Progress, do you want to disrupt this organization? What is your intention?"

These questions had little, if anything, to do with the actions the grand jury was investigating. The proceeding continued to go downhill when the grand jurors themselves had the opportunity to ask questions toward the end. Most of the grand juror participation at this point came in the form of hostile comments toward me such as "I bet his shoes are leather," and, in reference to my heavy use of the Fifth Amendment, "Yeah, he's got no vocabulary."

Despite my nervousness and terror inside the grand jury room, I was momentarily pleased to hear the faint sounds of drumming and chanting coming from the crowd of supporters outside. Surely, Peifer and the grand jurors also heard. I didn't know until later that Leslie was arrested by the Portland police outside the federal building during the grand jury session, allegedly for blocking traffic. Of course, by this time both the Feds and Portland police knew full well that Leslie worked at the ELF Press Office and was a vocal and visible political organizer in Portland—not to mention a good friend of mine.

After nearly an hour inside the grand jury room, I was instructed to go out and wait with my attorney. Peifer told me that he would come out and speak to us before I was released. When Peifer came out, he handed my attorney an order compelling testimony applying toward my future grand jury appearances. The order was specific to information surrounding the Boise Cascade fire and meant that if and when I was called back before the grand jury, I would be required to answer all questions relating to the Boise Cascade incident without Fifth Amendment protection. In other words, I had to either answer the questions or be immediately imprisoned on contempt charges. Before releasing me, Peifer also informed my attorney that he would be calling me back before the grand jury in a month or so.

In late March, I received notice through my attorney that I had been commanded back to testify before the grand jury on April 26.

Once again, the organizing began for another national day of action against state repression, and a call was put out internationally for actions on or around April 26 targeting US federal buildings and embassies. The response to the call was far greater this time, and not only from activists and supporters.

On April 20, I received a call from a reporter on the East Coast asking if I had a response to the press release issued by members of Congress the day before. I had absolutely no idea what the reporter was referring to, so he faxed me a copy of a press release that had been issued by Rep. George Radanovich, a Republican from California. Its headline read, "Federal Buildings Threatened by Environmental Extremist; Western Caucus Chairman Writes Reno Seeking Protection." The release continued,

> Rep. George Radanovich (R-California) joined Congressman Don Young (R-Alaska) and others in sending a letter to Attorney General Janet Reno seeking additional protection for federal buildings

following an e-mail received from the North American Earth Liberation Front. The e-mail called on "militant demonstrations targeting US federal buildings and embassies" on Wednesday, April 26th and was dated April 1, 2000.

"We are requesting that Attorney General Janet Reno institute a criminal investigation of those responsible for sending out this e-mail threat and we asked her to respond to us by 4 p.m. EST today with her intentions," said Radanovich, who serves as Chairman of the fifty-six-member Western Caucus.

"As we remember the fifth anniversary of the Oklahoma City bombing today it is important that we take every threat seriously. The Clinton-Gore Administration has aligned themselves with the organized national environmental extremists in the past, however I hope they do the right thing and investigate this email before somebody gets hurt," he concluded.

The Congressman seeks to have the Justice Department use the Racketeer Influenced Corrupt Organization (RICO) prohibitions against interstate criminal organizations. Copies of the letter sent to Attorney General Janet Reno and the e-mail sent by Craig Rosebraugh from the North American Earth Liberation Front are available upon request.

What the fuck? I thought as I read and then re-read the press release. *Could this be any more ridiculous?* I immediately thought of the email message that I had sent out advertising for a national day of action against state repression. I recalled it being somewhat tame in its wording compared to my usual inflammatory writing style. Just to reassure myself, I pulled it up.

New Grand Jury Date Set—Time to Organize

April 1, 2000

I received notice two days ago that I have been commanded to appear before the grand jury in Portland once again on April 26. They have already granted me immunity and are commanding my testimony regarding the burning of the northwest headquarters of Boise Cascade in Monmouth, OR, which happened on December 25, 1999.

As soon as I take the Fifth Amendment or refuse to answer any questions I will be immediately subject to a contempt hearing.

We are organizing a national day of action against government repression on April 26. All individuals and groups concerned about government harassment and/or who support the courageous work of the Animal Liberation Front and Earth Liberation Front are asked to hold militant demonstrations targeting US federal buildings, embassies, etc.

If you are interested in setting up a demonstration please contact us in Portland to coordinate actions. Literature on grand juries, the ELF, and government harassment is available upon request.

Craig Rosebraugh

North American Earth Liberation Front Press Office

I wondered what had prompted Congress to feel so threatened that they had to petition Janet Reno for action. My curiosity piqued, I searched for, and finally located, a copy of the actual letter sent by eight members of Congress to Reno. I found it quite interesting, to say the least, that these Congressional members (Don Young, Helen Chenoweth-Hage, Barbara Cubin, George Radanovich, Richard W. Pombo, Wally Herger, James V. Hansen, and Chris Cannon) were making such a fuss over this email that I had signed. I mean, if I was attempting to provoke major terrorist activity against the federal buildings and embassies, would I really sign my own name? Obviously this group of politicians believed so. I then wondered what the US Attorney General would think of my email and of the petition from Congress. As it turns out, either my announcement wasn't in violation of the law or Reno didn't want to waste the time and resources to investigate—either way, charges were never filed regarding this incident. Reno must have acknowledged some threat, though, as added security was called for at all US federal buildings on April 26.

A few days before the grand jury, my attorney put forth a motion in court to have my subpoena dropped due to a procedural error on the side of Assistant US Attorney Peifer. On February 29, Peifer had the order compelling testimony ready and waiting before I ever testified. I was told that the usual procedure is that the US Attorney's office waits to see what actions or inactions a witness takes before such an order is completed. Peifer was effectively able to argue that, based on my prior dealings with him and the grand jury, he had a reasonable suspicion that I would be invoking my Fifth Amendment right on February 29. Therefore, a judge declared that Peifer was not out of line by having the order completed ahead of time. I was still commanded to appear on April 26 and would be under the order compelling testimony for the Boise Cascade action.

When the day arrived, support protests were held in Portland, Sacramento, Los Angeles, Washington, DC, Denver, Minneapolis, London, and several other cities. Once again, the Portland demonstration attracted a sizable crowd, with over one hundred people carrying signs, banners, drums, and bullhorns. Walking toward the federal building with my attorney, I felt a strong sense of support from the protesters as they came into view.

Entering the grand jury room yet again, I knew I had a very slim chance of leaving a free person that day. Naturally, I was nervous as hell. In a two-hour session, I worked through each question, one by one. After each question was asked, I was able to go outside and discuss it with my attorney. While lawyers are not allowed inside federal grand juries, witnesses have the right to leave the room at reasonable occurrences to consult with counsel. Of course, the term *reasonable* is open to differing interpretations, and the US Attorney's Office can charge the witness with disrupting the proceedings, or with contempt, if it appears that this right is being abused.

To all of the questions falling outside the scope of the order compelling testimony, I took the Fifth Amendment. But to the questions about the Boise Cascade action, I told Peifer and the grand jurors that I could not recall the answers—the Reagan defense, as some news reporters referred to it. With all of the stress from the grand jury harassment and pressure from federal authorities, I simply had and continue to have a major memory problem. Of course, what this meant is that legally I could not be held in contempt of court for not answering the questions.

The answers I gave, frustrating as they were to Peifer, were the only responses I could give to the questions presented. Peifer became so frustrated with this outcome of his inquisition that his last questions to me were, "Does your memory lapse concern you? Have you seen a doctor about your memory? How do you function on a day-to-day basis with such a memory problem?"

After two hours had passed, and a considerable amount of smoke had issued from Peifer's flaming head, he told me that he needed to speak to my attorney before I could leave. Outside the grand jury room, Peifer informed my attorney that I would be called back again in a month or so for further questioning. Surprisingly, I was then released and was able to walk out of the US Federal Courthouse and back into the world. I was happy and relieved to discover that I had yet again managed to not cooperate with the grand jury without going to prison.

It was only a short while before I received the call from my attorney informing me that Peifer had set my next appearance date for May 24. This time, however, a second individual had been subpoenaed to appear on the same day and time in Portland. I was uncertain how this would work but figured one of us would just be made to wait outside while the other was being questioned.

Josh Harper, an activist in the Pacific Northwest who had been working with Ocean Defense International trying to stop the Makah whale hunt in the Olympic Peninsula, also had received a subpoena for May 24. While Josh had been a member of Liberation Collective and a friend and former roommate of mine, I was unclear as to why he had been served. Then I recalled that Peifer, in the February 29 grand jury session, had attempted to implicate Harper in a rabbit farm raid that had occurred in Philomath, Oregon. Josh also had been an outspoken advocate of both the ALF and the ELF for years and had promoted direct action in a video series he produced entitled *Breaking Free*. I assumed he had been commanded to testify for these reasons, along with Peifer's lack of success in indicting anyone from the Portland federal grand jury investigation.

In a dramatic show of force and intimidation, Josh actually received his subpoena on the water just off the Pacific Northwest coast. Coast Guard cutters surrounded his boat, and federal agents, after boarding the vessel, served the subpoena. This was Josh's first subpoena to a grand jury.

Prior to May 24, activists again organized to attempt to pressure the grand jury system to stop harassing people in barbaric proceedings. Once again, emails and letters were sent out internationally calling for militant action targeting US federal buildings. As the 24th drew near, protests were scheduled to be held in Portland, Los Angeles, Bloomington (Indiana), Minneapolis, and San Diego. Suffering from a serious lack of sleep, my stomach a nervous wreck, I spent May 23 trying to enjoy what could very well have been my last taste of freedom for up to eighteen months. I figured the more times I was called back to this grand jury, the greater chance I had of being held in contempt for not cooperating. *This time could be it*, I thought.

Late in the day, I received a call from my attorney, who unexpectedly informed me that my subpoena for the next day had been called off. Peifer's reason was that apparently the grand jury did not have time to deal with Josh and me on the same day at the same time. I wondered why Peifer hadn't figured this out a month before when he scheduled us for the same day. Perhaps he wanted to allow the agony of anticipation to build for as long as possible. Peifer told my attorney that I would be called back to the grand jury some time either in June or July. Josh, who had stated publicly that he would not be cooperating with this grand jury, was still scheduled to appear the next morning.

Nearly a hundred people gathered once again in front of the Federal Courthouse at 8:00 A.M. on May 24 to support Josh and protest against the ongoing harassment dished out by the grand jury system. When 9:00 rolled around—the time Josh was commanded to appear—he was nowhere to be found. Outside the Federal Courthouse, in front of protesters, reporters, and police, I read aloud a statement from Josh that summarized his opposition to testifying.

Why I Am Resisting the Grand Jury

My name is Josh Harper. I am a green anarchist currently residing in Seattle, WA. I was recently attempting to interfere in the killing of whales off of the Olympic Peninsula when the vessel I was aboard was surrounded by the Coast Guard. I was boarded and issued a subpoena commanding me to appear May 24 in Portland, OR. I have decided to defy this subpoena and wish to explain my decision to fellow activists. First and foremost, this world is dying. All that is beautiful about the world is being destroyed and paved over. The animals are being either killed or turned into machines for human consumption. Our society, which was for thousands of years egalitarian, is now filled with neurosis, discontent, and alienation. But there is more out there! All of our rage, all of our anger at this system can be focused into positive action. This grand jury wants to stop that positive action. Although the ALF and ELF are only small parts of a larger effort for autonomy, freedom, and a progression to an intact Earth, they are important because they show us that we can fight back, and WE CAN WIN! I will not betray them by speaking with their enemies.

Secondly, as an anarchist I would never willingly cooperate with the grand jury system. The very idea that this government presumes they can command me to do anything shows how very little they know me. My life is my own, my thoughts are my own, and what I decide to do will not be dictated to me by judges, attorneys, and their lackeys with guns. If they want me, let them come and get me. They can drag me to the grand jury room, but they can never make me speak.

I send Craig Rosebraugh all of my respect. He has faced down this grand jury, and even though he has chosen a different tactic than me, I understand his motivations. The media he is gaining is invaluable—he is awakening even more people to the path of resistance. To the ALF and ELF—I do not know you, but I send you my endless admiration. Keep fighting. You are my sisters and brothers, perhaps some day you can remove the masks so that we may celebrate victory together. Until then, let us all remain in utter defiance of those who would try to stop us.

I knew that reading Josh's statement aloud outside would piss Peifer off on top of Josh's not showing up. Later that afternoon, my attorney called me to say that Peifer was demanding that I hand over Josh's letter. I told him I didn't have it.

Peifer never did summon me back to the grand jury, so this interaction would be the last I would have with the grand jury system—at least for some time. Josh, on the other hand, would not be so lucky, as the Feds began searching for his whereabouts. Four months later, on September 27, Josh was taken into custody in Seattle. After being held at the SEATAC Federal Detention Center for two days, he was released on bail.

On October 27, over one hundred people showed up outside the US Courthouse in Portland in support of Josh and to demonstrate a continued objection to the grand jury system. At this arraignment date, Josh successfully asked for a postponement so he could obtain an attorney. The Court then rescheduled his arraignment for November 17, 2000.

When November 17 came, Josh's date was again set back due to his out-of-state attorney not being licensed in Oregon. At this particular appearance, the federal court placed a release order on Josh that prevented him from ideologically voicing support for the ELF or the ALF. Peifer pleaded with a federal judge to place these extra restrictions after submitting into evidence a copy of an email sent by Harper discussing his support of direct action. If he violated this order, Josh would be subject to arrest and held until his trial.

On December 1, Josh's arraignment finally concluded, and he was charged with criminal contempt. His attorney entered a not guilty plea and the case was set for trial on January 3, 2001. Fortunately for Josh, the trial would never take place. His attorney successfully managed to cut a deal with Peifer, trading Josh's appearance in front of the grand jury for the withdrawal of charges against him. Josh went into the grand jury room, pleaded the Fifth and, like me many times before, was released.

At this point, the federal grand jury investigation into the ELF and ALF had been in operation since 1997 and still not one individual had been indicted. Whether the Feds wanted to admit it or not, the ELF and ALF, by their sheer organizational structure, were continuing to grow while evading all attempts by law enforcement to stop them.

LONG ISLAND
HEATS UP

"If you build it, we will burn it."

—Spray-painted message left by the ELF on a new
home under construction, Long Island, New York,
December 2000

R efusing to allow the raid to weaken our attempts to form the NAELFPO, Leslie and I worked quickly to get the downtown office up and fully functional. Within a few days, we had located enough used office equipment and supplies to begin answering the numerous inquiries from news media, which had been piling up due to all the recent ELF activity as well as the February raid. Sitting at our desks inside the second floor of the Governor Building, Leslie and I took turns explaining to reporters—both in person and via telephone—the motives of the elusive ELF.

Media interest continued to build after the ELF struck at the University of Minnesota in St. Paul just seven days after the raid in Portland. On February 10, 2000, I received a communiqué from the group stating that they had, the day before, broken into the Green Hall greenhouse and destroyed eight hundred transgenic research crops. After just a few days in the new press office, it felt good to be able to publicize this action and demonstrate to the Feds that their raid had made me more determined than ever to speak out on behalf of the underground saboteurs. This action was also proof that the ELF was continuing to target the issue of genetic engineering. Urban sprawl was clearly on their minds as well, as the spring 2000 actions in Minneapolis and Bloomington showed.

Up to this point, the ELF had been an organization known primarily in the Pacific Northwest and a few other scattered local areas across the United States. While the Vail arson in 1998 surely sparked numerous national and local stories, the ELF had failed to make continual national headlines or to penetrate the largest news center in the country (and arguably the world)— the New York City media market. From a public relations perspective, coverage in New York meant international exposure and a dramatic rise in national publicity.

Leslie and I were well aware of this fact and constantly attempted to push the ELF story into the New York scene. Through direct calling, faxing, and emailing press releases, we were determined to saturate the market out East until we saw results. Thankfully, we received some assistance in the matter in July 2000.

In the middle of the month, communiqués were sent to both the NAELFPO and the GenetixAlert press office[71] from the ELF, claiming responsibility for an attack at Cold Spring Harbor Laboratories on Long Island, New York. The ELF had evaded security and destroyed two acres of genetically modified corn and several greenhouses. They had also damaged several trucks and left anti–genetic engineering messages in spray paint at the scene.

I expected this to finally break the group into the New York news media. For days after the press release went out, I scanned the internet for stories, with little or no luck. It simply didn't make sense to me that this action had received virtually no notice from reporters. Later in the year, I would begin to see this as an unnerving trend.

I was excited about the ELF activity spreading to the New York area and hoped that it would continue—that it wasn't just a one-time occurrence like the 1998 Boston Consulate action.[72] I felt that if the ELF was going to continue to grow in size and impact, frequent activity would have to be seen in multiple local areas across the country. Only in this way could the ELF ensure that not one person, business, or governmental organization that profited from the destruction of the environment would feel safe and untouchable. It was only days later, on July 20, when the ELF struck again, this time in Wisconsin. The target was the US Forest Service's North Central Research Station Biotechnology Laboratory in Rhinelander. A communiqué sent by the ELF to the NAELFPO stated,

71 Formed to report specifically on illegal anti–genetic engineering actions by all organizations.
72 See page 94

On behalf of native forests everywhere, we attacked the US Forest Service's North Central Research Station Biotechnology Laboratory in Rhinelander, Wisconsin last night. Over 500 research pine and broadleaf trees and saplings were cut down, ring-barked and trampled. Additionally, ten Forest Service trucks were defaced and calling cards were left behind. Due to an overzealous security guard, we had to make an earlier than anticipated exit.

In Rhinelander, the Forest Service is mapping the DNA of white pine and attempting to genetically engineer them to be resistant to pine rust. Why? To aid industry in creating disease resistant trees suitable for tree farms that will increase their profits. Despite the obvious threat of genetic pollution by GE trees, these fools aided by industry financing, plod ahead in the name of science.

Don't get us wrong—this action is against the Forest Service, not just one particular project or research program. What they do on a daily basis is sheer genocide: putting forth the notion that they are "managing" life, running an asinine timber program that destroys the last of the old-growth and mars everything else, cutting deep into roadless areas in Idaho, spraying biocides like Btk in forests in Eastern Oregon and Washington under the guise of "pest management," treating wildlife as some numbers on a graph. The list goes on.

On that note, we strongly advise our allies to cease their quibbling with the Forest Service over details of their genocidal plans i.e. roadless policy, promises of no logging on public land etc. The sooner we realize that the Forest Service, like industry, are capitalists driven by an insane desire to make money and control life, the better. Then we can start taking more appropriate action.

As for the feds—we know that you are stepping up the pressure by harassing press officers and other absurdities. What you don't realize is that we are infiltrating your ranks and gathering our own information. We could be that temp worker typing away on your disgusting computer. We could even be your secretary or intern. We are everywhere and nowhere and we are watching.

For wilderness and an end to industrial society,

ELF

Earth Liberation Front

The ELF drove home its message by leaving the spray-painted warning at the scene, "ELF IS WATCHING THE US FOREST SERVICE."

Damage to the trees located along Oneida County Highway K was estimated at between $750,000 and $1,000,000.[73] An estimated $20,000 in damage was also inflicted on the ten US Forest Service vehicles that had acid applied to their windows. Judy Isebrands, a scientist from the targeted US Forest Service facility, estimated that the action had set back the research project ten to fifteen years. "We feel personally attacked," Isebrands stated shortly after the incident.

With the phone at the press office ringing off the hook, this was the busiest and most productive year yet for the ELF. There was no disputing the fact that the organization was growing in size and geographical scope. I was truly amazed and inspired that this group of courageous unknown individuals had inflicted over $30 million in damages since 1997 and not one person had been captured by authorities.

Long Island then began to erupt in a series of unexpected actions. In late September 2000, the press office received a communiqué from the ELF claiming responsibility for continuing the work against sprawl that had started with Vince Scott's home in Bloomington eight months before. The message read,

73 The $750,000 estimate appeared in "Group says research-tree attack was against bio-engineering," Associated Press State Wire, July 22, 2000. The $1,000,000 estimate appeared in "Environmental Group claims responsibility for vandalism," Wisconsin Radio Network, July 21, 2000.

> Greetings Allies,
>
> Members of the Earth Liberation Front are glad to announce our late night visit to the construction sites along Whiskey Rd. in Coram, Long Island on September 26th. During the festivities a bulldozer and a house under construction were spray painted and damaged, and numerous survey stakes "disappeared." We will no longer allow urban sprawl to destroy what little of the environment we have left on Long Island, especially so close to a nature reserve. Urban sprawl has led to the virtual extinction of several animal species, such as the Blue Heron and the Box Turtle, from the island. So until next time???
>
> The elves

This is it, I thought after receiving the communiqué. *This is the action that will finally get New York's attention.* I figured that with all of the executives and even news people who owned homes on the Island, this latest act by the group would have to get noticed. But, similar to the Cold Spring Harbor attack in July, the media releases I sent out seemed to produce no results. Fortunately, although media coverage is always an added bonus, the ELF actions are effective in themselves.

When the ELF targeted a specific piece of property, substantial monetary damages were normally inflicted on the owner—be it an individual, business, or government agency. While most of these entities had insurance and were therefore partially, if not fully, covered from any financial losses, insurance companies are not invincible. Like any other business, they have to make their bottom line their priority. There is no feasible way, then, that an insurance company can suffer a substantial loss without raising the rates of the policyholder who was targeted. In theory, the more ELF strikes occur against a particular business or industry, the more insurance companies will have to raise rates across the board until they are either forced to refuse policies to potential targets or make their premiums so high that it forces them out of business. Of course, news reports of ELF actions also serve a productive purpose. For one, media stories always contain words or phrases—sometimes complete communiqués—that increase awareness of the group's ideology across the country and around the world. This distribution of the group's message is extremely crucial to its expansion and the creation of new cells.

Secondly, the media coverage also helps to spread ELF's messages and warnings to other potential targets. It allows people to understand that their property may also be attacked if they are destroying the environment purely for monetary gain. For a group as small as the ELF, this feature was quite important in making the organization's pressure far outweigh its size.

While the September 26 incident had gone largely unnoticed by East Coast reporters, the ELF wasn't discouraged. Just over a month later another action was taken on Long Island:

> In the early morning hours of November 11th, members of the Earth Liberation Front paid a visit to the construction sites off Whiskey Rd. in Coram, Long Island. This has been the third hit on the construction site and the worst yet. Several houses were spraypainted extensively and had their windows shattered. We here elves are waging an unending war against urban sprawl and will fight to our last breath to protect our environment from greedy corporate interests.
>
> ELF

After learning from the communiqué that this was the third strike by the group at this location, I was even further surprised at the lack of interest from reporters. After the usual routine of faxing out news releases with the attached communiqué, I began directly calling various news agencies, particularly on Long Island, to attempt to find out the reason for the apparent blackout. Most of them finally got me off the phone after saying they would look into the story. Yet, with only a few exceptions, the Long Island actions remained untouched by the print, television, and even radio media. It was during this time that I first realized that I obviously wasn't the only one who had grasped the importance of spreading the ELF ideology. Federal agents and industry groups must also have known that it would serve their interests to keep the ELF actions out of news stories. Whether this was the case with the Long Island actions, we'll probably never know, but it would take several more actions to finally burst the bubble of silence.

Amazingly, the ELF returned to Long Island on November 24 and again on December 1, 2000. With each action came another communiqué reiterating the ELF's dedication to stopping sprawl on the Island. The November 24 incident was similar to the prior three but caused more damage. The communiqué received by the NAELFPO stated,

On November 24th, members of the Earth Liberation Front did a 4th action against the construction sites along Whiskey Rd. in Coram, Long Island. During the action over 17 windows were smashed along with the spraypainting of various slogans. The ELF then proceeded to another site of urban sprawl in Miller Place. They then created some havoc including the decommissioning of earth raping equipment. On a property sale sign and post that was stuck through a Bulldozer, our mark was left, "EARTH NOT FOR SALE—ELF."

Earth Liberation Front

While still fairly minor in terms of actual property damage (as compared with say, Vail), these actions were gradually becoming more destructive as the saboteurs became increasingly frustrated that the warnings to developers in the area were not being taken seriously. It seemed they were also becoming more confident and able to conduct increasingly complex missions.

The December 1 action by the ELF continued along this gradually increasing path of tactical severity. The communiqué read,

Greetings,

On December 1st, members of the Earth Liberation Front executed a massive strike on a large construction site building over 40 luxury houses in Middle Island, Long Island. During the action, an immense number of windows, totaling over 200, were smashed, survey stakes were ripped out of our earth, slogans were spray painted profusely, and various other forms of ecotage were performed on the houses. The workers were kind enough to have lined up all their vehicles the day before to facilitate our monkeywrenching. An assortment of equipment ranging from backhoes to bulldozers sustained crippling damage. The final number ranged to a little more than a dozen.

Urban sprawl not only destroys the forest and green spaces of our planet, but also leads directly to added runoff of pollutants into waterways, increased traffic that causes congestion and air pollution, and a less pleasing landscape. These luxury homes are being built precariously close to the 320 acre Cathedral Pines County Park. Long Island has the 2nd largest pine barren ecosystem in the world. Our greedy and corrupt politicians are more than willing to provide subsidies and allow construction in any area not under current protection by the Long Island Pine Barren Protection Plan. Our forests also lay [sic] on top of our aquifer which provides a large expanse of drinking water that is easily contaminated by pollutants and runoff. We will not stand by idly while our Earth is butchered for the monetary gain and the luxury of the wealthy elite. As long as our planet continues to be raped, we will be out there.

We are everywhere.

Earth Liberation Front

Finally, with this latest action, some news stories began to appear in the local Long Island media. New York City media still had yet to pick up on the growing number of ecodefense actions in its own backyard, but this would soon change. While this had already constituted the most focused and intensified campaign the ELF had ever undertaken, the group still had not used its most popular weapon—arson.

Eight days later, the ELF struck again—this time ensuring that New York City and the rest of the United States heard their message. One two-story condo was burned to the ground and three others were damaged at the Spring Lake housing development in Middle Island, Long Island. While authorities and news media claimed the action caused $200,000 worth of damage, the ELF had attempted to inflict losses well into the millions. According to the communiqué received by the NAELFPO, the ELF tried to burn a total of sixteen houses under construction. However, according to local authorities, most of the incendiary devices failed to ignite.

The communiqué appeared as follows:

Greetings,

The Earth Liberation Front claims responsibility for the fires that ravaged the Birchwood at Spring Lake housing development in Middle Island, Long Island. During the night of December 9th, members of the ELF crept into the construction site and placed incendiaries in 4 rows of condominiums. The structures were checked thoroughly for the presence of any occupants (human or animal) before being set. All of the incendiaries ignited successfully and the resulting fires gutted almost 16 nearly completed luxury homes which were to be sold at several hundred thousand dollars each. Messages denouncing urban sprawl were scrawled on many of the remaining future dens of the wealthy elite. Survey stakes were also pulled up to prevent the planned expansion of the housing development along the border of a New York State Conservation Area. The actions of those who orchestrated the construction are absolutely intolerable, so we are now declaring an unbounded war on urban sprawl. As the stakes of the struggle continue to expand, so will our methods and tactics. Window breaking and disabling vehicles can only do so much, and in a battle with our earth in the balance we can not hold back or go soft on those pillaging the planet for profit. Hopefully, the several million dollars in destruction will provide an unmistakable message to developers that their land rape will now be more costly than ever before.

Earth Liberation Front

With fires burning homes in Long Island neighborhoods, the New York news media could no longer keep the ELF out of the national spotlight. As the group's tactics escalated to arson, the press office back in Portland—on the opposite side of the continent—was bombarded with interview requests. While Leslie and I were struggling just to keep up with all the interest from the East Coast, the ELF continued with its bold string of actions.

On December 19, another home was burned on Long Island, this time in Miller Place. The communiqué from the ELF stated,

Greetings from the Front,

The Earth Liberation Front claims responsibility for the torching of a luxury home under construction in Miller Place, Long Island on December 19th.

Anti-urban sprawl messages were spraypainted on the walls, then accelerants were poured over the house and lighted. Let there be no mistake that this was a nonviolent action, and the house was searched for any living thing before being set alight. This is the latest in a string of actions in the war against urban sprawl.

Urban sprawl not only destroys the forests and green spaces of our planet, but also leads directly to added runoff of pollutants into our waterways, increased traffic that causes congestion and air pollution, and a less pleasing landscape. Our earth is being murdered by greedy corporate and personal interests. The rape of the Earth puts everyone's life at risk due to global warming, ozone depletion, toxic chemicals, etc. Unregulated population growth is also a direct product of urban sprawl. There are over 6 billion people on this planet of which almost a third are either starving or living in poverty. Building homes for the wealthy should not even be a priority.

Forests, farms and wetlands are being replaced with a sea of houses, green chemical lawns, blacktop, and roadkill. Farmland is being bought out by land developers because of [farmers'] inability to compete with cheap, corporate, genetically engineered, pesticide-saturated food. The time has come to decide what is more important: the planet and the health of its population or the profits of those who destroy it.

The purpose of sloganeering is not self righteous posturing as has been reported, but a direct warning to the Earth's oppressors. Apparently, Long Island's growing smog and cancerous water is not a good enough warning to those directly responsible for it. The site of this recent action was warned twice of impending actions with the monkeywrenching of several vehicles and spraypainted messages. It's time for the people of Long Island to put their foot down and no longer passively tolerate our island's rape. It is time for Nassau and Suffolk County Police to realize we are but the symptoms of a corrupt society on the brink of ecological collapse. Law enforcement should be directing their time and resources towards the real terrorists. Those who commit murder and theft upon our populace daily. Big business is the enemy of the people, yet most people remain blind of [sic] it due to the massive propaganda and the power they wield. Every major media outlet on Long Island is in their pockets. The time for action is upon us. We are watching.

Earth Liberation Front

This second arson attack by the ELF, the group's ninth major action in five months on Long Island, kept the media interest piqued. I was amazed at the series of actions, especially since it appeared so focused and still no one had been arrested. *If this could only happen simultaneously in cities all across the country*, I thought. Perhaps then corporate America would be forced to stop killing to feed their greedy wallets.

Toward the end of the year and into 2001, the ELF actions on Long Island climaxed with two more impressive arson attacks. On December 29, the group burned four more luxury homes under construction. The ELF's message forwarded by the NAELFPO to media outlets nationwide read,

As an early New Year's gift to Long Island's environment destroyers, the Earth Liberation Front (ELF) visited a construction site on December 29 and set fire to four unsold luxury houses nearly completed at Island Estates in Mount Sinai, Long Island. Hopefully, this caused nearly $2 million in damage. This hopefully provided a firm message that we will not tolerate the destruction of our island. Recently, hundreds of houses have been built over much of Mount Sinai's picturesque landscape, and developers now plan to build an additional 189 luxury houses over the farms and forests adjacent to Island Estates. This action was done in solidarity with Josh Harper, Craig Rosebraugh, Jeffrey "Free" Luers and Craig "Critter" Marshall, Andrew Stephanian, Jeremy Parkin and the countless other known and unknown activists who suffer persecution, interrogation, police brutality and crappy jail conditions, yet stand strong. Whether it's denying a prisoner vegetarian or vegan food or phone calls (which is a right), or inflicting even the terrorism of the grand jury, they stand strong. Oppression of our brothers and sisters will only make us uproot [sic] our tactics, by means, frequency and cost. The more brutality you give our brothers and sisters, the more money we cause the oppressors. Our hearts go out to all of them. Keep up the fight. Never give in.

In what would be the last in this series of arson attacks on Long Island, the ELF struck again on January 14. The group burned an articulated loader and a pickup truck at Melo's Construction Corporation in Miller Place. This was the eleventh major action taken by the group since July 2000.

This surge of activity by the ELF was unprecedented at the time and was unmatched as far as the number of consecutive actions occurring in one local area. While other areas of the United States have witnessed more financially damaging actions by the group, the repetitive and concentrated nature of the ELF attacks on Long Island during this time remains unique. The beauty of the campaign was that it could have been anywhere. While Long Island represents a clear example of problematic sprawl,[74] the Long Island actions could just as easily have taken place in Oregon, California, Washington, Colorado, Utah, Arizona, Minnesota, etc.

Eventually, national news media picked up on this phenomenon—the ELF could be anywhere, attacking anyone deemed to be making money by killing the planet. Nearly all of the New York media seemed quite hostile to the ELF, its actions and ideology, no doubt due in part to the realization that the battle to save the environment had just come home to their backyards on Long Island. Perhaps the best illustration of this media behavior can be found in an interview I gave to John Stossel on ABC's *20/20*. Of course, at the time of the taping, neither Stossel nor his producers informed me that the interview was for one of his "Give Me a Break" segments, which have typically existed for the specific purpose of attempting to make fun of and discredit progressive causes.

When I arrived at the makeshift set inside a Portland hotel suite, Stossel's producer was friendly and welcoming, the usual behavior of the producers I'd dealt with, whose only job was to get the story. When Stossel walked in, he was even worse in person than he appeared on television, smug and eager to deliver his makeshift brand of derogatory and snide comments. The purpose of the interview was not to give the American public insight into the ELF, its motives, and its ideology, but rather to aggressively attack the organization and its spokesperson. It was by far the worst interview I had sat through, consisting primarily of Stossel insulting me repeatedly and trying to make me angry.

"You're just a kid who doesn't know anything," Stossel barked at me over and over. "You're just a thug." I had to bite my lip to keep from punching him. Weeks later, when the segment aired, it was obvious that Stossel was, unsuccessfully, just trying to get a rise out of me—to demonstrate that the ELF and its spokesperson are just an angry bunch of kids and thugs. The most memorable moment of the program came at the end of

---

74 In 1998, 34,000 acres of agricultural land existed in Suffolk County. Land experts suggest that, at the current rate of development, only 9,000 acres will be left by 2015.("Group claims responsibility for fires," *USA Today*, January 4, 2001.)

Stossel's segment when, after watching my interview from the studio, Barbara Walters stated, "I find him absolutely chilling."

While the *20/20* piece was by far the worst of the media that the Long Island actions attracted, the tone was fairly similar throughout most of the interviews. Leslie and I did our best to remain positive in relaying facts about the ELF, knowing that each and every line of reported ideology provided an opportunity for the group to grow. This six-month spree of actions had finally opened up the gates of the New York media market, and exposure for the ELF began to spread internationally. With millions of dollars in losses attributed to the group, and a growing frustration felt by law enforcement, the pressure against the ELF was beginning to build.

The following actions were also claimed by the ELF during this time period:

September 9, 2000, Bloomington, Indiana: Attempted arson attack at the GOP headquarters.

October-November, 2000, Courtenay, British Columbia: Greens and Fairways at Crown Island Golf Resort were destroyed in protest of the destruction of Green Space.

November 27, 2000, Boulder, Colorado: A $2.5 million mansion was torched in response to sprawl.

December 7, 2000, Long Island, New York: Ten windows smashed and slogans painted at McDonald's corporate offices (Joint claim with the ALF).

10

JOHNNY LAW
TRIES TO
MAKE A DENT

*O*ne of the most remarkable facts about the ELF up to this time was that no one had been arrested or charged with any crime relating to the organization. While politicians and law enforcement attributed this fact to their own lack of finances and personnel, those within the ELF knew their covert structure was very difficult to penetrate and stop. By the middle of 2000, the group had accumulated over $30 million in damages and gave no sign of slowing down.

After the FBI raid on our home in February, Elaine and I were forced to find a new place to live. We decided to try living alone for privacy and also because we couldn't think of too many people we trusted completely—or who would want to live with us in our police state. By April, we had settled into a basement apartment on Southeast Hawthorne Boulevard in one of Portland's trendier sections.

I was now working at the press office nearly full-time and at the vegan bakery over full-time. After the many grand jury appearances that year, I still came across federal agents frequently in my neighborhood or knocking on my front door. Somehow, I managed to ignore them and carry on with my day-to-day activities of defending politically motivated arsons to the national news media. Interruptions to my routine almost became routine in themselves. Special Agent Daniel Feucht, whom I now considered a veteran enemy, continued with his sporadic psychological games. Sometimes Feucht would appear on our doorstep early in the morning and knock endlessly for minutes. When we refused to answer the door, he would go and sit in his SUV, parked in our driveway, for a short period, and then resume his knocking. He would repeat this performance several days in a row.

One morning, when Elaine's mother Val was staying with us for a visit, all three of us awoke to Feucht and his knocking. Not sure how she would react, I instantly apologized to Val (like it was my fault!), but the situation didn't seem to faze her much. In fact, while Feucht was banging on the door, Val brainstormed possible exit routes for my escape.

Sneaking out of my house became another habit. For weeks at a time, I would leave quickly through back and side paths after checking to make sure no one was awaiting my appearance. We had figured out that Feucht wasn't after Elaine, so she was able to provide crucial help with the scouting missions. On only a couple of occasions did I observe them actually noticing my departure.

One of these occurred on my way to take Elaine's old car to the mechanic. After Elaine had been in a serious accident that had totaled my truck, she had let me use her beater for the baking company deliveries. Just after I pulled the car out onto Hawthorne Boulevard, I noticed a forest green Chevrolet Suburban pull out a couple of cars behind me. After a dozen or so blocks, I noticed the vehicle staying right with me so I decided to wind my way through side streets to see if it was really following. Sure enough, after I turned off into a residential area and zigzagged through many streets, the SUV was still in my rearview mirror. As I looked closer, I could tell it was Feucht. *The bastard*, I thought, wondering, as I often did, what in the hell he wanted this time.

Without giving the matter much thought, I made it down to an industrial area and began gunning the engine around corners, attempting to lose Feucht. By this time, however, it wasn't just his green SUV behind me; it appeared that a total of three cars were on my tail. Miraculously, after running countless stop signs and flying around numerous corners, it looked as though I had lost them. I made my way back to the mechanic's shop and parked a few blocks away. Fearing that they were still on my trail, I sprinted into the shop and, out of breath, attempted to explain to them why I had parked so far away. Thankfully, Elaine had volunteered to pick me up, and when she arrived, I raced out of the shop and jumped into her new car.

I knew that if the matter was that important to the government, the agents would simply knock down my front door again to find me. It was odd, though, to say the least, being chased by the Feds and passing people in cars and on foot who were just going about their everyday lives. *Would they even believe this is happening?* I wondered.

As the ELF actions across the country grew in frequency, the pressure from the federal government to stop the organization also increased. While I had already faced my share of heat—and it always seemed to be on the rise—I was no longer alone. Johnny Law was trying to make a dent in the ELF, anywhere it could.

Tree Spiking in Bloomington

Shortly after the ELF burned Vince Scott's home in Bloomington, the FBI and BATF began visiting and attempting to question Frank Ambrose, an outspoken and highly visible local environmental advocate. Ambrose was a community organizer and a member of Earth First!, Industrial Workers of the World, Speak Out for Animals, and the American Lands Alliance. As had often been the case with the investigations into the ELF, the Feds seemed to have no leads into the arson on Vince Scott's home, so they chose to lean on a known aboveground local activist.

The pressure on Ambrose and his wife, Marie Mason, also a dedicated and visible labor, environmental, and animal advocate, continued on July 19, 2000, when five Indiana Conservation Officers (COs) and one FBI agent raided their Bloomington home. At 6:30 A.M., the state and federal agents knocked on Ambrose and Mason's door and announced that they had a warrant to search the apartment and their car. After entering the apartment and showing the warrant, the agents began ransacking the place, looking for any evidence of a tree spiking incident that had recently occurred in Bloomington.[75] According to the warrant, the agents were authorized to seize hammers, nails, nail heads, metal cutting tools, computers, boots, and any communication linking Ambrose to the ELF.

Not surprisingly, the vast majority of the materials taken in the raid were not on the warrant. The primary property seized consisted of organizational literature and address books belonging to Mason. In addition, spray paint, a crowbar, Mason's family photo albums, two household hammers, tin snips, and a Leatherman tool were taken. While the agents left Ambrose's

---

75 On June 26, officials from the Department of Natural Resources discovered 20 ten-inch long spikes driven into 17 trees in a section of the Monroe State Forest destined for logging. ELF claimed responsibility.

boots untouched on the floor, they photographed the soles of all the shoes in the closet. When Ambrose and Mason confronted the agents about taking items not listed on the search warrant, they were simply told that the items were being taken and there was nothing they could do about it.

According to the couple, it was obvious which agency was in control of the raid. The five COs primarily stood around and kept an eye on them while FBI agent Rob Woesner did the majority of the searching. Furthermore, any time the COs had a question, they went to Woesner for advice—which usually amounted to, "Take it."

Near the end of the raid, the COs separated Ambrose and Mason and attempted to get them to talk. Ambrose was told that he should cooperate with the state so that the Feds would not get involved. The Feds, the COs told Frank, were much worse and would not give him any deals. With Mason, the COs tried to convince her to pressure her husband to turn himself in. Both told the agents that they were not going to talk, and that if evidence existed to arrest either of them, they would already be in custody.

Upon leaving the apartment, the agents promised they would return later in the day with an arrest warrant for Ambrose. They also announced that they would be speaking with "everyone" in the local environmental community and that someone would "rat" on Ambrose eventually. Neither the FBI nor the COs returned to the apartment that day, however, and only a few other individuals in the local environmental movement were harassed.

This harassment of other Bloomington activists typically entailed attempting to get them to say that Ambrose had been involved in illegal activities. Agents also demonstrated an interest in Mason's activities and visited Heartwood, a local forest protection organization where she had been employed. Unfortunately, when Heartwood director Allison Cochran was questioned about Mason, she cooperated and, without a warrant, agreed to hand over Mason's old computer.

Both Ambrose and Mason felt this search and questioning was just harassment in response to their non-ELF-related activism. Just after the raid, they stated, "It was clear the FBI was targeting us because of our political beliefs and our involvement in the takeover of a State Forest office in protest of the logging they were planning, and the COs were there just because the crime being investigated was a state-level crime and therefore their jurisdiction under the law." Unfortunately for Frank, as the ELF activity in Bloomington continued, the pressure against him was also stepped up.

In late January 2001, the story broke nationwide that federal agents had made their first arrest in connection with ELF activity. On January 25, 2001, Frank Ambrose was taken into custody and charged with tree spiking in relation to the June 2000 ELF action in Indiana. Ambrose quickly learned that tree spiking was a Class D felony, which carries a sentence of up to three years in prison and up to a $10,000 fine. For federal agents, this marked an incredible public relations opportunity to demonstrate that they were finally making some progress in tracking the ELF. But to Ambrose and Mason, this was just the latest step in what appeared to be a constant campaign of harassment.

Immediately upon his arrest and after being let out on bail, Ambrose released the following statement to the public:

Press Statement for Frank Ambrose

January 25, 2001

Today I was arrested for allegedly spiking trees that were scheduled to be logged in our publicly owned State Forests.

First, I want to assure people of my innocence. I have not committed the act that the Indiana Conservation Officers and the FBI are accusing me of, nor do I know who did. I am only guilty of being outspoken about the issue of logging on our public lands. I am committed to the protection of these treasures. Although I have publicly supported groups that have at times engaged in clandestine campaigns, I do not myself participate in property destruction. I believe in and am committed to nonviolent direct action and civil disobedience as has been practiced for years by the civil rights, peace, labor, and environmental movements.

This country's police agencies have made my arrest a media spectacle, as they have been trying to catch someone from the Earth Liberation Front. In their zeal to catch someone, anyone, they have conveniently forgotten about civil rights. They have used a number of underhanded tactics to destroy any support I may have as an activist and citizen in this community. The police had raided our house in July looking for implements of tree spiking, and came away with family photo albums, address books, and organizational files about the groups my wife and I have worked with in the past. Conservation officers have also called upon charity organizations that have helped me and my family out in times of need and told them I was a "terrorist," even though I have not been convicted of any crime and deny this allegation.

I am sure they will continue to label me a "terrorist" in their media spectacle, even though there has been no trial and I have not been convicted of anything. I urge the media to consider what they are printing and how they label me and others. Remember, even though the FBI calls what the ELF does "terrorism," it does not mean that it is terrorism. The ELF has widely publicized guidelines that preclude any actions that endanger life, human or otherwise. Terrorism is random, bombs exploding in crowded shopping plazas and actions of that nature. Terrorism seeks to frighten and demoralize by causing harm or even death. I do not engage in these kinds of actions and do not belong to any terrorist organizations. I have always been a peaceful activist and have attempted to change governmental policies through peaceful means.

The FBI and other police agencies have run over innocent citizens' civil rights looking for the few people who have committed acts of nonviolent property destruction, while overlooking the real criminals. Real criminals, like Burny Fischer (the director of the Indiana Division of Forestry), break Indiana's statutes. Mr.

Fischer allows logging to occur on our State Forests without any sort of environmental review, as is required. This results in massive "property" destruction (i.e. the forests, which belong to us all) and loss of life. Moreover, the "property" that is destroyed is something that has been set aside for the enjoyment of all. Why is he not being charged with felonies and threatened with years in prison, while I am having these threats leveled at me for only speaking my mind and taking part in one nonviolent civil disobedience?

Innocence is no protection against the harassment and financial burdens being foisted upon me, as I have learned. These irresponsible accusations have cost me and my family greatly. I hope the media will be ethical and responsible, and not participate in continuing to print specious and slanderous statements about me. Though, this will be a difficult time for me while I am forced to prove my innocence, I am confident that I will be found innocent in a court of law.

The probable cause affidavit filed in Monroe Circuit Court that led to the charges being filed against Ambrose details the primary evidence allegedly linking him to the tree spiking. According to the affidavit, Department of Natural Resources employees saw a car registered to Ambrose at the Monroe State Forest about the same time the trees were spiked. On June 26, State Division of Forestry employees found a nail box on the ground and later witnessed a man walking near some of the damaged trees. Police determined that only one hardware store in the area, Lowe's, carried the ten-inch spikes used in the ELF actions, and that Lowe's had sold four boxes of the same type of spikes three days before the nailed trees were discovered. The store's video surveillance allegedly showed a man buying the spikes, and State Forestry employees identified the buyer as the person they had observed at the location of the tree spiking.

In response to the affidavit containing the alleged evidence of his guilt, Ambrose suggested that this evidence could have easily been manufactured to make nearly anyone appear guilty. "I've said this before and I'll say it again: The FBI's the best agency in the world at convicting innocent people," he stated after his arrest in January.[76] With a first court date scheduled for February 2, 2002, Ambrose and Mason prepared for the months of mental and physical stress that lay ahead.

Arson on Long Island

Simultaneously, investigators on Long Island obtained the break they had been searching for to stop the spree of local ELF actions. On January 16, FBI agents raided a house on the Island in connection with the ongoing investigation into the ELF. While the identities of the homeowner and occupants were not released, the FBI Joint Terrorism Task Force seized computer files and "piles of other material."[77]

Shortly thereafter, it was announced that a Long Island teenager had been taken into custody in relation to ELF activity. George Mashkow III, known as "Kci" to friends, was arrested in February 2001 after boasting to schoolmates about his involvement with ELF arson attacks. After his arrest, Mashkow agreed to cooperate with the FBI and handed over the names of three other young men who, he claimed, made up the cell of the ELF responsible for many of the crimes on Long Island. Upon receiving this statement from Mashkow, the FBI took into custody Jared McIntyre, Matthew Rammelkamp, and Connor Cash.

Jared McIntyre was quite familiar with environmental issues, especially those pertaining to the local Long Island area. Growing up in the Long Island suburb of Coram, McIntyre was an honors-level student at Longwood High School who frequently contributed to the school newspaper—writing stories critical of the prison system, industrialized farming, and other social issues.

McIntyre also worked as a paid intern at the Brookhaven National Laboratory, researching global warming. Now, in addition to arson and conspiracy charges relating to ELF activity

---

76 Steve Hinnefeld and Doug Wilson, "Frank Ambrose Says He's Innocent," *Bloomington Herald-Times*, January 26, 2001.
77 "FBI Raids House On Long Island in Connection With ELF," Associated Press, January 16, 2001.

on Long Island, McIntyre also pleaded guilty in February to planning another arson attack at a fast food restaurant and at a duck farm.

Just days later, Matthew Rammelkamp pleaded guilty to burning down four partially built homes. A sixteen-year-old high school junior, Rammelkamp was also an honors student, successfully juggling a full course load of advanced placement classes. He and McIntyre had first met at an environmental rally in the fall of 2000.

Connor Cash, a nineteen-year-old human rights and environmental activist, was arrested on February 15. His bail was set at $250,000, but his family, after putting a lien on their home, successfully bailed him out. A very visible activist on Long Island, Cash had co-formed the Food Not Bombs hunger relief program in Port Jefferson Station in the spring of 1999. Additionally, Cash was a member and key organizer of the Modern Times Collective. This autonomous youth activist network focused on a broad spectrum of social and political issues, from educating the public about sweatshops to counseling sessions for at risk or suicidal teenagers. As Cash grew to be an effective and well-known activist on Long Island, he began to catch the attention of law enforcement.

Trouble for Cash and Modern Times began on May 6, 2000, when the organization held a street party in the town of Huntington. The goal of the demonstration was to take over the town's main street in protest of the World Bank, International Monetary Fund, and globalization. A total of fourteen protesters were arrested that day, including Cash, who was taken into custody after erecting and climbing up on a twenty-eight-foot tripod, effectively blocking the road.

When Modern Times then went to Philadelphia to protest the Republican National Convention on August 1, Cash was arrested with fifty other protesters. Shortly thereafter, Cash and others involved with Modern Times began receiving visits from the FBI, who attempted to question them about the ELF actions on Long Island. According to three witnesses, Cash was one of several group members who were threatened with reprisal if they did not cooperate.[78] The FBI told Cash, "It's going to be your ass if you do not cooperate."

In response, Cash immediately hired civil rights attorney Fred Brewington and refused to give any statements to the Feds. As a result, Cash and other members of Modern Times were routinely followed by photographers and videographers—federal agents attempting to track their every move.

In early February 2001, Modern Times printed a lengthy statement in its newspaper responding to the harassment. Members of the organization believed that the FBI was not just after information about the ELF but was trying to obtain information on young social justice activists and disrupt their work. It stated in part, "The FBI was not just interested in intimidating and investigating those involved in the ELF, but 'fishing' into the activities of youth community activists."

Surprisingly, the statement also declared an opposition to the ELF actions: "Creating an environment of fear and intimidation by means of arson is not conducive to the development of an empowered community. Furthermore, arson puts at risk the lives of volunteer firefighters and innocent community members who are not profiting from urban sprawl." It was only a few days later that Cash was arrested.

Within days, a press release was issued by the US Attorney's Office in the Eastern District of New York. The title of the release alone was enough to earn the story a place in national and, by this time, international media: "Earth Liberation Front Member Arrested on Long Island and Charged with Arson— Three Members of Suffolk County, Long Island 'Cell' Plead Guilty to Arson Conspiracy."

This announcement marked the first-ever conviction of an ELF member in the United States. The news media seized upon the story, and the press office was flooded with requests for interviews. "Do you have any comment on the convictions of three teenaged ELF members on Long Island? Have federal investigators finally stopped the ELF? Is this the typical age range for ELF members?"

---

78 Eric Laursen, "Hard Times for Modern Times," *In These Times*, Issue 25, May 14, 2001.

It was truly a media frenzy. Unfortunately for the public image of the ELF, the arrests of these four young men appeared to have confirmed the stereotypical belief held by many reporters that ELF members are just a bunch of misguided young kids. The interviews became so pointed in this direction that, after a while, Leslie and I refused to give any comment on the Long Island arrests. We both supported the actions that were under investigation and were horrified that people had gotten caught. Mostly, though, we were pissed that Mashkow had been foolish enough to discuss his activities publicly, then ratted out his so-called friends.

Mashkow, McIntyre, and Rammelkamp—all minors—pleaded guilty in a New York federal court to charges of arson conspiracy. While McIntyre and Rammelkamp admitted guilt and their involvement in ELF actions, they refused to cooperate with law enforcement—unlike their cohort Mashkow. Unfortunately for McIntyre, Rammelkamp, and Cash, Mashkow had handed the FBI a victory that had eluded them for the last four years—the breakup of an ELF cell.

Cash, the only adult among the four to be arrested, was faced with the brunt of the charges. Investigators asserted that Cash was the ringleader of this ELF cell and had talked the three minors into conducting the actions, believing if they were caught they would not face the same penalties as adults. It is also alleged that Cash purchased the gasoline that was used to set fire to five homes under construction in Mount Sinai in December 2000. Additionally, authorities accused him of driving the three other teens to unspecified locations where acts of vandalism and arson occurred. As a result, charges of arson conspiracy and aiding and abetting arson were added against Cash. Together, these charges could have put him behind bars for forty years. Unlike the other three youths involved, Cash immediately pleaded not guilty to all charges and waited for his trial, which would not occur until May 2004. After three years of anticipation and being labeled a terrorist, Cash was found not guilty on all charges.

With court dates scheduled throughout 2001, Cash, like Ambrose in Bloomington, anticipated a stressful and intimidating time before his trial. The September 11, 2001, attacks on the

Pentagon and World Trade Center, which directly or indirectly affected so many people, had unusual repercussions for Cash: in late September, he had one count of aiding terrorists added to the charges already against him. This meant that if found guilty on all charges Cash could have spent the rest of his life in prison. His attorney, Fred Brewerton, called the new charge "absolutely absurd" and stated that it was an attempt by the government "to force the young man to plead guilty" when, he maintained, there was not a shred of evidence that Cash had broken any law or done anything improper.[79]

Law enforcement investigators made an additional, though minor, breakthrough in their pursuit of the ELF in Nebraska in July 2001. In a period of less than a month, four golf courses were heavily vandalized in and around Omaha. Fairways were dug up and spray-painted messages were left on buildings at the various locations that included the letters "ELF." On July 19, three college students, all nineteen years old, were charged with damaging the golf courses, indicted on multiple counts of fourth-class felony charges of criminal mischief. All three men, Jason Thiemann, Kraig Schjodt, and Brian Hindly, claimed to have connections with the ELF, a link allegedly made through the internet.[80]

Bail for each of the three men was initially set at $10,000; they were later released on $5,000 bond. On August 14, 2001, all three of the men pleaded not guilty, but they changed their pleas to guilty on November 8. They were then sentenced to diversion and restitution of $1,883.34 each.

Back in Bloomington, in the post–September 11 atmosphere, a move was also made in the case against Frank Ambrose. Just one day after the East Coast attacks, Ambrose's charges were dismissed. Of course, with the entirety of the news media's attention focused on Washington, DC and New York, this move received little in the way of publicity beyond one or two local stories.

---

79 Ibid.
80 Shannon Henson and James Ivey, "Vandalism Suspects Say They're Part of ELF," *Omaha World-Herald*, July 20, 2001.

In a prepared statement read on September 12, Monroe County Prosecutor Carl Salzmann asserted, "As a result of further investigation, it appears that the conspiracy involving the spiking of trees in Monroe and Brown Counties is more extensive than it first appeared. Therefore, we believe that it is in the interests of justice to dismiss this case at this time." My own belief is that prosecutors lacked evidence implicating Ambrose and, therefore, chose to drop the charges at a time when they would receive the least publicity. With all the hype stirred up in the national news media about the arrest of Frank Ambrose— "the first ELF member taken into custody and charged"[81]—in the end, there simply was no case.

Despite the arrests in Long Island and Nebraska, the vast majority of ELF actions—including the most spectacular and financially devastating (Vail, Vince Scott's home, Boise Cascade, Michigan State University, etc.)—had yet to be solved. More importantly, even though law enforcement agencies had increasingly stepped up the pressure against the organization, they had clearly failed to make a dent in the activities of the ELF, who had only increased their opposition to actions that threaten the world we all live in.

---

81 "Indiana man arrested for ELF attack," *UPI*, January 26, 2001, upi.com/Archives/2001/01/26/Indiana-man-arrested-for-ELF-attack/6949980485200/.

A
BUSY
YEAR

> We torched Superior Lumber in Glendale, OR on January 1, 2001. Superior Lumber is a typical earth raper contributing to the ecological destruction of the Northwest. What happened to them should shock no one.
>
> This year, 2001, we hope to see an escalation in tactics against capitalism and industry. While Superior Lumber says, "Make a few items, and do it better than anyone else," we say, "choose an earth raper and destroy them."
>
> ELF
>
> Earth Liberation Front

The ELF's momentum continued to grow, making 2001 the most active year in the group's history. On January 1, the ELF set Superior Lumber on fire, causing an estimated $800,000 in damages. The communiqué above marked the third consecutive year that the ELF had struck a logging enterprise in Oregon. But one particular phrase in this message—"This year, 2001, we hope to see an escalation in tactics against capitalism and industry"—seriously concerned law enforcement agencies. And as the year went on, the ELF showed that it was as good as its word.

Superior Lumber was targeted in part because it was the largest contract holder of the Bureau of Land Management in the state of Oregon.[82] In operation since 1951, the company now runs approximately eighty million board feet of timber annually at its mill in Glendale, located in the southern portion of the state. Superior Lumber also operates another mill on the western outskirts of Eugene that employs eighty people. Nearly 60 percent of Superior's board feet comes from milling timber for the US Forest Service, the BLM, and other state and private timberlands. The rest comes from the harvesting that Superior alone engages in.

Superior Lumber had become an increasingly controversial company after it created its own helicopter logging operation in the late 1990s. The helicopters allowed the company to harvest

---

82 Janine Jobe and John Sowell, "Extremists Admit Mill Arson," *The News Review*, January 9, 2001.

timber in roadless areas where conventional logging is not allowed, thus increasing the company's opportunities for new contracts and revenue.

The ELF targeted Superior Lumber just a short time after Seattle US District Judge Barbara Rothstein made a ruling in the company's favor. Rothstein declared that Superior could resume harvesting trees in the Isabella and Poor Bishop sales on BLM land south of Jacksonville, Oregon. These sales constituted two of 180 that were halted after the National Marine Fisheries Service (NMFS) failed to follow environmental regulations when it erred in releasing biological opinions supporting federal timber sales in Washington, Oregon, and Northern California.[83] Superior Lumber had resumed harvesting timber from these sales just two days before the ELF attack.

Steve Swanson, president of Superior Lumber, told news reporters that the building was a complete loss, as most of the rooms were gutted by the flames. The heat was so extreme in some areas—estimated at over two thousand degrees Fahrenheit—that light fixtures and computer monitors melted. Law enforcement investigators concluded that two fires were started on opposite outside walls of the two-thousand-square-foot building. The fires then raced up the walls and ignited the attic. Swanson commented, "It's a tactic where you can have the entire roof burning, but the alarms in the rooms below haven't gone off."

"We're not surprised," he said after hearing the news that the ELF had taken credit for the arson.[84] Clearly, he understood at least this much of the ELF's message: "The mill will be paying more for security and look [sic] at our security strategy, but there is no way to totally protect yourself."[85]

The ELF spread even further geographically near the end of January with a minor act of vandalism in Louisville, Kentucky. A communiqué sent to the NAELFPO, claiming responsibility for the act, stated that on January 23 five windows had been broken

83 Jobe and Sowell, "Extremists Admit Mill Arson."
84 Brian Denson, "Earth Liberation Front takes credit for Glendale mill fire," *The Oregonian*, January 9, 2001.
85 Jobe and Sowell, "Extremists Admit Mill Arson."

and another eighteen damaged at two new commercial buildings under construction. Like the Bloomington and Long Island actions, sprawl appeared to have been the inspiration for the vandalism. The communiqué stated in part, "The once beautiful farmlands of Eastern Jefferson County, KY are being destroyed by earth rapers for corporate profit."

Planting Seeds

Just under one month later, the ELF struck again—this time in California. The communiqué sent by the ELF to the NAELFPO stated,

The Earth Liberation Front takes credit for torching the Delta & Pine Land Co. Research cotton gin in Visalia, California, on February 20.

D & PL continues to pursue its "Terminator technology" despite global opposition to the genetic engineering of plants to produce sterile seeds. Engineering a suicide sequence into the plant world is the most dangerous new technology since nuclear power and needs to be stopped.

We chose this warehouse because it contained massive quantities of transgenic cotton seed in storage. But now, this seed will no longer exist to contaminate the environment, enrich a sick corporation, or contribute to its warped research programs.

After cutting through a padlock on a door to get into the warehouse, we placed 4 five-gallon buckets and half diesel in strategic locations. Windows were broken to provide the fire with oxygen and timers were set. Within just a few minutes the operation was complete.

We are the burning rage of a dying planet.

Earth Liberation Front (ELF)

… Terminate D & PL, cremate Monsanto, burn biotechnology.
. …

Delta and Pine Land Company had become known within both the biotech industry and the environmental movement for their controversial Terminator seed technology. Using this scientific procedure, D & PL genetically engineered seeds that are sterile and therefore unable to reproduce. Farmers who used these sterile seeds must purchase new seeds regularly from corporations such as Monsanto (now Bayer), which clearly benefit from the increased profit potential. For many generations, farmers have been saving the best seeds from the harvest to plant as the following year's crop, a technique that could steadily improve yields over the years. But seeds saved from hybrid crops, which may produce substantially larger yields, rapidly diminish in quality, forcing farmers to purchase new seeds often.

Farmers who choose not to use hybrid seeds often suffer because, even though their crops may be healthier than the hybrids, they often do not appear as large or brightly colored. In this way, a market is created that forces farmers into a position of dependence on hybrid seed producers. Obviously, healthy seeds that do reproduce are not as economically pleasing to biotech corporations as the sterile seeds that bring in annual dollars from farmers.

The D & PL arson received virtually no publicity in California or across the United States. As with the news media blackout of the first Long Island actions, this particular strike by the ELF would have gone largely unnoticed by the public had it not been for the release of the communiqué and the efforts of NAELFPO. Although only two mainstream stories covered the arson,[86] we surely alerted the environmental movement and industry that this important strike had occurred.

Old Growth

Early in March, I headed to Eugene, Oregon, where I had been invited to take part in the ELAW environmental law conference once again. At past ELAW conferences, I had spoken on panels dealing with government repression, direct action, and the ELF.

---

86 "Fear of Vandals Crops Up in Valley," *Fresno Bee*, March 13, 2001, and Sam Stanton, "Eco-terrorism Group Claims Tulare Attack," *Fresno Bee*, March 4, 2001.

This year seemed to be no different, as I had been scheduled to participate in a couple of sessions dealing with the same subject matter. Just hours before I was to begin presenting, I received another communiqué from the ELF claiming responsibility for tree spiking in the Umpqua National Forest. I couldn't think of a better venue to receive and promote an ELF communiqué.

It appeared that, sometime in late February or early March, members of the ELF had conducted their action just outside of Eugene. The message from the saboteurs stated,

Units 6 and 8 of the Judie Timber Sale in the Hardesty Wilderness Area (Umpqua National Forest) have been spiked. Also, survey stakes have been pulled and destroyed on the road cutting into Unit 8. We inserted 60-penny nails and 8- and 10-inch spikes both high and low in the trees to prevent cutting of this native forest.

This Salvage Rider sale threatens the Laying Creek watershed which provides water to the nearby town of Cottage Grove. Scarred early in the century by fire, this vibrant forest provides habitat for rare plants, tree frogs, and elk (which we saw herds of during our excursion).

All responsibility for worker safety now lies with the owner of the sale, Seneca Jones Corporation and their accomplices, the Forest Service.

Cancel this sale immediately.

ELF

Earth Liberation Front

Conservationists had been attempting to protect the area, located eleven miles northwest of Oakridge, Oregon, for decades. In 1998, environmentalists, with assistance from a state representative, were able to temporarily preserve a section. Arguing that most of the cutting would take place in roadless areas, activists managed to delay the work. The Seneca Jones Corporation had been recently preparing to cut approximately 1.3 million board feet from the unprotected area of the Judie timber sale.[87]

When a tree spiking action reaches the news media, reporters and industry representatives commonly argue that the act seriously endangers the lives of loggers and mill workers. Yet the rationale behind the pounding of nails or spikes into trees is to preserve that section of the forest. The spiking is announced out of concern for the workers who may have to handle the cut logs; it now becomes the logging company's decision whether or not to put their employees at risk.

Just a couple of days after ELAW was finished, the NAELFPO received notice of another action on Long Island, putting to rest the notion that the Feds had caught the only active "cell" in the area. (Thanks to the organization's nonhierarchical structure of anonymous cells, if one cell is infiltrated or captured by authorities, the members cannot provide any information that might lead to the capture of other cells.) At approximately 11:55 P.M. on March 5, the ELF targeted the Old Navy outlet store in the "Big H" shopping center located in Huntington Station. Over eight ten-foot by ten-foot windows and a large neon sign were destroyed in this small but newsworthy mission.

While the damages to the store were estimated at only $1,800,[88] the communiqué revealed to the public, through the national news media, the largely unknown fact that the family that owns Old Navy, The Gap, and Banana Republic was also involved with clear cutting old growth forests in the Pacific Northwest. The communiqué appeared as follows:

During the evening of March 5th, members of the Earth Liberation Front descended upon the Old Navy Outlet Center in downtown Huntington, Long Island, NY. We smashed over 8 10′ x 10′ insulated plate glass windows and one neon sign. This action served as a protest to Old Navy's owners, the Fisher family's involvement in the clearcutting of old growth forest in the Pacific Northwest. These actions will continue until the

87 Lance Robertson, "ELF Says It Spiked Trees in Timber Sale," *The Register Guard*, March 6, 2001.
88 "Old Navy the Latest Target of ELF," *Long Islander News*, March 6, 2001.

Fisher family pulls economic support from the lumber industry, regardless of whether with the Pacific Lumber Company or otherwise.

In the past week, mother nature has blessed the Northeast with snow, and we are reminded of our brothers and sisters in the Northwest, and their struggle to preserve what mother nature has blessed them with, the forests in the land that they call home. We will not sit idly by, and will do our best to amplify their voices, so that their message will get through to the Fisher family in the only language they know—economics.

Old Navy, Gap, Banana Republic care not for the species that call these forests home, care not for the animals that comprise their leather products, and care not for their garment workers underpaid, exploited and enslaved in overseas sweatshops. As more and more minds continue to be exposed to the true nature of their greed, fewer and fewer will sit idly by, and the cries of the earth will not fall upon deaf ears. We will not stop.

Love, The Elves

With this one minor strike, the ELF was able to focus national attention on the Fisher family's practices, and potentially increased the public pressure for them to stop their unjust business operations.

Swoosh

On their own, small-scale acts of vandalism such as the action at the Old Navy store would not have generated massive attention from the news media. At most, they might receive a mention in the local paper or police log. But because they were attributed to an international, politically motivated organization, these previously minor acts became national news items.

Such was the case once again on April 2, when the ELF attempted to burn down a Nike outlet store in Albertville, Minnesota. While they failed to do this (intact incendiary devices were found, undetonated, on the roof of the building), the release of the communiqué directed national attention to the international movement against the Nike corporation. The communiqué stated,

Take actions against globalization now!

The Earth Liberation Front has very recently paid a visit to a Nike outlet in the town of Albertville, MN. This visit was in solidarity with all people of all nations to fight globalization, and to support the growing anti global sentiment. This is also a call for direct action against globalization in solidarity with all of the anti FTAA [Free Trade Area of the Americas] actions scheduled in Canada later this month.

After witnessing first hand the treacherous conditions that Nike workers experience daily in sweatshops around the world, it was decided that no NGO organization [sic] could have the immediate impact necessary to end conditions that exist currently at any sweatshop.

Instead, direct action is a more efficient tactic to stop Nike in their footsteps. Unfortunately, due to weather conditions, the visit was short, and although the plan was to destroy the roof, only minor damages were sustained.

Although the roof of this Nike outlet did not go up in flames as planned, this action is still a message to Nike they cannot ignore. In fact, there are only two options for Nike at this point. Option 1.—you can shut down all of your sweatshops immediately, and immediately place all assets into the communities that you have stolen from. Along with this, you must close down all Nike outlets, starting with the Albertville, MN location (you are especially not welcome in this town!!!) . . . or, Option 2.—People across the globe will individually attack Nike outlets, as well as retailers that sell Nike (including college campus shops) until Nike closes down or adheres to demand #1. It is important to point out to Nike that the violence they use against the poor, and especially those that do all the work for them, will only be met with violence towards what they hold dearest . . . their pocket books. All ELF actions are non violent towards humans and animals. But if a building exists which perpetrates, and sponsors violence towards people or animals (such as a Nike outlet, or a Gap outlet, etc.), then by God, it's got to be burned to the ground!!! The ELF wholeheartedly condones the use of violence towards inanimate objects to prevent oppression, violence, and most of all to protect freedom. Direct action is a wonderful tool to embrace on the road to liberation.

Sincerely, Philip H. Knight, Chairman and CEO

Nike, Inc. One Bowerman Drive Beaverton, OR 97003–6433

Fax: (503) 671–6300

In response to this action, the public relations department at Nike issued a slick announcement designed to make the public feel that the attack was against them as well as the corporation— an obvious attempt to further build the bond between the corporation and the consumers they rely on for financial success. The message stated in part, "Terrorism aimed at our employees, consumers and other innocent people in the community is absolutely unacceptable. . . . [We] encourage activists to express their concerns through constructive dialogue and meaningful action."[89] This was an intelligent public relations move on the part of Nike, effectively diverting all attention from the true motives of the ELF attack to a rallying cry against terrorism.

The Feds Return

By this time, Leslie and I had moved the press office into a house we rented with Vanessa and Elaine in March 2001, since we had run out of funds to pay the rent for the office downtown. With both of us living there, it seemed like even more work could be done in support of the ELF.

Along with conducting interviews and publicizing the actions of the day, one of the first activities Leslie and I involved ourselves in after moving to the new location was to organize a national day of support for Frank Ambrose prior to his case being dropped. Ambrose faced a court appearance on April 5, and Leslie and I decided to organize as much public support for him as possible.

89 "ELF Claims Attempted Arson Attack on Minnesota Nike Store," Associated Press, April 5, 2001.

In the two weeks leading up to Ambrose's appearance, the NAELFPO called for a national day of action against state repression to fall on April 5. We encouraged communities across the United States to hold rallies and protests at US federal buildings to show support for Ambrose and the ELF while denouncing governmental harassment of those working to protect the Earth. As at every event we promoted, we encouraged "militant direct action," a phrase that always excited news reporters and frustrated law enforcement agencies, since neither knew precisely what we meant by it. Technically, it could mean anything from legal activism to civil disobedience to property destruction and even violence. Of course, we always maintained when questioned that we were simply encouraging people to do whatever it takes to stop the unjust state and its policies.

Leslie and I had scheduled a press conference to begin at 10:00 A.M. in front of the US federal building in downtown Portland. Rather than organizing a protest or a rally, we both thought it would be strategically wise to stage a simple media event to discuss the details of Ambrose's case in order to raise public awareness and support for him. We spent the two weeks before April 5 sending out mailings, plastering posters all over Portland, and alerting local and national news media to the events scheduled across the country.

I went to bed early that night, since I had to wake up especially early the next morning to deliver all the baking company orders before the press conference began. Still, it felt like I had closed my eyes for only a split second when my alarm went off at 5:15 A.M.

Driving across town to the bakery, located on Foster Road in Southeast Portland, I struggled to keep my eyelids cracked open. Pulling into the parking lot of the Temple Ballroom, the building that housed my Calendula Baking Company in the basement, I noticed a couple of random cars in the parking lot. I didn't pay them much attention as I staggered toward the front door, fumbling with my keys. *Fuck! I forgot the key!* I muttered to myself as I sprinted back to Elaine's Mazda 323. Since I had to go back across town to the house to find the key, there was a good chance I would be late for the press conference. *If I'm late, Leslie can just start without me, and I'll speak after he's done*, I thought, yanking open the car door and jumping back behind the wheel.

I had only traveled a couple of blocks when I noticed a car trailing me. It was still only 5:45 A.M., and there weren't too many cars on the road. Fighting back paranoia, I just ignored the car and kept speeding along, trying to get home as quickly as possible. When I turned right onto Southeast 39th Avenue heading north, I could see at least two vehicles now obviously following me. *Jesus Christ, what now?* I wondered. Since I was fairly used to being followed, my first instinct was to try to lose them. I turned quickly onto side streets, weaving in and out of blocks. Looking constantly into my rearview mirror, I could see I was having no luck this time.

When I came back to 39th Avenue and turned right again, a Portland police car joined in the chase, taking the lead in front of the other cars. Reaching Northeast Broadway Street, I turned left and sped west towards my house. Just as I rounded the corner the cop turned his lights on. I pulled to the side of the road with the policeman and three other unmarked cars following me. Two of them turned onto a side street and parked out of my sight, while the third pulled up directly behind the police car. *This is not going to be a routine patrol stop*, I thought, certain I'd be screwed no matter what the outcome.

The officer approached my vehicle and cautiously asked to see my license and registration. When I asked him why I had been pulled over—even though I had just broken numerous traffic laws—he told me I had a tail light out on my vehicle. As I knew this wasn't true, I tried to argue the fact with him, but he immediately fled back to his patrol car with my identification.

Ten to fifteen minutes later, I found myself still sitting in the car on the side of Broadway, wondering what in the hell the cop was doing. Looking in my rearview mirror, I then noticed a few men walking toward my car, and I knew the answer was coming.

"Mr. Rosebraugh, step out of the vehicle," said one man, approaching my driver's side window. It was the FBI. Instantly, I thought they must have come to arrest me for something. Ever since the 2000 grand jury appearances, when the US Attorney's office had threatened to file federal charges against me, I had been waiting for this day.

Stepping out of the car, I was led over to the sidewalk and thoroughly searched. An FBI agent presented me with a warrant signed by US Magistrate Judge John Jelderks ordering the search of myself, Elaine, Leslie, our home in North Portland, the Calendula Baking Company and Temple Ballroom building, Leslie's 1970 Volvo station wagon, and Elaine's Mazda, which I had been driving. I was then informed that I had been made to wait for so long by the Portland cop because the search warrant had not yet appeared on the scene. *Wonderful*, I thought.

With my arms and legs spread and my body shoved against a vacant building, I was ordered to empty all of my pockets. While an FBI agent tore through all of the items in my wallet and scraps of paper in my pockets, I managed to get a call off on my cell phone to let my housemates know what was happening and to find out if there was a raid in progress at home.

When Elaine answered the phone, I could tell by her voice that agents were inside the house. While she remained calm, I told her what was happening to me and that I hoped to see her after this ordeal was over. I looked at my watch—it was only 6:00 A.M. The very early morning commuters had just begun to appear in the streets, and, as I looked around Broadway, a few employees of nearby businesses stared at this most peculiar scene. *It probably is not every day they get to see the almighty FBI in action*, I thought.

Looking over the warrant further, I saw that it also called for the seizure of any property relating to a recent arson that had occurred in Eugene, Oregon. The list of property to be seized was so extensive that it covered nearly everything one would expect to find in an office or vehicle. I was familiar with the arson attack under investigation, as I had received a communiqué regarding the incident from anonymous sources. While the fire was not claimed as an ELF attack, the perpetrators seemed to share at least some aspects of the ELF's ideology.

On March 30, 2001, an unknown group of people had set at least thirty-six new SUVs on fire at the Joe Romania Chevrolet dealership in Eugene, causing well over $1 million in damages. The communiqué received by the NAELFPO stated,

Claim for Romania Arson

1 million dollars worth of luxury SUV's were torched at Romania Chevrolet. Sucking the land dry, gas-guzzling SUV's are at the forefront of this vile imperialistic culture's caravan towards self destruction. We can no longer allow the rich to parade around in their armored existence, leaving a wasteland behind in their tire tracks. The time is right to fight back.

Romania Chevrolet is the same location that was targeted last June, for which two earth warriors, Free and Critter, are being persecuted. The techno-industrial state thinks it can stop the growing resistance by jailing some of us, but they cannot jail the spirit of those who know another world is possible. The fire that burns within Free and Critter burns within all of us and cannot be extinguished by locking them up.

In this continuous assault on both the planet and ourselves, SUV's destroy the earth while the prison system tries to destroy those who see beyond this empty life. We must strike out against what destroys us before we are all either choking on smog or held captive by the state. Take power into your own hands. It's your life.

In the past, I had occasionally received communiqués that were not associated with the ELF but claimed responsibility for actions in defense of the environment. I chose to release this information to the media for the same reasons I passed along ELF messages: the public has a right to know the political motives behind these acts of economic sabotage. This communiqué represented the most costly non-ELF act I had ever helped to publicize.

As it states in the communiqué, this act was a protest not only against SUVs, but also against the jailing of Craig "Critter" Marshall and Jeff "Free" Luers. These two men had been charged with setting fire to three SUVs at the same dealership during June 2000 and attempting to burn a gasoline tanker in May 2000.

Craig Marshall pleaded guilty to conspiracy to commit arson and possession of a destructive device, and in exchange for his plea received a reduced sentence of five years and six months in the Oregon State Prison. Jeff Luers, who pleaded not guilty, was never offered the same deal and after a trial received an unheard-of sentence of twenty-two years and eight months. Luers still maintains his innocence on the charge of attempting to set fire to an oil tanker, and neither he nor Marshall has ever admitted any association with the ELF.

The fire of March 30, 2001, sent a definite message not only to Joe Romania Chevrolet, but also to investigation agencies nationwide. It demonstrated that this movement to protect life on Earth was daring enough to attack a target twice, and powerful enough to make the second strike ten times worse than the first. With over thirty-six SUVs torched this time, federal investigators surely felt pressure to take some retaliatory action themselves.

Of course, the retaliatory target was our home, the NAELFPO, my business, and our vehicles. Police and federal agents told at least one newspaper that evidence collected at the site of the Joe Romania arson in March assisted the FBI in obtaining the search warrant signed on April 4 and executed not even twenty-four hours later.[90] Of course, this alleged evidence was never made public.

As I waited there on Broadway Street, a second federal agent grabbed my keys and began the search of Elaine's car. After tearing out all the back seats and ransacking the glove compartment and the rest of the interior, the agent walked away with a few scraps of paper containing useless scrawled notes. Other than a few similar items from my wallet, that is all that was taken in the first phase of the search.

Next, the agents took me back across town to the bakery, where I was told that the owner of the building, Bruce Clark, would not cooperate and open the doors. This instantly brought a smile to my face. Bruce, who had been a good friend of mine for

---

90 "Agents raid eco-terrorist group's press office for clues to arson attack," *The Oregonian*, April 6, 2001.

years, despised the Feds, and I had wondered on the ride over just how far he would go to resist them.

Arriving at the building, I could see that Bruce had locked all the exterior and even interior doors and was screaming at the agents through the thick wood of the antique front doors. Just to make sure he realized the warrant appeared "legitimate" (or as legitimate as a warrant can be) I yelled through the door to him and asked if he knew they were planning on breaking in. The agents had already removed a door ram from their vehicle and were preparing to use it. Bruce's only reply was "Fuck 'em, let's see how far they are going to go." *Excellent*, I thought, knowing full well that the agents would break in one way or another.

After another few minutes, I watched as a side window was smashed and the agents, with guns drawn, jumped into the building and threw Bruce down at gunpoint. Incredibly, Bruce at that very moment had been on the phone to KBOO community radio in Portland. The station had put him on live, and he was giving a play-by-play account of the situation all the way up until he was taken down. I would love to have heard that broadcast. This brilliant move also alerted the news media to the situation, and, within half an hour, media trucks began arriving at the building.

Once the agents had searched Bruce, I was taken into the building and seated next to him on a front stairway. In a scene reminiscent of the 2000 raid, we waited with a police officer guarding both of us while the agents tore apart the three-story building. I felt horrible for Bruce, since my baking company only ever used the basement, and here his entire building, including his office, was also being searched. He was a very good sport about the whole situation, though, and, instead of being frustrated with me, he directed his anger toward the law enforcement agents, who we felt were the real enemy.

Sitting with Bruce on the stairs, I pondered what a mysterious coincidence it was that this raid had just happened to occur on the very same morning that Leslie and I had called a national day of protests in support of Frank Ambrose. As the press conference in Portland was scheduled to begin at 10:00 A.M. downtown, I knew that this maneuver was meant, at least in part, to disrupt the media event Leslie and I had planned. Looking at my watch, it was just past 8:00 A.M., and I had a feeling these agents were not going to be finished with the search of Bruce's building anytime soon.

During the search of the Temple Ballroom, I was handed another subpoena to testify before a grand jury. This time, I would have to appear not in Portland but in Eugene, where a grand jury was seeking information on the arson at Romania Chevrolet.

According to the subpoena, I was commanded to appear before the grand jury on April 18. By this time, I was feeling like I should be admitted into the Guinness Book of World Records for the most grand jury subpoenas received, as I had already been served six previous times. They already knew I wouldn't answer their questions—it felt like nothing more than harassment.

Sometime after 9:00 A.M., an FBI agent came out and took Bruce back into the men's bathroom. There, Bruce was subjected to all kinds of questions regarding his business, what went on in the building, his association with me, and the Romania arson. Soon afterward, another agent attempted to question me, once again getting only my tight lips in response.

Finally, I could see that the agents—who by now I had learned consisted of members of the BATF, FBI, and Oregon State Police—were finishing up with the search of the building. After the many hours Bruce and I had been made to wait on the stairs as state and federal agents ransacked the building, only a small handful of items were seized, including some paperwork from the Calendula Baking Company and from Bruce's property business, some of Bruce's notes, and a random tool used in the kitchen. If the whole process had not been so dehumanizing and immoral, this moment would have almost been comical, with all the effort put into conducting simultaneous raids to investigate the Romania SUV arson, and the ultimate seizure of a few largely useless items. Of course, I had not taken into consideration the property that would be seized from the house. At approximately 10:30 A.M., half an hour after the press conference was supposed to have started, the search of the Temple Ballroom was completed. I was immediately driven back to Northeast Broadway Street, where my car had been abandoned earlier that morning. The FBI pulled up behind the car, and without saying a word I jumped out of their vehicle and was free. For a second, I felt like the ordeal was over—but then I realized I had no idea what was occurring back at the house on North Gantenbein Street.

Since the FBI had seized my cell phone, I couldn't call home, so I jumped into the car and raced to the house. As I turned the last corner onto Gantenbein, I could see news media trucks and a small crowd in the middle of the block in front of the house. I jumped out of the car and ran up to the crowd to find Leslie outside talking to reporters. Elaine and Vanessa, I quickly learned, were still inside and the raid here was still in progress.

I made my way through the reporters' barrage of questions to Leslie, who informed me that he had made it to the press conference. Apparently, the same rules were in effect that I remembered from the 2000 raid—the residents of the house were free to leave, but anyone who did step outside would not be permitted to return until the search was completed. Leslie had jumped onto his bicycle and ridden down to the federal building just in time to make the 10:00 A.M. press conference. Upon arriving there, he immediately alerted all the reporters present that there was a raid in progress at the NAELFPO and at the Calendula Baking Company. Nearly all of the media representatives present loaded into their vehicles and drove over to the house. News helicopters were even sent to the scene and were flying above when I arrived.

Looking around the small gathering on the sidewalk in front of the house, I recognized a few familiar faces, friends who had heard about the raid on the news and come to offer support. This was quite a contrast to the 2000 raid, when I had felt so isolated. A friend from the local cable access station had arrived, as always, with a camera in hand. I was told that he had been there for a while, walking around the house trying to get pictures—especially facial shots—of the federal agents inside. I knew the agents typically tried to stay away from cameras so they could not be identified later by the public. I hoped my friend from the cable station could obtain everyone's photo, and I vowed to make posters of them and plaster the entire Portland area.

As the media satellite trucks prepared for their live noon feeds from the sidewalk in front of the house, all we could do was wait for the raid to be completed. I wondered how Elaine and Vanessa inside were coping with this intrusion. As if she had received my warm thoughts, Elaine suddenly appeared in the living room window. Waving to her, I fought off my anger long enough to smile. When she waved back, I knew at least she, and most likely Vanessa, were safe.

A moment later, I glanced over at the same window and Elaine was still waving. *Is she playing some game?* I thought. Interesting timing. As I waved back again, I noticed she wasn't waving so much as motioning. *She's trying to tell me something. Go around.*

"I think Elaine is telling us to go around to the back of the house in the alleyway," I told the crowd of observers. I ran around the block and from a few houses away could see the Feds beginning to bring boxes out the back door. I yelled back to the small crowd in front, and my friends and the reporters raced back to the alley. When we all arrived, an FBI SUV was just pulling into the alley directly behind the house. *They obviously don't want the news media to capture them on tape*, I thought. Unfortunately for the Feds, my friends and supporters and the group of reporters were there to witness the theft of hundreds of items from the house.

One by one, agents emerged from the back door carrying closed moving boxes. Along with the boxes came computer monitors, printers, and other office equipment. Giving in to my anger, I began to join others in screaming obscenities at the Feds as they walked back and forth to the SUV. Many of them covered their eyes with large black sunglasses. I was pleased to see these images on the local television news late that night. I had an urge, largely for my own gratification, to smash the FBI SUV as it passed me in the alleyway, but I held back. As the SUV inched past us, the remaining Feds cleared out of the front of the house and hurried to their vehicles. By the time I came around to the front, they had all disappeared.

When I entered the house, Elaine and Vanessa were shaken up but otherwise fine. Elaine handed me the property receipt that allegedly stated what the agents had seized. I noticed that the list was quite long, with far more items taken than in the 2000 raid. As I read through the document, I began to think the entire NAELFPO had been taken. Racing up the stairs to the second floor office, I found my impression confirmed.

The office was practically empty. Piles of dust outlined the patterns on the two desks where CPUs, monitors, keyboards, printers, scanners, a fax machine and other equipment had been. Opening up the filing cabinets, once filled with copies of media releases, communiqués, NAELFPO literature, and address lists (for resistance, organizing protests, etc.) I found only a few scraps of paper. The desk drawers had been similarly ravaged.

This is ridiculous, I thought, shaking my head and rereading the seized property list. Unlike the 2000 raid, in which the federal agents had primarily seized computer items such as CPUs and external drives, this time they had taken the entire office. They had seized equipment that could not possibly offer any form of evidence in the investigation into the Romania arson. Hardware such as monitors, keyboards, scanners, etc. have no ability to hold memory, and yet they had been taken along with everything else. Clearly, the raid—investigation or not—was just another attempt to shut down the NAELFPO. Furthermore, as personal address books and belongings had been stolen, it looked like a definite attempt to disrupt our lives.

The search warrant had been signed by the US District Court at 3:10 P.M. on April 4, just fifteen hours before the raid—leading me to believe that the raid had been a last-minute effort to disrupt our press conference. Furthermore, because so many useless items had been taken, I was certain that the US government knew the important role the press office played in the direct action environmental movement. The agencies tracking the ELF and other economic saboteurs knew that politically motivated property destruction was on the rise. They also surely realized that the ideologies driving these groups, which were heavily distributed in part by the NAELFPO, were spreading rapidly and resulting in a dramatic increase in both large- and small-scale actions. Using the Romania arson as a legal motive, the Feds served a dual purpose with the raid—investigating the arson attack and making another stab at destroying the NAELFPO.

There was no way in hell that Leslie and I were going to let some thugs of the state pressure us into stopping the crucial work of publicizing the ELF actions. Already, the national news had reported on the attempted arson at the Nike outlet store in Minnesota. After the live satellite feeds all day in front of the house, the raid also became a featured news item across the country. The interest only continued to grow after Leslie and I sent out a press release about the situation on some borrowed and backup equipment.

Over the next few days, we received calls of support from all over the US and even internationally. People wondered how they could help, what we needed, or just called or emailed to thank us for our perseverance. I will always be truly thankful to those people who, out of the kindness of their hearts and their support for the ELF, helped the NAELFPO in this time of need. Within a couple of weeks, Leslie and I had received enough donations from around the world to fully resume our press office functions. This experience was a definite sign to me that support for the ELF and direct action in the form of property destruction was growing.

While we had survived another raid, I still had the grand jury appearance on April 18 to deal with. The prospect of traveling to Eugene to face a grand jury investigating the Romania arson didn't thrill me, to say the least. Eugene was known as a police state, a city where protesters had been brutalized repeatedly. It was in Eugene that Rob Thaxton was sentenced to over seven years in the state prison for tossing a rock at a cop during a demonstration. Eugene is also the city where Craig Marshall and Jeff Luers were caught, charged, and convicted. The fact that the grand jury, which I already felt would be ridiculously unjust, would be held in Eugene just made it that much worse.

As the day of my appearance neared, I learned that my attorney was going to be out of town and could not represent me. Following his advice, I called the US Attorney's office in Eugene to ask for a postponement so my lawyer could make the date. To my surprise and relief, I was told over the telephone that I could disregard the subpoena. The Assistant US Attorney stated that if his office needed me they would contact me through my attorney. Just to make sure I had some documentation of this decision, I asked for a confirmation letter to be sent to my lawyer. A few days later, I was thrilled to receive a call from my attorney stating that his office had indeed received the fax from Eugene. I was off the hook.

While I still had not been charged with any crime relating to my activities as a spokesperson for the ELF, this raid was a clear sign that the pressure was still increasing against the NAELFPO. Simultaneous raids—a four-hour search at the bakery combined with a six-hour siege at our home by over sixteen agents in all— demonstrated the frustration and pressure that federal agencies were feeling over their lack of success in stopping the ELF. But, like the ELF itself, the NAELFPO was not going to be easily stopped, especially by opposing interests and/or law enforcement.

With the stakes for both the ELF and the NAELFPO being raised, the Feds hoped the movement would begin to crack, that mistakes would be made and a hierarchical leadership would be found and stopped. To their disappointment, the ELF continued on in its aggressive style with the press office at its side, giving a voice to the underground fighters.

A
MOVEMENT
CLIMAXES

Only a couple of weeks after the Nike action, the ELF struck again, giving me perhaps one of the best birthday gifts of my life. On April 15, my twenty-ninth birthday, the ELF conducted their first-ever action in Portland, Oregon. A message received by the NAELFPO stated,

> The Earth Liberation Front claims responsibility for the fire that took place at Ross Island Sand and Gravel on Sunday, April 15th. For many years Ross Island Sand and Gravel has been guilty of stealing soil from the Earth, specifically the lagoon on Ross Island. Further, the recent acknowledgment of the dredging of toxic disposal cells has drawn our attention to the exploitation that Ross Island Sand and Gravel commits against our Earth. In their Easter basket we decided to leave four containers with gasoline and a time delayed fuse placed under two of their cement trucks. If Ross Island Sand and Gravel mines in the Columbia River Gorge, then the ELF will take necessary action. Let this be a warning to all greedy corporations who exploit our Earth's natural resources, especially those who plan on doing it under the FTAA and the title of "free trade."
>
> the elves and the Easter bunny

With the primary office of the investigation into the ELF based in Portland, this first local act by the group was bold, to say the least. The action caused an estimated $210,000 in damages to Ross Island Sand and Gravel, which has one location just across and up the Willamette River from the downtown Portland FBI office. In a *60 Minutes* segment on the ELF that aired on January 15, 2001, Dave Szady, then head of the Portland FBI location, had admitted that the ELF had gotten the better of the FBI. Now, just a few months later, in his own town, the ELF was thumbing its nose at the investigatory agency and getting away with it.

For years, Ross Island Sand and Gravel had been making news headlines with its environmentally destructive practices. Just prior to the ELF attack, the news went public that the company was responsible for the dredging of toxic disposal cells the Port of Portland had placed in the Willamette River lagoon. In fact, Ross Island Sand and Gravel had received so much scrutiny that they had recently made public statements in regards to cleaning up their act. "We've tried to take a meaningful public position in terminating our mining at Ross Island and furthering the reclamation as good corporate citizens," stated Chuck Steinwandel, the company's general manager.[91] But for the ELF, this action by Ross Island Sand and Gravel was too little and too late. The company's failure to change its practices in response to public opposition marked it for an attack.

Leslie and I were both extremely pleased to observe this escalation in ELF activity in 2001, and decided that, in addition to our regular work of dealing with the news media, we would develop new projects during the year to help promote and further spread the ELF ideology.

First, we planned to improve the design of a quarterly magazine we had begun publishing early in 2000, entitled *Resistance—Journal of the North American Earth Liberation Front Press Office. Resistance* listed recent ELF actions along with communiqués, news, and ideological rants from both of us. We sent out between five and ten thousand copies of each issue to organizations, individual subscribers, stores, infoshops, and even libraries internationally.

We also decided to produce a booklet, titled *Frequently Asked Questions about the ELF*, that would promote the ELF and its ideology by answering a set of questions that Leslie and I had been commonly faced with over the years. After a few weeks of writing and designing, the finished product contained twenty-two questions and answers. We published it ourselves and distributed it internationally using the *Resistance* contacts we had established.

In May, Leslie and I began work on an educational video about environmental destruction and the motives of the ELF. The twenty-two-minute video consisted mainly of highlighted segments taken from the answers to many of the questions in the booklet we had completed earlier in the year. Specifically geared toward the concerned but not-yet active environmental advocate,

91 "Eco-terrorist Group Says It Was Behind Arson Attack," *The Oregonian*, April 24, 2001.

the video served as a visual primer on the ELF, its ideology, and its structure.

Leslie and I decided to mix voiceover narrations in front of environmentally destructive scenes with direct on-camera headshots of both of us. For our on-camera scenes, we felt it was crucial to involve on-location backgrounds that would add further meaning to our dialogue. After debating various locations, and after taking into consideration our practically nonexistent budget, we jumped into my truck and headed out to begin the project.

We spent a few weeks shooting scenes for the video, from locations around the Pacific Northwest all the way to southern California. We filmed forest and lake scenes by Mt. Hood in Oregon, old growth redwood forests in northern California, smog, traffic, and Disneyland in the Los Angeles area, and more. Anxious to get the video released, we headed back to Portland only to be immediately faced with another first for the ELF.

Simultaneous Fires

For the first time ever, the group had conducted simultaneous arson attacks in two different states—a clear sign that the ELF was growing in strength and efficiency. On May 21, phone calls began coming into the NAELFPO from both Seattle and Portland reporters, asking Leslie and me about two fires that had occurred the night before. According to the news media, two separate fires had burned down the Center for Urban Horticulture at the University of Washington and buildings at Jefferson Poplar Farms in Clatskanie, Oregon, an hour or so outside of Portland. Apparently, FBI and BATF crews on location at both sites had instantly suspected the ELF.

One reason for this was that genetic researcher Toby Bradshaw—who had been previously targeted by anti-genetic-engineering vandals just prior to the WTO protests in 1999—had his office at the University of Washington Center for Urban Horticulture. Bradshaw suspected he might have been the target for this fire after noticing that two plastic boxes from his office had been displaced. These boxes, which contained a pair of corn snakes Bradshaw used for biology lectures, were found under a serviceberry tree, safely away from the fire. In addition, the parties who had burned two buildings and several vehicles belonging to Jefferson Poplar Farms in Oregon had left "ELF" written in paint on the side of one of the structures. The phrase "You cannot control what is wild" was also found scrawled at the scene.

After I had talked to a number of reporters from Oregon and Washington, Leslie and I decided to head out to Clatskanie to see for ourselves firsthand the aftermath of a sizable ELF attack. Over an hour into the trip, it became clear to us that we were lost. This was a rural farming area with back roads winding around into who knew where. Finally, after rounding yet another turn, we could see the large satellite news vehicles parked up ahead.

We parked on the road directly in front of Jefferson Poplar. Even before getting out of the vehicle, we saw the smoke still rising out of a torched building a hundred yards away. Within seconds, a couple of news reporters recognized me and walked over to ask what in the hell both of us were doing there. I told them Leslie and I were there for the same purpose as the news crews, to get firsthand information about the possible ELF attack.

While I was giving a couple of interviews, the Feds on the scene spotted us and began driving by slowly, taking pictures and just outright staring. I still wonder to this day what the FBI and BATF agents on the scene there in Clatskanie thought when they looked up and saw the press officers for the ELF standing directly in front of the site of a massive arson attack that had just occurred the night before. After the interviews were over, a few FBI agents came over and attempted to question us about the fire, the motive for setting it and our presence at the scene. At that point, we decided it was time to leave. Driving away from Jefferson Poplar, I could see the federal agents staring at the back of our vehicle as it pulled away. Like Leslie and I, they were waiting to see if the notorious eco-sabotage group would indeed claim responsibility.

Sure enough, on June 1, I received the much-anticipated communiqué from the ELF.

Part 1

At 3:15 A.M. on Monday, May 21, the research of Toby Bradshaw was reduced to smoke and ashes. We attacked his office at the University of Washington while at the same time another group set fire to a related target in Clatskanie, Oregon, 150 miles away.

Bradshaw, the driving force in GE tree research, continues to unleash mutant genes into the environment that is [sic] certain to cause irreversible harm to forest ecosystems.

After breaking into Bradshaw's office at the Center for Urban Horticulture, we inspected the building for occupants and set up incendiary devices with a modest amount of accelerant. Although we placed these devices specifically to target his office, a large portion of the building was damaged. This extensive damage was due to a surprisingly slow and poorly coordinated response from the fire department, which was evident by their radio transmissions.

As long as universities continue to pursue this reckless "science," they run the risk of suffering severe losses. Our message remains clear: we are determined to stop genetic engineering.

From the torching of Catherine Ive's [sic] office at Michigan State University to the total incineration of GE seeds at the D & PL warehouse in Visalia, CA, the Earth Liberation Front is growing and spreading. As the culture of domination forces itself into our very genes, wild fires of outrage will continue to blaze.

ELF

Part 2

Early Monday morning, May 21, we dealt a blow to one of the many institutions responsible for massive hybrid tree farming in the Northwest. Incendiary devices at Jefferson Poplar in Clatskanie, Oregon burned an office and a fleet of 13 trucks. Unfortunately, due to a design flaw, one targeted structure was left standing. We torched Jefferson Poplar because hybrid poplars are an ecological nightmare threatening native biodiversity in the ecosystem. Our forests are being liquidated and replaced with monocultured tree farms so greedy, earth raping corporations can make more money.

Pending legislation in Oregon and Washington further criminalizing direct action in defense of the wild will not stop us and only highlights the fragility of the ecocidal empire.

As we wrote in Clatskanie "You cannot control what is wild."

ELF

Earth Liberation Front

This dual action stunned investigators, reporters, and much of the Pacific Northwest. At Jefferson Poplar farms, the ELF had inflicted at least $500,000 in damages, and the University of Washington in Seattle sustained losses of over $2 million. Next to the Vail arson in 1998, these latest simultaneous strikes were some of the largest and most damaging ever attributed to the ELF.

As expected, the biotech community rallied around the victims of the attack, especially Toby Bradshaw. Every attempt was made to portray Bradshaw as a saint conducting research crucial for the health and welfare of humankind. Bradshaw himself actually stated just after the blaze in Seattle, "Burning crosses did not stop the civil-rights movement, and burning buildings won't stop the tree-genetics research programs around the country."[92] I could hardly believe that this lunatic was equating the civil rights movement with genetic research. This unfortunately appeared to be another case of "If I convince myself I am doing good, then I must be doing good."

One of the main figures who came immediately to Bradshaw's defense was his friend and colleague Steve Strauss, director of the Tree Genetic Engineering Cooperative at Oregon State University in Corvallis. Strauss worked hard to paint Bradshaw as the innocent victim of an attack by uneducated fanatics. This attempt to win public support by asserting that opponents of genetic engineering are anti-science and anti-human is common

---

92 Hal Bernton, "Eco-Terrorists suspected in UW horticultural fire," *The Seattle Times*, May 22, 2001.

practice in the biotech industry, and plays upon the perception that "the white lab coats know better, and we must trust them." Yet, isn't that how both DDT and the atomic bomb were created?

Strauss was able to successfully convince *The Oregonian* to run an editorial he had written, which appeared on June 7, 2001, condemning the ELF attack and promoting genetic engineering. I was so furious when I read this industry puff piece—not an uncommon sight in *The Oregonian*—that I spent two days working on a rebuttal. I figured the paper would have to run my submission—I mean, who better to write a response than the spokesperson for the group that had been verbally attacked?

Thrilled with this opportunity to tell the other side of the story, I emailed my submission to *The Oregonian* and assumed they would jump at the chance to print it—controversy sells! After a couple of days without hearing from the newspaper, I called the commentary editorial staff, only to find out they were still deciding whether or not they wanted to run the piece. Politely, I asked them why I should not be granted the same space as Strauss to reply to his attack on the ELF. The response I finally received was that they were thinking of running something—just not from me.

As for Bradshaw and Strauss, they clearly have felt the effects of the ELF and the anti-genetic engineering movement. Strauss, himself targeted by vandals who destroyed three poplar plots at OSU in March 2001, admitted in a *New York Times* article that "he planned to cut back on genetically engineered trees, in part because of the attacks."[93]

Scrambling to Keep Up

Not long after claiming responsibility for the simultaneous actions, the ELF struck again in Idaho and then in Michigan. At the University of Idaho, located in Moscow, the ELF claimed credit for sabotaging the school's biotechnology building in protest of genetic engineering. Among other GE

---

93 Sam Howe Verhovek with Carol Kaesuk Yoon, "Fires Believed Set as Protest Against Genetic Engineering," *The New York Times*, May 23, 2001, nytimes.com/2001/05/23/us/fires-believed-set-as-protest-against-genetic-engineering.html.

research projects, the University of Idaho, in partnership with Monsanto's Naturemark, was genetically modifying potatoes to be resistant to various viruses and pests. The university was collaborating with Naturemark and the Idaho 4-H in a so-called "educational" program called "Biotechnology and Potatoes." This joint effort was aimed at teaching students of all ages about plant biotechnology and included hands-on genetic engineering. In the Young Enterprise Program, another outcome of this partnership, students participated in the marketing of genetically engineered potatoes. Naturemark supplied its genetically modified NewLeaf potatoes to students, who then marketed them to local communities. These projects aimed at propagandizing students with industry myths and no doubt failed to include discussions on the serious threats posed by genetic engineering to the natural environment.

The message from the saboteurs read,

Biotech Out of Our Community!

ELF Claims Attack on University of Idaho Biotech Building

The University of Idaho Biotechnology building, currently under construction, was targeted in the early hours of the morning on June 10th by a cell of the Earth Liberation Front calling themselves the Night Action Kids. Survey stakes were removed and the exterior of the new building painted with such sentiments as "NO GE!" and "Go Organic."

This is the second action against the Biotechnology building. The first of which [sic] individuals entered the building and caused an unknown amount of damage.

An anonymous ELF Night Action Kid compares research in Genetic Engineering and Biotechnology to the scientific studies which led to the creation of the nuclear bomb. "Biotechnological research may be intended for good ends by the scientist, as was nuclear research, but in our free enterprise police state society it will be used almost solely for greed and control. With Genetic Engineering we are creating another nuclear bomb."

Monsanto and other large corporations are patenting seeds and forcing farmers to sign contracts that they will continue buying these GE, and many times pesticide resistant, seeds from the same corporation year after year, effectively taking control over our food sources. Genetically Engineered food on our grocery store shelves is not labeled as such, so the individual does not know what he or she is eating. Genetically Engineered fish are escaping into the wild populations with the chance of killing off entire species. Genetic testing for predisposition to certain diseases, such as cancer, may soon keep you and your children from getting insurance or a job.

"GE corporations and their supporters have claimed that we [anti-GE activists] are using scare tactics to further our viewpoint. The fact is that Biotechnology and Genetic Engineering are scary prospects when placed in the hands of large corporations who care only about profits and not about the health and safety of the people, or the effects they are having on the environment. Through the University of Idaho Biotechnology Program we are teaching our children to work in a field which is developing faster than its effects, both physically and ethically, can be monitored and has the potential for causing catastrophic harm to all humans and the planet," claims another Night Action Kid, who continues, "Get Biotech out of Moscow! It is not wanted in our community."

Then, on June 11, a message arrived at the NAELFPO claiming responsibility on behalf of the ELF for three actions during June and early July in Michigan. The communiqué read,

To whom it may concern,

Greetings from the Great Lakes nation-state of Michigan. Not so long ago we had informed the ALF press office of an action against Butcher Boy Meats where six trucks had been vandalized: windshields and side windows broken and abrasives introduced into the lubricating systems. We'd also reported on some monkeywrenching of heavy machinery utilized in the erection of yet another industrial complex; these two actions were only a humble genesis.

Approximately four weeks ago a newly built McDonald's was vandalized. Two large plateglass windows and a drive-thru window were broken, and the drive thru order unit was destroyed. This action was in solidarity with the actions of women farmers in Brazil against "worldwide neoliberal economic policies," not to mention the clearing of rainforests to raise cattle for fast-food hamburger patties. Considering "the golden arches" are a nefarious symbol of economic globalization, ecological destruction and worker exploitation, we felt they were an appropriate target (even though a small one), and we left graffiti and flyers stating our motives and vision.

Two days later, eight SUVs were torched at Roy O'Brien Ford Dealership. Four incendiary devices were placed amongst eight Ford Expeditions causing an unknown amount of damage. All that's known is that eight Expeditions had been removed from the lot the following day. This action was a snarl of rage directed towards the planet rapers who construct these unregulated petroleum guzzlers and the capitalist whores who pander them and profit off the pollution caused by fuel emissions and the needless use of natural resources. This was our sounding of class war in Macomb County. We have just begun!

Finally on July 4th, at approximately 2:45 am, an office of Weyerhaeuser Co. was torched. Amount and extent of damage unknown. We believe only one executive office was gutted, but we're uncertain. This action was taken in protest of the company's part in funding O.S.U. and the University of Washington's poplar and cottonwood genetic engineering research. TGERC [Tree Genetic Engineering Research Cooperative, at Oregon State University] and PMGC [Poplar Molecular Genetics Cooperative, at the University of Washington] are more evidence of negligent corporate executive backing of profit motivated research in agricultural biotechnology. Their complete disregard for the Earth and the humans and nonhumans that inhabit it is not only reprehensible but totally unforgivable. To risk our planet and life upon it in exchange for profit is deserving of the most extreme measures in stamping genetic modification out. GE testing must be systematically and strategically eliminated wherever and whenever possible. We are striking the financiers and supporters of GE testing in support of and in solidarity with all the nighttime gardeners and ecowarriors everywhere. We cannot be stopped.

In love and struggle,

the Elves

ELF

As Leslie and I scrambled to keep up with all of the incoming communiqués and interview requests, a location in Kentucky was hit in the early morning hours of July 21. This time the target was the Dynegy power plant located in LaGrange.

Press Release to the General Public

On early Saturday morning (July 21, 2001), eco-activists committed sabotage against the Dynegy power plant in LaGrange, Kentucky. Fifteen vehicles designed to rape the earth had their tires slashed and flattened. Along with various spray-painted ELF slogans and a dozen broken windows. This action was done in solidarity with all the people effected [sic] by this corporate wasteland. We wanted to send a clear message to Dynegy that the people will not sit around idly while our earth and health is put into jeopardy for the sake of a few fat wallets in Houston. It was clear that the citizens of the community did not want this in their backyard, and that they were spoon-fed lies by corrupt politicians. The power is in our hands to take direct action against the power plant and other forms of corporate imperialism. It is the last means to take, for all other options (legal and peaceful) have been exhausted.

No compromise in defense of mother earth.

The elves of the Earth Liberation Front

Long live the ELF!

Dynegy, like many polluters of the natural world, has joined the trend of attempting to appear "green" and environmentally concerned. However, while Dynegy's natural-gas-powered plants may be cleaner than coal-burning plants, they still release nitrous oxide, one of the main ingredients in ground-level ozone and smog. Dynegy stated that they intended to follow all laws in relation to the release of emissions. However, in the year 2000, Dynegy faced penalties for violating Texas air quality standards in four counties. Under a court settlement, Dynegy spent $500 million between 2005 and 2012 to install pollution controls to decrease emissions.[94] In 2001, the state of Illinois sued Dynegy over its coal ash discharges that caused groundwater pollution.[95] With corporations such as Chevron being Dynegy's primary investors, it is no wonder that the energy company is an ecological nightmare and thus a perfect target for the ELF.

After dealing with the explosion of news media attention regarding these latest acts by the ELF, I concentrated my efforts on editing the video and preparing it for release to the public. I had been invited to premiere the new video, entitled *Igniting the Revolution: An Introduction to the Earth Liberation Front*, at a national conference on animal rights in Washington, DC. While I could not afford to go myself, I finished up the editing with just hours to spare and shipped the video across the country overnight. I wanted to be there in the room the first time it was shown, to see the reaction from the audience, but I settled for hearing decent reviews hours later over the telephone.

I did look forward, however, to a West Coast premiere, and what better place than Portland, the city that is home to the NAELFPO, in the state where the US ELF actions originated? I contacted the North Portland campus of Portland Community College (PCC) and asked what the procedure was for renting a room to show a video to the public. After finding out that it was as simple as filling out a reservation form and paying a small fee, I raced over to the campus and reserved a space for July 27, 2001.

94 "Illinois Power Company and Dynegy Midwest Generation Settlement," EPA.gov. epa.gov/enforcement/illinois-power-company-and-dynegy-midwest-generation-settlement
95 Stephen Joyce, "Illinois Sues Dynegy for Causing Alleged Coal Ash Pollution," *Bloomberg Law*. news.bloomberglaw.com/environment-and-energy/illinois-sues-dynegy-for-allegedly-causing-coal-ash-pollution

With the date set, I designed and produced a large number of eleven by seventeen inch posters advertising the event. These were displayed in local businesses and on college campuses, telephone poles and other community bulletin boards. When officials from PCC saw the posters—which showed an enlarged picture of Vail in flames—they freaked. Even though I had filled out the contract as a representative of the North American Earth Liberation Front Press Office, officials at PCC called me and suddenly acted as though I had tricked them into allowing a known terrorist to show a recruiting video on their campus. They informed me that my event would now require a $1 million insurance policy and that I would personally have to hire a number of off-duty police officers for security. If these requests were not met, the event would be canceled.

There was no way I was going to hire police officers to come to the screening. Furthermore, I did not (as I am sure PCC officials suspected) have enough capital to foot the bill for the enormous insurance policy—so I was left with no choice but to reschedule the showing. I finally decided to show the video the same night, but on the sidewalk directly in front of the school. Numerous reporters, along with over one hundred local Portland residents, turned out to see the first West Coast showing of the so-called "recruiting video" displayed on a battery-powered portable video unit.

National news media picked up the story, increasing the controversy and sales of the video, which had been made available by mail order. While US Assistant Attorney Stephen Peifer in Portland contended that the video advocated committing serious crimes, including arson and extortion, neither Leslie nor I ever faced charges from its production.

ust under one month later, a roar of activity was again heard from Long Island, where the ELF continued to thrive despite the increasing pressure from authorities. The message appeared as follows:

Statement for Aug 21st ELF action

On Tuesday August 21st members of the Earth Liberation Front paid [a] visit to the newly built bio-tech building for Cold Spring Harbor Laboratories, located on Sunnyside Blvd., in Plainview, Long Island. Here activists inflicted heavy damages to their exterior air filtration and coolant systems by smashing thermostats and computer instruments, and damaging extensively insulation to coolant pipes. The building was donned [sic] with slogans denouncing genetic engineering, one reading "tampering with biodiversity = extinction," the other reading "Love ELF." Upon retreat windows were also smashed.

This was a warning shot from the Long Island community to the Labs, that the technologies they develop have potentially drastic and lethal consequences. Be forewarned that we are watching your every move, and if you thought for one second you could keep your new Plainview lab location under wraps you were gravely mistaken.

We watch your every step.

ELF /

This was the second time that the ELF had targeted Cold Spring Harbor Laboratories in just over one year. After the communiqué reached the NAELFPO on September 2, the group would go into one of its first dormant periods of the year. Meanwhile, the events on the East Coast were about to turn the United States and the rest of the world upside down.

Additional actions taken by the ELF in 2001 include:

June 13, Long Island, New York: ELF and ALF joint action against five Bank of New York Branches in protest of the bank's association with Huntingdon Life Sciences, a notorious animal testing company.

July 16, Macomb County, Michigan: Fire destroyed the first floor of the headquarters for Spencer Oil Co.

POLITICIANS
SEEK
ACTION

"This is a weed that has come into the lawn and if you don't cut it out, it will spread."

—Congressman Scott McInnis, referring to the ELF,
March 7, 2002[96]

Long before the September 11, 2001 attacks on the Pentagon and the World Trade Center and the attendant backlash against progressive groups at home, politicians increasingly felt pressure to take action against the ELF. ELF hits were becoming more frequent across the United States, and industry victims naturally had an interest in halting the attacks. Since local, state, and federal law enforcement agencies were clearly having no effect on the organization, various industries turned their sights to politicians for assistance.

As early as 1999, legislation began to include provisions dealing specifically with politically motivated environmental or animal advocacy crime. One example of this came with the Juvenile Justice Bill, passed in May 1999 shortly after the Columbine High School shootings. While not related to "juvenile justice" in any direct sense, animal rights and environmental protection provisions were included. The Bill made it legal to come down harder on people who commit politically motivated nonviolent offenses, allowing for longer prison terms.

Additionally, the Juvenile Justice Bill did the following:

- Made it a federal crime to distribute information on how to make pipe bombs (over the internet or otherwise) or other weapons of mass destruction if the teacher intends for the information to be used to commit a federal crime, or knows that the recipient will use the information to commit such a crime.

- Enhanced penalties under the Animal Enterprise Terrorism Act by changing a minimum sentence from one year to a mandatory five years.

---

96 From McInnis's presentation during a meeting on "Stopping EcoExtremism: A Conference on Legislative, Legal and Communications Strategies to Protect Free Enterprise, Private Property, and American Business," held in Washington, DC on March 7, 2002 and sponsored by the Competitive Enterprise Institute.

- Created a National Animal Terrorism and Ecoterrorism Incident Clearinghouse to accept, collect, and maintain information on crimes against animal enterprises or commercial activities due to their perceived impact on the environment. Records of such incidents are available to all law enforcement agencies.

During the same month, Senators Diane Feinstein (D-CA) and Orrin G. Hatch (R-UT) made a proposal to amend the Racketeer Influenced and Corrupt Organizations (RICO) Act. Historically, the RICO Act had been used to target organized crime, but Feinstein and Hatch were successful in changing it to include "Animal Enterprise Terrorism and Ecoterrorism." The RICO Act specifically targets criminal activity that is organized across state lines. Therefore, activists who use the telephone or internet and are caught for illegal activity could easily be charged with RICO provisions.

In February 2001, then–FBI director Louis Freeh announced publicly that the ELF was considered to be the number one domestic terrorist threat in the United States. This official designation led to a surge of national news stories. But the declaration also allowed for an increase in the FBI's budget and a growth in the number of personnel assigned to track and stop the elusive ELF.

This announcement by Freeh came just over a month after the ELF's January 2001 communiqué calling for an "escalation in tactics against capitalism and industry." As the year progressed, the FBI designation of the ELF as a pressing domestic terrorist threat appeared to have virtually no effect on the organization. In fact, it almost seems as if the ELF affirmed Freeh's announcement that year by living up to their goal of escalating tactics. His announcement came only a few months before the simultaneous actions at the University of Washington and at the tree farm in Clatskanie, Oregon.

The following month, in March 2001, two bills aimed at increasing penalties for "eco-terrorists" were approved by the Oregon House of Representatives. With HR 2344 and 2385, the legislature attempted to expand Oregon's organized crime laws to include such activities as sabotage of animal research, livestock, or agricultural operations and even tree spiking. Convictions under the laws would have been punishable by up to twenty years in prison and a $300,000 fine. In late May to early June, these "eco-terrorist" bills were passed by Oregon lawmakers.

Similar to the enacted Oregon bills, the Maine legislature introduced an "Act to Deter Environmental Terrorism in the State." Presented by Senator Kilkelly of Lincoln, the act sought to criminalize the "destruction of property or the interference with a place of business's normal course of business by individuals or groups for the primary purpose of making a political statement on natural resource and environmental issues." The proposed Act also categorized "environmental terrorizing" as a Class C felony, punishable by up to a $5,000 fine and a maximum of five years in prison. This would not only affect underground groups such as the ELF but also individuals conducting legal aboveground protests.

In America's dairyland, the Wisconsin legislature was also presented with new proposed "anti-eco-terrorist" laws in June 2001. The proposed legislation would have made vandalizing or terrorizing agricultural property into a Class C felony—punishable by up to ten years in jail and a $10,000 fine.

As politicians moved to act on their corporate constituents' requests to stop the ELF, I eventually found myself brought into the political game. On June 27, 2001, I received a letter from Rep. Scott McInnis (R-CO) asking me to voluntarily come and testify at a Congressional hearing in Washington, DC on the "emerging threat of ecoterrorism." The initial letter didn't state what the goal of the hearing was or who else was being invited to participate. In fact, it was extremely vague, offering few details about the subject matter of the hearing. Rather, the bulk of McInnis's letter contained information on policies and rules of Congressional hearings in general.

I have to admit, I got a big kick out of receiving this letter. I found it hilarious that any member of Congress would, even for a moment, think that I might come and voluntarily testify at a hearing so obviously biased in favor of industry and law enforcement. But, just to give Congress the benefit of the doubt, I sent McInnis a response asking him to clarify the intentions of the "ecoterrorism" hearing. I asked him if what he meant by ecoterrorism was actually the terror and destruction inflicted on the natural environment by industry. If the intent of the hearing was truly to investigate and stop this industry-driven destruction and terror, then I would be delighted to participate. Of course, I knew full well that the chief purpose of the hearing was to investigate and stop organizations such as the ELF from operating. There was no way, I informed McInnis, that I would help with such an effort. "I have no desire," I wrote, "to cooperate with the same State that is directly responsible for the ongoing murder and exploitation of life both within this country and internationally." By the time I learned of McInnis's next move, it was October, and the political climate had intensified beyond anyone's expectations.

As the news of the September 11 terrorist attacks on the World Trade Center and the Pentagon hit, I wondered how this event would affect resistance politics in the United States. I further wondered how it might influence the political and legal efforts to stop organizations such as the ELF. According to the FBI, the rest of the US government, and most mainstream news media, the ELF had already been considered a terrorist organization well before September 11. *Now,* I wondered, *would there be a calculated effort to publicly link the ELF to groups such as Al-Qaeda?*

I also wondered how the events of 9/11 would affect the ELF and its actions of economic sabotage in defense of the Earth. Would the organization continue its aggressive spree of actions? Would the group find the post–September 11 political atmosphere in the United States too oppositional and give up?

In one month's time, on October 17, I heard the news that answered many of my inner questions. The ELF had struck again—targeting a US government agency, the Bureau of Land Management. Two days before, on October 15, the ELF had set free two hundred wild horses from a BLM facility near Susanville, California. After the horses were a safe distance away, the group went on to set four timed incendiary devices that destroyed two barns, two vehicles, and an office building. This bold move was naturally criticized even more harshly than usual by the corporate news media.

The ELF didn't stop there, either. The group finished up the year in revolutionary style, claiming responsibility for one further action on November 5. The message stated,

> Hello; this is a communiqué from a nameless Earth Liberation Front Cell. We claim no issue or area as our own, we just act. This is to announce we have spiked countless trees in the Otter Wing Timber Sale, located in the Nez Perce National Forest. For too long, the forests of Central and North Idaho have been under assault from industrial forestry. The Boise, Payette, Clearwater, Idaho Panhandle, and Nez Perce are some of the National Forests in Idaho that have been scarred from excessive logging. The timber sale program—nothing but a financial drain as well as an ecological disaster—must end. The Otter Wing Timber sale has destroyed a once pristine ecosystem on the South Fork of the Clearwater River. It is an area which hosted abundant wildlife such as fish, birds, mammalian predators, ungulates and a beautiful mosaic of different forest vegetative patterns. Now most of that area has been logged—aside from the spiked units. We are serious. This is our first act of sabotage in Idaho. We may feel compelled to act again. The forest service of Idaho should know that as long as they continue to destroy Idaho's last remaining wildlands, they risk action on behalf of the ELF.

In keeping with the ELF's promise to escalate "tactics against capitalism and industry," the year 2001 had been by far the most active in the group's history.

•   •   •

On October 3, 2001, a strange call came into the NAELFPO from a Washington, DC–based reporter. He asked if I had any response to the announcement by the House Resources Committee that they planned to subpoena me to testify at an "ecoterrorism" hearing scheduled for February 2002. Surprised, I prodded the reporter for more information. It turned out that after receiving my response to his letter, McInnis had asked the Resources Committee to approve subpoenaing me for this February hearing. On October 3, the Committee on Resources authorized Chairman James V. Hansen to issue a subpoena requiring me to attend the Subcommittee hearing scheduled for February 12. The title of the hearing organized by the Congressional House Subcommittee on Forests and Forest Health was "Ecoterrorism and Lawlessness on the National Forests."

Wonderful, I thought, hanging up the phone. Apparently seven grand jury subpoenas weren't enough; now it appeared that I was going to have to stand up to the US Congress. I couldn't believe this display of government waste. I had already shown how little I would cooperate with any attempt to stop the ELF and ALF over the years, and now, as if they hadn't been paying attention, I would have to travel all the way to Washington for another round of Craig says nothing.

The one thing I was thankful for was that the reporter had tipped me off to an incoming subpoena. Knowing it was on its way, I vowed to delay receiving it as long as I could—comfortably. Now, I obviously could have immediately taken an extended vacation after hearing this news, one that would have lasted until some time after February 12. But after weighing the circumstances— this sort of thing had happened seven times before, I had survived each time without cooperating and had never been indicted with a single crime related to my spokesperson work, and, since it was the House, I would only risk one year in jail for not cooperating. I decided to carry on with my regular life as much as possible, while trying to make those serving the subpoena earn their pay.

Just as I had many times before, I began monitoring all activity in my North Portland neighborhood. I watched out for cars that didn't appear to belong in the economically depressed area, as well as any that suddenly showed up parked nearby. As an added security measure, I also began to use the back alley when leaving or returning home, always careful to check it first for signs of agents. Just a few days after I received the phone call about the subpoena, the knocking began at the front door. Looking out my bedroom window, I could see it was not the FBI or the BATF (or any of the other agencies I had become familiar with over the years) but rather the US Marshals. After knocking for a while, the two men walked back to their vehicle and left. This scenario was replayed many times over the next few weeks.

Sometimes the Marshals stopped knocking to ask for me through the door by name. After it was clear I didn't want the damned subpoena, they started saying things like, "This is your big opportunity, Mr. Rosebraugh; this is your chance to voice your concerns in front of Congress." Compelling—or comical—as this argument may have been, I was not in any way convinced that Congress wanted anything but to lock me, the ELF, and the ALF up for eternity.

As the Marshals' visits became increasingly intense and frequent, we covered all the windows on the main floor of the house to prevent unwanted eyes from peering inside. Elaine, Vanessa, Leslie, and I became even more cautious about ensuring that all doors were locked at all times. Everyone at the house was also quite helpful in scoping out the neighborhood when I had to go out. I took the bus even more than usual to avoid being seen in my vehicle, and often boarded and deboarded at different stops to prevent any routine from being observed.

In the middle of the month, after the Marshals had been coming for a couple of weeks, I was almost caught. I was driving my car home and, as usual, entered the neighborhood with caution. As I slowly drove up North Gantenbein Street, I didn't see anything out of the ordinary, but just as our house came into view, I saw a man dressed in civilian clothing (no US Marshals jacket) on the front porch. Glancing over to my left, I noticed another individual in an unmarked white car, obviously waiting for the person on the porch. Figuring it was the Marshals, I continued driving straight past the house and down the street. After a block and a half, I turned the car around and parked on the street where I could see when, and if, the Marshals left.

Just as I parked, I saw the man sprint off the porch and jump into the white car. It pulled out, skidded around, and headed back in my direction. I drove forward slowly, then floored the gas and passed the car, separated from the Marshals by only a few inches. I flew down toward the next block as the white car turned again and sped toward me. Making a quick left and then another right at the next block, I headed straight for the freeway. Pushing the rpm near the red zone, I jetted up the freeway. To my amazement, I had lost them. I took the first exit on the other side of the Willamette River, then pulled into the Food Front parking lot and, with my adrenaline pumping, walked in to get some snacks. I waited until nightfall to return home.

After this incident, I was sure that the house was going to be raided again, if for no other reason than to obtain access to subpoena me. Surprisingly, the Marshals instead cut back their visits, and, by the last week in October, it seemed as though they had given up. At least that is what I expect they wanted me to believe. While I knew I had not seen the last of the Marshals, I did relax my vigilance slightly.

Around 5:00 P.M. on Halloween, Vanessa put some carved pumpkins on the front steps of the house and began lighting the candles inside them. Wanting to watch her scary faces light up in the dusk, I stepped onto the front porch and walked toward the pumpkins. Just as I raised my eyes to the street, I saw two men running toward the house yelling, "Mr. Rosebraugh!" Before I could think to run back inside and lock the door, the anticipated white sheet of paper was handed to me. I had been served. The two Marshals had been sitting in a car down the block just waiting for me to slip up, and I had.

While I knew the subpoena was coming, and that I would eventually be served, I was pissed that the Marshals had caught up with me when I had only been on my porch for a few seconds. Signed by House Resources Committee Chairman James V. Hansen, the subpoena commanded me to appear in room 1324 of the Longworth Building in Washington, DC at 3:00 P.M. on February 12, 2002. I immediately contacted my attorney, Stu Sugarman, to notify him of the situation and ask for his assistance. Excited at the opportunity to take on Congress, Stu immediately began work on the case.

Feeling like I could use all the public support I could get, Leslie and I quickly sent out news releases nationally about the hearing and my subpoena. While the news would have gained attention on its own, certain statements in the press release itself also sparked considerable media interest:

> The legal forms of objection and attempts at changes in environmental policy since the 1960s have not worked. Our environment is more polluted and destroyed now than ever before. More actions, like those of the ELF, are needed to stop the destruction of life caused by greedy, corrupt corporations and politicians. . . .

> In light of the events of September 11, my country has told me that I should not cooperate with terrorists. I, therefore, am refusing to cooperate with members of Congress who are some of the most extreme terrorists in history. Currently, they are responsible for allowing the slaughter of now over an estimated 1,500 Afghan civilians. They are responsible for the Sept. 11 attacks due to horrendous US foreign policies of imperialism, and they are responsible for the current ongoing genocide against the innocent people of Afghanistan. This alleged war on terrorism has largely been conducted to allow the US to attempt to oust the Taliban, and put in place a new puppet regime in Afghanistan who would allow the US to build their much sought after pipeline from the Turkmenistan oil reserves through southern Afghanistan, Pakistan, and to the Gulf. These sorts of practices, mixed in with domestic policies of racism, classism, and further imperialism at the expense of life, demonstrate the truly terrorist reality of the US Congress and Government. I could not live with myself if I cooperated with that injustice.

Naturally, the response this press release received from the news media was intense. Many of the stories focused on my condemning the government as terrorists, and it appeared a showdown was building for February 12.

On November 2, I received a few calls from reporters asking if I had any comments regarding the press release issued by Scott McInnis earlier that day. Locating a copy of the release, I was amused to find that McInnis was directly asking environmental groups to publicly condemn the ELF. The media release stated,

McInnis Challenges Environmental Groups to Disavow Eco-Terrorism: Colorado Congressman to Hold Hearing on Eco-Terrorism Next Year

Washington, DC—Representative Scott McInnis (R-Colorado) today sent a letter signed by himself, Representative James Hansen (R-Utah), Chairman to the House Resources Committee, and other Members of Congress to key environmental organizations, calling on them to publicly disavow the actions of eco-terrorist organizations like Earth Liberation Front (ELF) and Animal Liberation Front (ALF), terrorist cells that have exacted a substantial financial and personal toll on scores of individuals and enterprises throughout the United States.

On October 30, 2001 ELF claimed responsibility for the radical firebombing of a US Bureau of Land Management wild horse corral near Susanville, California. The incendiary device set a blaze and caused nearly $85,000 in damage.

McInnis, who chairs the Resources Subcommittee on Forests and Forest Health, has scheduled a hearing to probe the threat of eco-terrorism early next year. One of the witnesses scheduled to testify is Craig Rosebraugh, the self-appointed spokesman of the Earth Liberation Front (ELF). Rosebraugh was subpoenaed earlier this month after rejecting earlier offers by McInnis to testify voluntarily.

"In probing the threat of terrorism, it only stands to reason that Congress should probe the threat of eco-terrorism as well," McInnis said. "It is crucial that key environmental organizations join with us in combating these underground eco-terrorist organizations."

The phrase "key environmental organizations" is important to note, since McInnis, or more likely his aides, only sent the letter to a small handful of organizations. Those that received the letter were primarily among the mainstream organizations, such as the Sierra Club that had already gone out of their way to publicly condemn the ELF.[97] The letter appears below:

October 30, 2001

As our Nation begins the recovery and healing process following the tragedy of September 11, we believe it is critical for Americans of every background and political stripe to disavow terrorism in all its forms and manifestations. No matter its shape, source or motivation, Americans simply cannot tolerate, either overtly or through silence, the use of violence and terror as an instrument of promoting social and political change.

With this understanding, we are calling on you and your organization to publicly disavow the actions of eco-terrorist organizations like the Earth Liberation Front (ELF) and Animal Liberation Front (ALF). Eco-terrorist cells like these have exacted a substantial financial and personal toll on scores of individuals and enterprises in all corners of the United States. In the dark of night and under the cover of anonymity, environmental radicals have firebombed government offices, research centers, schools, homes, and businesses. In so doing, they have sent a ripple of fear though all the many communities in their destructive path. While the attacks of eco-vigilantes have not yet reached the magnitude of what America experienced over the last several weeks, their tactics are no less deplorable, their methods of pursuing political change no less appalling, and their use of fear and terror no less repugnant.

In February, then FBI Director Louis Freeh identified radical eco-terrorist organizations like ELF and ALF as one of America's leading domestic terrorism threats. The FBI's announcement came on the heels of a January 1st ELF communiqué proclaiming, "This year, 2001, we hope to see an escalation in tactics against capitalism and industry." In the time since, ELF has made good on its

---

97 The Sierra Club had even gone so far as to work with the FBI in the Colorado Vail arson investigation.

threat to ratchet up the violence in 2001, using incendiary devices to, amongst other things, level the University of Washington's Center for Urban Horticulture, torch an entire fleet of trucks owned by a private timber company,[98] and burn the Oregon Offices of Superior Lumber Company. Alarmingly, ALF arsonists struck a biomedical lab in New Mexico just nine days after the horrors of September 11, destroying property estimated at $1 million. This year's attacks, together costing local businesses and taxpayers upwards of $5 million, are in addition to the over $40 million in damage that ELF and ALF have inflicted since their inception. Even during this hour of national crisis, ELF and ALF continue to terrorize Americans in pursuit of their militant agenda.

We trust that you will join us in publicly condemning this source of domestic violence. Your statement would send a profound and powerful message to these organizations: Americans of every background and political persuasion repudiate the use of terror in every form, including environmental terrorism.

Thank you in advance for your attention to this important issue. We look forward to receiving a timely response to this letter.

Sincerely, Scott McInnis, Chairman James V. Hansen, Chairman House Committee on House Resources

Forests and Forest Health Committee

Even though Congressman McInnis insisted that every group he contacted did indeed publicly denounce the ELF, at least one—WildLaw—wrote an excellent response letter in support of action taken to stop the real "eco-terrorism." The letter stated,

The Honorable Scott McInnis

United States House of Representatives

320 Cannon House Office Building

Washington, DC 20515

---

98 This particular incident was never claimed by the ELF.

Dear Congressman McInnis:

I am in receipt of your letter of October 30, 2001, which you sent to numerous environmental organizations "calling on you and your organization to publicly disavow the actions of eco-terrorist organizations." On behalf of WildLaw, the nation's foremost (and best looking) non-profit environmental law firm, I am pleased to extend our thanks to you for your courageous stand and to set forth our strong condemnation of "environmental terrorism."

We have long fought against those secretive multi-national organizations that have sponsored "environmental terrorism" in America. Throughout our great land, these groups are poisoning our air, our water and our food supply. Children have been hurt. People have been killed. Landowners have had their property and profits taken from them. Rivers have had all their fish and other life killed, being rendered so unfit that no one is allowed to swim or fish in them. Law-abiding corporations have been damaged by these outlaws who do not follow the laws of the United States. Often, these "eco-terrorist" organizations are state sponsored. Indeed, here in Alabama, the State itself defends every group that citizens have tried to stop from committing these acts of "environmental terror."

These international organizations have cells in many countries and in many places here in the United States. Most of them have active and heavily-financed operatives right there in Washington, DC. These groups often do not recognize the rule of law. In their fundamentalist view of the world, they claim that they have more rights than US citizens, and they threaten that people must do their bidding or suffer great consequences. They target innocent citizens and even politicians who do not agree with them and their goals, and they use their vast resources to destroy the lives of those who dare question them. Therefore, knowing that these international organizations have the ability to take even you out of office, I must applaud your heroic effort against these groups by calling them "environmental terrorists" and looking for the support of the environmental community.

As part of our work against terrorism, I also wish to report two acts of extremely costly and illegal sabotage that should be investigated as soon as possible. One involves the destruction of corporate property in Massachusetts. In complete defiance of law and international treaty, a number of disguised men boarded several ships at night and destroyed the goods on board, causing a great deal of pollution. I do not know their identities other than the ringleader who used the name "Sam A." Also, in Rhode Island, a ship by the name of Gaspée was destroyed by arson by saboteurs who took the law into their own hands, contrary to everything you wrote in your fine letter. Please pass this information along to Attorney General Ashcroft and the FBI so that they can look into these illegal acts.

Thank you. It is completely un-American to terrorize the environment.

Sincerely, Ray Vaughan, Executive Director

Congressional Hearing

After discussing the matter further with my attorney, I decided to attend the hearing as commanded, taking a personal vow of noncooperation. Stu Sugarman agreed to represent me during the proceedings and immediately acquired as much information as possible on the hearing from various Congressional aides. While McInnis had attempted to convince the public that this hearing was called to focus on all threats posed to the natural environment, I was the only "pro-environment" person either asked or subpoenaed to attend. We also both soon learned that McInnis didn't just have a deep personal concern over the so-called "eco-terrorist" crimes being waged within the United States. Whether he even cared is perhaps only really known to him, but he was surely influenced by a couple of other, outside, factors.

In addition to pressure from corporations such as Boise Cascade or Vail Resorts, Inc., to crack down on the ELF, McInnis, as Chairman of the House Resources Subcommittee on Forests and Forest Health, was facing political pressure from a trio of Congressional members whose constituents had been hit by the ELF. George Nethercutt, representing the Fifth District in Washington state, became quite vocal after the University of Washington was targeted in May 2001. Darlene Hooley, from the Fifth District in Oregon, and Greg Walden, from the Second District in Oregon, represented areas in the state where the most ELF activity had occurred.

At this time, McInnis was also vying for the Chairmanship of the Resources Committee. In an atmosphere of heightened antiterrorism hysteria, McInnis surely thought that a Congressional hearing on "eco-terrorism" would gain him political points and the needed backing from industry. If all went well for him, I surmised, he would be able to use September 11 and the ELF actions for his own personal gain.

As the new year came, I prepared myself for the long trip to the East Coast. At the time, I was enrolled in an off-campus master's degree program at Goddard College in Vermont, and my residency was scheduled for the week prior to the Subcommittee hearing. So I made arrangements to travel first to Goddard and then to Washington, DC directly after the residency. By law, witnesses subpoenaed to testify at Congressional hearings get reimbursed for travel expenses. As I do everything in my power to avoid airplanes, I was able to get a round trip train ticket from Portland to DC compliments of US taxpayers. If nothing else positive came from the trip, at least my school travel expenses for this residency would be considerably lower.

As on the many occasions when I was faced with grand jury subpoenas, Leslie, Elaine, Josie—a local Portland activist—and I attempted to organize a National Day of Action Against Government Repression. Naturally, this day of action would fall on February 12 to coincide with the Subcommittee hearing. The goal of the national protests was to demonstrate support for the ELF, ALF, and direct action in general, while denouncing attempts by the US government to indict anyone involved in these activities.

On this particular occasion, we even formed an ad hoc organization to sponsor the national day of action. The Mobilization for the Protection of Civil Liberties (MPCL) was created not only to provide support for the February 12 hearing and protests but also as an information source on the US government's domestic repression that came with its insulting Operation Enduring Freedom war on terrorism. I immediately launched a website for the group and listed on it information about the Patriot Act, military tribunals, grand juries, and the February 12 "eco-terrorism" hearing.

In addition to the website, we sent letters and advertisements about the day of action to organizations across the United States. While the response was fairly slow, a few weeks before the hearing, Portland, Boston, Detroit, Los Angeles, Olympia, Salt Lake City, and Washington, DC had confirmed that they would be holding demonstrations. I hoped this might, at least, be a small counter to McInnis's asinine attempts to divide the environmental movement by getting groups to speak out against one another. A strong national show of support for both the ELF and the ALF, and against the Subcommittee hearing, might just be enough to make the hearing backfire politically on McInnis.

Before I boarded the train in Portland, I learned that I would not be alone in Washington, DC. In addition to Stu, I would also have Elaine, Josie, my sister Keri, and my father there for support. I was amazed and thankful that they all had agreed to come. While I have a handful of friends in the DC area, I counted on these familiar faces from home to make me feel more at ease.

Before I left, Stu informed me that I had the opportunity to submit written testimony to the House for the hearing. This testimony would be read by the entire Subcommittee and would eventually be included in the permanent Congressional record. At first, I dismissed the idea, not wanting to participate in the hearing in any way. Stu agreed that the safest move for me—if I wanted to get out of the hearing without going to jail—was not to submit any testimony. Any words I might write would be that much more information for law enforcement and the Subcommittee to scrutinize and question me about. When I left Portland, however, I still had not made up my mind about whether to enter any testimony and told Stu I would let him know before the upcoming deadline.

Riding across the snowy Rocky Mountains and through the upper Midwest, all I could think about was what might happen on February 12. I was still trying to decide whether to submit written testimony. I knew for certain that I was not going to provide any verbal testimony, but I thought that entering something in writing might give me the opportunity to voice my opinion against the state's terrorism and its support of environmental destruction. Additionally, as I was the only pro-environmental representative included in the hearing, I felt some responsibility to at least make an objection to the hearing and take a stand in support of the ELF and ALF. While I knew anything I submitted might bring me closer to facing at least one year in jail on contempt charges, by the time I arrived in Vermont, I had decided to enter in written testimony. The only problem was, I hadn't written anything yet.

During the rigorous week of scholarly sessions at Goddard, I somehow found time to draft an eleven-page objection to the US government, its terrorist policies, and the attempts by politicians and law enforcement to stop the ELF and ALF. When I first emailed a copy to Stu, he advised me not to submit it, since some of my statements fell a bit too close to what might constitute treason. After reviewing his comments, I edited the submission down a bit, making sure it still retained its primary messages. After my residency was completed, I traveled to Washington, DC where a friend helped me to edit the final draft.

I had no idea what the response was going to be from Congress, but I felt compelled to enter in my written testimony. On February 7, Stu officially submitted my testimony to the House. Now all I had to do was wait five more days to see what wrath might fall upon me in response.

A few days before the hearing, I had some last-minute speaking engagements at the University of Pennsylvania in

Philadelphia and at Vassar College in Poughkeepsie, New York. At both schools, I showed the ELF video to packed audiences and explained the rationale and need for direct action. The attendees seemed pleased with my presentations, and many told me they would try to come to DC for the February 12 hearing and protest.

On the evening of February 10, I met Elaine and Josie at Dulles International Airport and took them back to a motel in Georgetown. Elaine was naturally feeling stressed over the entire situation and had taken it upon herself to help organize the protest there in Washington. This was to be a difficult task, especially flying in only two days before the hearing.

The next day, Stu and I met to discuss last-minute details before the hearing. We also decided to go and look at the hearing room so that we would be better prepared for the next day. Entering the Longworth Building was eerie, to say the least, as this was during the period when anthrax was being found in various government buildings around the capital.

Walking down the hallway, we came upon Room 1324, only to find it locked. There appeared to be an office next door, so we went in and asked to see the room. When we told the clerk who we were, her eyes immediately widened, her jaw dropped, and she fled the room, saying she would be right back. Within minutes, a small handful of people flocked down to "greet" us, obviously taken aback that a "terrorist" spokesperson was in the building. Stu and I held back our laughter. If this was any indication of the next day's proceedings, the entire event was surely going to be a spectacle.

Since the room had a hundred seats, many supporters planned to go inside and watch the hearing. People began lining up in the hallway of Longworth early the next morning for the 3:00 P.M. hearing. Stu and I had agreed to meet that day in the Library of Congress and then walk over to the hearing together. Laughing hysterically about the entire situation, we almost were late. At ten minutes to three, we headed for Longworth.

Walking up the street, I could see people in front of the Longworth Building distributing literature and holding protest signs. While it wasn't a sizable number of people, I soon learned that the bulk of supporters were inside, waiting to enter Room 1324. As Stu and I walked down the hallway toward the room, we passed what appeared to be about two hundred people waiting to get into the hearing. Nearly everyone was being denied access because there were not enough seats in the room. A friend who had been standing in line told me that just as the room had opened, a large group of people in suits had come walking up the hallway and been let in before the people who had been standing in line all day. They were obviously seat fillers, utilized so that the hearing wouldn't be filled with people who supported civil liberties and/or the ELF and ALF.

Cold stares and flashbulbs greeted me as I entered the room. Other than Stu and Elaine, it appeared that no other supporters were inside. The three of us took our reserved seats in the front row and awaited the beginning of the hearing. Everywhere I looked around the room, I saw law enforcement agents, politicians, and reporters who had come to view the spectacle. I even noticed some excellent enlarged pictures of ELF actions that I assumed some presenter would be using as a visual aid. Security at the hearing was extremely high, and each time I looked toward the left or right end of the aisle, some law enforcement agent was staring back at me.

Sitting directly in front of me at a long table were the Congresspeople comprising the first panel: George Nethercutt, Darlene Hooley, and Greg Walden. I was scheduled by myself to make up the second panel. The third panel would consist of James F. Jarboe, Section Chief, Counterterrorism Division of the FBI; Porter Wharton III, Senior Vice President of Public Affairs for Vail Resorts, Inc.; Michael S. Hicks, Northwest Oregon Area Logging Manager for the Boise Cascade Corporation; and Richard Berman, the Executive Director of the Center for Consumer Freedom. The fourth and final panel would include William Wasley, Director of Law Enforcement and Investigations for the Forest Service, Gloria Flora, from the Public Employees for Environmental Responsibility, and Dr. Michael Pendleton, from the Government Accountability Project.

Within minutes, the fun began with McInnis, seated in the center of the half circle, giving the opening monologue. When he turned the floor over to the first panel, George Nethercutt started reading his prepared testimony. Nethercutt used this opportunity to attempt to compare the ELF to Al-Qaeda and to gain support for his Agroterrorism Prevention Act. In HR 2795, Nethercutt argued for an expansion of the RICO statutes, and for broadening the Animal Enterprise Terrorism Act to include all commercial or academic entities that use plants or animals. Nethercutt's act also sought to allow access to the death penalty if a death occurs as a result of "agroterrorism."

Darlene Hooley spoke next, also reading from written testimony. Hooley, like Nethercutt, had an act to promote: HR 2583, the Environmental Terrorism Reduction Act. I had already heard of Hooley's attempts at introducing this legislation on the local television news. The Congresswoman had traveled to the Boise Cascade offices in Monmouth, Oregon, for a symbolic press conference announcing her commitment to stopping the environmental advocates. HR 2583 offered federal assistance at the local level to combat "ecoterrorism," and authorized the Attorney General to designate specific locations as "high-intensity environmental terrorism areas." This would, in theory, allow for more federal dollars to be allocated to areas with this designation.

Greg Walden, the last to speak on the panel, also voiced his support for HR 2583, which he was sponsoring with Darlene Hooley. Naturally, since the bulk of ELF activity had occurred in Oregon, an increase in federal funding to stop it would likely impress Hooley's and Walden's corporate constituents. Thus, when the election time rolled around again, this act might just pay off for the careers of the two Oregon representatives.

Once these three had completed their testimonies, McInnis called me to the panel table. As Darlene Hooley got up from her chair, she slammed it into my knees before hobbling off. My natural reaction was to slug her in the back, but I hesitated, taking a moment to find the humor in the incident. I still wonder to this day if the Hooley chair maneuver was intentional.

As soon as Stu and I sat down at the table, McInnis stated that my attorney would not be able to sit with me. According to McInnis, I could converse with him; he just couldn't sit at the table. So Stu walked half a step back and sat down behind me. McInnis then began his questioning.

Before the audience of reporters, law enforcement personnel, and Congresspeople, I took the Fifth Amendment in response to each and every question. After my first response, McInnis appeared shocked, as though he hadn't been told what I had done in numerous grand jury appearances. I had assumed that they would be prepared, expecting me to take the Fifth, and that they would have the contempt paperwork ready. Instead, McInnis now called on his staff attorney to begin researching the Fifth Amendment and contempt.

The longer the questioning went on, the more ridiculous the proceeding appeared, not only to me but also to the crowd of obviously amused reporters. Finally, McInnis turned the floor over to other members of the Forest and Forest Health Subcommittee.

After an hour or so of constant Fifth Amendment responses, Greg Walden asked if I was related to Kenneth Lay.[99] Walden's comparison of me to Kenneth Lay prompted roars of laughter from the audience and reporters. One of the next questions was whether or not I had submitted the written testimony held up by a Congresswoman. I responded that I had indeed supplied written testimony, but I had no idea if that particular testimony was the one I had submitted. This just seemed to anger the Congresspeople even more.

The only other question I answered was whether or not I was a US citizen. I affirmed that I was indeed a US citizen, a fact obviously known to the Committee and only asked to see if I would take the Fifth when it was not applicable. To the other fifty-some questions I was asked during the proceeding, I relied upon the Fifth Amendment and remained silent. McInnis was sure I had violated the Fifth Amendment privilege by taking it when it was not applicable. If this was indeed the case, I could be charged with contempt of Congress. Just before he was finished

---

99 At the time, Kenneth Lay, Chair and CEO of Enron, was being investigated for his role in the scandal that sank the energy giant corporation. Lay repeatedly relied upon his Fifth Amendment protection during questioning.

with me, McInnis told Stu and me that he would be sending a list of follow-up questions that would need to be answered to avoid contempt charges. In the meantime, he would decide whether or not I would be charged with contempt for my conduct in the hearing.

As Stu, Elaine, and I stood up to leave, all of the reporters flocked outside in the hallway behind us. Out of the corner of my eye, I saw my sister and father walk out of the room and was relieved they had made it inside. A crowd of reporters encircled us, and I let Stu respond to their questions on his own. At this point, I had nothing to say to them; I felt my written testimony fully summed up my beliefs and stances on all matters under discussion that day.

Behind the reporters, I could see that McInnis and another Subcommittee member had come out to see the spectacle and listen to what incriminating information I might leak to the press. The more Stu talked, the more I thought I could see smoke rising out of McInnis's head. He obviously knew the hearing had been a complete failure. After ten or so questions, Stu put an end to the spontaneous press conference, and we slowly walked down the hallway past the two hundred people still waiting to get in.

Reaching the outside front stairs of the Longworth building, I took a deep breath and felt relieved that I had survived another bout with the US government. I then learned that my father and sister were the only two people from that long line of supporters who had been let in. According to a friend, just before the hearing began, the security had announced that there was room for two, and since my relatives had traveled across the country, my friends let them cut to the front of the line and go inside.

Both Stu and I were pleased with the outcome of the hearing, and along with Elaine, Josie, my sister, my dad, and other friends, we celebrated over dinner that evening. Since all of us had one more day before we were scheduled to leave town and head back to the West Coast, the six of us spent the next day touring the Holocaust Museum.

On the train ride back to Portland, I couldn't believe the hearing had gone so well. Once again, I had managed not to provide any information to the Feds about the ELF or the ALF—and to stay out of jail. While this was by far the most intense action that the government had taken politically against the direct action organizations, and me personally, I knew it would not alter my support for politically motivated illegal activity—or the determination of those underground.

While I wasn't by any means sure that the entire situation was resolved, I didn't expect McInnis to follow up on his promise to send additional written questions. I figured that what he wanted was a show in DC, to give the appearance of trying to do something against the "eco-terrorists." For all I knew, just having the hearing take place might have been enough for him to feel confident about acquiring the Resources Chairmanship.

To my surprise, Stu received fifty-four additional questions on March 1. McInnis directed me to send him my answers no later than the fifteenth of the month. After spending many lengthy hours with Stu debating the best strategy to take in response, I finally decided to honestly answer thirty-nine out of the fifty-four questions. The questions I did choose to answer asked specifically for my opinion or were theoretical in nature. For the remaining questions, which pertained to sensitive information, I relied upon various Constitutional rights.

Of course, I had more time now than I had had in the hearing to discuss the legality of each answer with Stu.

In the news media release sent out by MPCL about the follow-up questions, I stated, "I decided to answer questions asking for my opinion because I am not ashamed of my personal political beliefs. As I have repeatedly stated, the US government is the most extreme terrorist organization in planetary history. I would not be honest with myself or the public if I did not acknowledge the desperate need for massive political and social change within this country."

When Stu sent my responses off on March 15, I thought there was at least a decent chance that McInnis at this point might pursue contempt charges. My answers were aggressive and provocative, and I felt his decision would really depend on what he intended to accomplish by the entire hearing. Yet Stu had done an excellent job of researching the legalities of all my responses, and we were fairly convinced that any contempt hearing would be difficult for us to lose.

So, after Stu sent the responses in, I resumed my "normal" life. As the days passed, Stu and I became increasingly convinced that McInnis would never respond. Stu even found some evidence that McInnis had given up on the "eco-terrorist" political pursuit. On McInnis's website, all of the information about the "eco-terrorist" threat just seemed to disappear one day.

There is no evidence that increased political efforts to stop the ELF and ALF had any effect on those who take direct action to protect the environment and life. Nearly all of the legislation introduced in these efforts had been geared toward deterring the eco-saboteurs. Politicians seemed to believe—or to hope their constituents would believe—that direct action can be stopped by lengthening sentences for "eco-terrorist" crimes. But in the case of the ELF, law enforcement up to that time had no effect whatsoever in slowing the progress and growth of the organization—and neither had politicians' attempts to boost careers and please constituents.

IS
THIS
TERRORISM?

Ter•ror•ist /tererist/ n. person who uses violent methods of coercing a government or community.[100]

*T*n the mid-1990s, the term eco-terrorism began to be used to refer to acts of sabotage committed in defense of the environment. This label was not used within the environmental movement itself, but rather by mainstream news media, law enforcement, and politicians who were acting deliberately to reduce public support and increase condemnation of such acts. Do acts of property destruction taken to further the environmental movement constitute a form of terrorism? It all depends on whom you ask.

When I first heard the eco-terrorist label attached to ALF and ELF actions back in 1997, I was troubled for a couple of reasons. First, I had always equated the term terrorism with the threat of or actual injury to human life. Both the ELF and ALF had in their codes of conduct specific requirements that members take all necessary precautions against harming life, and in the history of both organizations in North America, not one person had been harmed by their actions.

I also found the eco-terrorism label ridiculous because actions by US corporations and the government that have caused massive terror, murder, and destruction on a global scale are never referred to as terrorism.[101] Yet groups of unpaid, nonviolent activists—who are fighting to protect the factors that enable all life on the planet to exist—earn the label of terrorists.

From the beginning of my time as a spokesperson for both the ALF and the ELF, I dedicated myself to attempting to tear apart the myth that these environmental preservationists were actually

---

100 Definition taken from the Oxford American Desk Dictionary and Thesaurus, New York: Berkeley Books, 2001.
101 Throughout the history of the country, the US government has engaged in terrorist activities to further its own agenda. While the sheer magnitude of this terrorist activity is far too extensive to list here, examples in modern times are contained within my testimony presented to Congress on February 7, 2002. US corporations also throughout history have been routinely guilty of prioritizing their quest for monetary gain ahead of protecting the life of humans, nonhuman animals, and the natural environment. Whether it be Shell, Chevron, McDonald's, Monsanto, Dow, automobile manufacturers such as Ford, clothing companies such as Nike, Banana Republic/Gap/Old Navy, logging companies, etc., US corporations have commonly engaged in terrorist activities without hesitation to protect their financial gain capabilities.

terrorists. This, I quickly learned, was not an easy task, since nearly all of the reporters I faced daily just took it for granted that I was an eco-terrorist spokesperson. Most never asked, "Is this terrorism?" but simply applied the label automatically. "Regarding the October 1998 terrorist act against Vail . . ." "Are there going to be more terrorist acts committed by the ELF?" "Has the ELF been successful with its terrorism?"

In attempting to combat this negative stigma, I shared with reporters my own interpretation of the eco-terrorism label. I argued that eco-terrorism to me meant some form of terror that is caused to the natural environment. I suggested that those actually deserving of this label were those directly responsible for environmental destruction: corporations like Pacific Lumber, Monsanto, Boise Cascade, McDonald's, Ford, etc.

By and large, the multitudes of reporters with whom I shared this view ignored my rationale and continued to use the eco-terrorist label to refer to ELF actions. Most were not at all convinced that there was a clear difference between terrorism, which aims to injure or kill people, and the actions of the ELF, who are committed to protecting life. Even after I compared the ELF brand of politically motivated property destruction to more "respected" forms of sabotage—such as the Boston Tea Party— there remained a heavy reluctance among the news media to admit that ELF actions differ substantially from classical forms of "terrorism."

As time went on, it became even more apparent to me just how biased this eco-terrorism labeling had become. When David "Gypsy" Chain was killed in northern California on September 9, 1998, after being hit by a falling tree cut by a Pacific Lumber employee, none of the various news reports that covered the tragedy ever indicated that this was an act of terrorism. The international news media again failed to identify terror tactics in the police response to a civil disobedience action inside Rep. Frank Riggs's office in Eureka, California. On October 16, 1997, a group of nonviolent protesters, demonstrating against the destruction of redwood trees in the Headwaters Forest, had pepper spray–soaked cotton swabs applied to their eyes by law enforcement. The videotape of the incident is gut-wrenching; the small group of protesters had locked together and were unable to protect themselves as the police repeatedly stuck the swabs into their eyes. The media even failed to identify as terrorism the May 24, 1990, car bombing that disabled activist Judi Bari and injured activist Darryl Cherney.[102] And perhaps most recently, there is the case of the Atlanta police assassinating Manuel Esteban Paez Terán, known as "Tortuguita," in 2023.

Yet each of these examples fits perfectly within the US government's definition of terrorism. The FBI defines terrorism as "the unlawful use of force or violence against persons or property to intimidate or coerce a government, the civilian population, or any segment thereof, in furtherance of political or social objectives." In the case of Judi Bari, she had demonstrated herself to be a powerful and respected force within the growing environmental movement, able to galvanize large masses of people and place increasing pressure on the timber industry. Both the federal government and various industries certainly had motives to act against her. Even though the individual, group, corporation, or government agency that planted the bomb still has not been "officially" determined, Cherney, along with Bari's estate, won a landmark court case against the FBI and Oakland Police Department in 2002.[103] This bombing of Bari and Cherney's car, no doubt politically motivated and illegal, constituted a clear example of terrorism.

David Chain had proven himself to be a strong component of the environmental contingency fighting to preserve the

102 At the time, Bari and Cherney were on a concert and speaking tour to gain support for Redwood Summer, a nonviolent civil disobedience campaign against logging. While driving through Oakland, California, a bomb exploded in their car, disabling Bari and injuring Cherney.
103 Evidence presented at the trial, which concluded on June 11, 2002, showed that the FBI and Oakland Police Department had (1) falsified, fabricated, and manipulated evidence; (2) perjured themselves under oath to get search warrants and high bail; (3) conducted a sustained media smear campaign to fool the public; (4) blamed the victims despite clear evidence of their innocence; (5) conspired to frame and demonize Judi Bari and Earth First! for political reasons; (6) spied on nonviolent environmentalists in a phony investigation of the bombing; (7) failed to investigate fingerprints and other evidence pointing to the real bombers; and (8) covered up their own wrongdoing and obstruction of justice. At the end of the trial both Bari and Cherney were vindicated of any wrongdoing and, along with Bari's estate, Cherney was awarded $4.4 million for damages. Eighty percent of this sum was awarded strictly for First Amendment violations.

forests of northern California. Corporations such as Pacific Lumber, guilty of some of the worst environmentally destructive practices in the area, surely found the efforts by Chain and other local environmentalists troublesome. The cutting of the tree that killed Chain while protesters stood in the area underneath was clearly a terrorist act, intended to force the environmentalists to stop getting in the way of industry-driven greed.

The same can be said for the pepper spray incident in northern California. The locked-down protesters by no means constituted any threat to the office or law enforcement on the scene, but rather, as the videotape demonstrates, were displaying peaceful, completely nonviolent behavior. It was a deliberate choice by the law enforcement on the scene to use pepper spray–soaked cotton swabs to attempt to forcefully stop the protest while sending a message to the environmental movement. Through the use of force and intimidation, the law enforcement representatives in this incident sought to coerce environmentalists into stopping their pressure against the federal government and timber industry.

And more recently, Tortuguita was peacefully protesting the proposed $90 million police training complex dubbed "Cop City" when officers swept through an activist camp, fatally shooting him fifty-seven times—even as his hands were raised in the air in a surrender gesture. Not only was this blatant and deliberate act of violence not considered terrorism by the media or government, the officers involved faced no charges from this execution.

With incidents such as these on the rise, and continued mislabeling by the mainstream media, I further devoted myself and my work at the press office to educating the public on the real meaning of terrorism and showing how the term is wrongly applied to the ELF. Terrorism shouldn't be equated with property destruction against corporations—but rather the very acts of those corporations engaging in business practices that threaten the environment and the ability for all of us to survive on this planet. Yet, as time went on and the ELF actions increased—both in numbers and severity—this task of making this distinction became more difficult and discouraging. I was confirmed in my belief that the decision to label the ELF as a terrorist organization was completely deliberate. What would be the motive for labeling the ELF a terrorist group?

Corporations, law enforcement, and the US government at all levels have strong motives for using any means in their power to stop organizations such as the ELF. First and foremost, all three of these entities wish to control any opposition. For corporations, who want to effectively predict and neutralize any serious infringement on financial gain, an elusive group such as the ELF introduces uncertainty and the possibility of a loss in profits.

For law enforcement, not having the ability to control, capture, and stop a criminal organization leads, at minimum, to frustration. But law enforcement also takes direct heat from the general public and, in this case, corporate executives who become angry that the "criminals" are not captured and the "crimes" continue. Certainly, from the perspective of law enforcement, the inability to control the ELF also means that corporations and the government itself, at least to some degree, are vulnerable.

The US government, throughout its history, has been determined to control any opposition both domestically and internationally. While normally this determination is masked behind national security propaganda, or the commonly spouted rhetoric of "protecting democracy," the ability to control opponents means not only a superficial feeling of personal security but also, more importantly, business security for US economic interests. The ELF, however, has proved to be an opponent the government cannot control. Corporate interests, in addition to pressuring law enforcement, have taken their anger to government representatives. Politicians have, at least in part, attempted to take action against the ELF to save or further their own careers. Since many political campaigns are paid for by corporate interests, politicians who want to continue playing the game often are left with little choice but to succumb to pressure from financially contributing constituents.

Taking into consideration these most obvious reasons why corporations, government, and law enforcement oppose organizations like the ELF, it is not a far stretch to conclude that the eco-terrorist label is an application of the number one strategy in military and domestic affairs—propaganda—in an attempt to minimize public support. From the side of law enforcement and the US government, the heavy propaganda campaign is a very intelligent move. It applies the weighted label of terrorism to acts well before the public has an opportunity to decide for themselves whether each incident is justified.

What do Americans think of when they hear the word *terrorism*? I am truly ashamed to admit it, but, growing up, I learned a set of racist assumptions from the news and entertainment media: that terrorism was related only to the Middle East, to Arabs, to men in headdresses who hijack airplanes. In my mind, a terrorist was a person who committed horrendous crimes and had to be locked up for life or killed.

These associations are extremely potent. When the eco-terrorist label began to be applied to acts of economic sabotage committed in defense of the Earth, its connotations of horrific atrocities crowded out any consideration of the eco-saboteurs, motives, and choice of tactics. Politicians such as George Nethercutt began arguing for the death penalty for "eco-terrorists."

Like the Americans targeted as Communists during either of the "red scares" of the last century, once the ELF had this label attached to it, the group arguably could not be accurately judged by members of the mainstream public. Unfortunately, the mainstream news media—where the overwhelming majority of Americans obtain their news—has played a key role in this labeling process. Instead of even attempting to provide any level of neutrality in news reporting, the mainstream press has repeatedly bowed to its corporate owners and sponsorship. Thus, each and every day, labels specifically designed to influence public opinion are purposely contained within news stories. To the unsuspecting eye, these labels appear commonplace and are simply accepted.

As time went on, I began to wonder whether I had chosen the best strategy in attempting to combat the eco-terrorism label. I had spent many long hours debating the subject with members of the news media and began to realize I was beating my head against a brick wall. Usually, all I received for my efforts were splitting headaches. Meanwhile, no matter what logic I used, the mainstream press still printed whatever the hell it wanted to. In the case of the ELF, the eco-terrorism label would not be dropped.

STEPPING
DOWN

*A*s the ELF began to rely on me, almost exclusively, as its go-between or messenger, the spokesperson persona started to take on a life of its own. As ELF actions increased in frequency and severity, significant media attention focused on me, the only known link to the mysterious group. Since the news media could not actually locate an ELF member to interview, I served as the next best source to represent the growing organization. I became the public face of the eco-saboteurs, someone for the media to use and abuse and for the public and industry to despise. The more I was referred to as the spokesperson for the ELF, the more the position became formalized in the eyes of the public, news media, and law enforcement.

This had both positive and negative effects. On the positive side, as I was further drawn into the "role" of spokesperson, I felt an increasing responsibility to do my best to promote the group and its ideology as clearly and effectively as possible. While I had begun in 1997 merely conducting a few interviews here and there, as time passed, I began to proactively seek out publicity for the organization in addition to creating methods of distributing the ideology to far greater numbers of people. The official opening of the North American ELF Press Office in 2000, the publication of *Resistance* and *Frequently Asked Questions about the ELF*, the creation of the *Igniting the Revolution* video, and numerous speaking engagements across the United States all assisted in ensuring that the ELF and its ideology were known not only throughout the United States and North America, but around the world. The growth in ELF actions, the publicity, and the distribution of the group's ideology worked together to engender new cells operating in previously inactive areas of the country.

The downside to all of this was that Leslie's and my efforts also served to more substantially establish the position of spokesperson. Around 2000, I began to think that this spokesperson role seemed almost contrary to the autonomous nature of the ELF. In this group, which has no known hierarchy or commander, the spokesperson—if for no other reason than sheer default—was made out to have the appearance of a leader.

While this serious misconception amused us at first, Leslie and I began to realize that our actions, despite our sincere motives, did have negative effects.

For me personally, the most serious effect came with being a central target for law enforcement repression. Since the ELF members could not be caught themselves, the federal government repeatedly placed pressure on me, the "spokesperson" who was constantly deemed to "know far more about the group than he is saying." Since there were no other spokespeople to share in the responsibility, I took the brunt of the assault. I thought of these personal troubles as a tradeoff for the crucial work I felt I was doing for the ELF's mission to protect the environment.

The negative effects of my role as spokesperson unfortunately extended beyond me to other activists. The responsibility I, and then Leslie, took on allowed others to ignore the necessity of becoming involved publicly in support of underground action. *Since someone else is doing it*, others must have thought, *that means I don't have to.*

Additionally, many saw the spokesperson position as something they could never do, either because they feared government repression or because they felt they lacked the skill to conduct news media interviews. Yet Leslie and I were by no means experts in media relations, propaganda, or dealing with repression. Now, certainly, I have had years of experience in all three categories, but that experience was acquired directly through activism. Just as I lived through numerous grand jury appearances, the Congressional hearing, two raids, constant monitoring, and physical and mental brutality, so do many others—and many more could if they were placed or put themselves in those situations.

I was not born with the ability or the desire to deal with news media or governmental repression. This is something I learned, partly by choice and partly from being thrown into vulnerable positions. I have always maintained that if I could do this sort of work, then virtually anyone could if they so desired or were forced. By no means was I an outgoing, confident, and self-assured individual growing up. On the contrary, I was extremely shy and had never thought I would be able to speak to hundreds or even thousands of people at a time, let alone appear repeatedly on national television. But once I decided to devote my life to the struggle to right social and political wrongs, I was able to more easily challenge and overcome many of my own personal fears and insecurities.

During my years as spokesperson, I realized that in order for the movement to continue to grow, more people would need to speak out on behalf of the ELF. Not only would this demonstrate to the government, corporations, and the public that the group was gaining support, but the more people who publicly spoke out on behalf of groups such as the ELF, the less able the government would be to repress and neutralize the supportive efforts. And if the public support was viewed as significant enough, various corporations and governmental organizations might conclude that it would be in their best interests to stop engaging in destructive practices rather than face the increasing pressure.

While I, and then Leslie, had both advocated for an increase in public support for the ELF over the years, few, if any, were willing and able to take on the responsibilities of serving in a spokesperson role. After many discussions, Leslie and I decided that the best scenario might be to simply stop conducting the media relations for the ELF and hope that someone would feel the responsibility to step up and resume the needed task. We felt that if we stepped down, the necessity for public ELF support might become more apparent. The only decision left for us to make was when to do it. As the year 2001 ran its course, my frustration level grew with each additional interview. Each and every time a story appeared focused largely on me, rather than the group, I knew it only added to the "spokesperson" phenomenon. By the time September came,

I knew I had to go.

On September 5, Leslie and I publicly released a statement officially declaring our resignation from duties as press officers for the North American ELF. The statement appeared as follows:

Effective immediately, Craig Rosebraugh and Leslie James Pickering will no longer be running the North American Earth Liberation Front Press Office. Both feel that if the Earth Liberation Front is to be a viable movement, public concentrations of support must not be centered on one or two individuals.

Since 1997, Rosebraugh has acted as a spokesperson for the Earth Liberation Front in North America. During this time, the group's activities have increased steadily and as a result have received widespread media attention. Due to the ELF being a covert, underground, and anonymous organization, much of the focus of the media attention has centered on Rosebraugh since he has been one of a few who have spoken out and supported the group within the legal realm.

Likewise, when the North American ELF Press Office was officially formed in 2000, Pickering also began to be singled out as a focal point of the group. Both Rosebraugh and Pickering have always maintained that the aim of the ELF is not to create martyrs, fame, or leadership but to inspire a people's movement of generous support and participation. By Rosebraugh and Pickering removing themselves from the media spotlight, this will allow others to step forward and demonstrate the truly diverse and powerful support behind the ELF in North America.

In no way is this to be interpreted as Rosebraugh and Pickering losing faith or support in the ELF. On the contrary, the two have maintained that ELF is one of the greatest demonstrations of the power the people can have if they so desire to take it. They sincerely wish to express their gratitude to all those who have expressed some form of support over the years. And to the courageous individuals that have been involved in ELF actions, they wish to express their love and thanks . . . for it is you who have given hope and inspiration in this world hell bent on making profits at the expense of life. Please continue your honorable work, as it is incredibly worthwhile and needed.

Leslie and I worded this resignation letter carefully to ensure that any reader would realize that we were not attempting to stop the ELF Press Office, website, or other related support activity. Rather, we wanted people to know that they needed to take on the press officer role, to take on some responsibility for publicly supporting efforts to protect life on Earth. Though we couldn't be sure what would happen, we waited for someone, preferably many people, to step forward to speak on behalf of the eco-saboteurs.

Upon hearing the news of the terrorist attacks on the twin towers and the Pentagon on the morning of September 11, I knew Leslie and I had, unknowingly, bypassed a major media nightmare by stepping down. If we had stayed even one week longer, we surely would have taken a severe beating from the news media and general public, who undoubtedly would have used the September 11 events to further criminalize the actions of the ELF. (A terrorist is a terrorist is a terrorist, right?) Fortunately for us, anyone trying to contact the press office telephone line that day, week, or month reached only a recording: "I'm sorry, you have reached a number that has been disconnected or is no longer in service."

Within the radical environmental movement, our resignation letter was taken fairly well. People seemed to understand our motives and, for the most part, supported our decision to stop working at the press office. As could be expected, much of the news media reported the story inaccurately, stating, for example, that I couldn't take the pressure anymore, or that I had left to pursue a master's degree. (While I was working on my master's at the time, this in no way contributed to my decision to leave the press office.) Regardless, the news had spread around the country that Leslie and I had stepped down, and we hoped this would spark others into action.

It was over six months later, after much contemplation, that I decided to come out and begin to speak publicly about why I had actually given up my role as a spokesperson. In fact, the explanation offered in the public statement was only a partial contributor to my personal decision to leave. The other reasons for leaving were, and still are, controversial and especially unpopular in the post–September 11 hysteria.

One of the most important reasons I left the press office had to do with the fact that many of the ELF communiqués I had received over the years suggested that the group considered itself to be nonviolent. The very guidelines of the organization insist on taking "all necessary precautions against harming life." While I accepted this belief when I started serving as spokesperson, my own ideas began to change as I studied and contemplated the subject further.

When I began representing the ELF to the news media and the public, the violence that the ELF was working to prevent so clearly overwhelmed and outweighed the destruction undertaken by the group itself that it didn't make sense to me to attack the ELF as a violent organization. However, a required component of nonviolence ideology, as I interpreted it, was the ability to display compassion, respect, and decency toward the opponent. The opposition is supposed to be weaned from error by sympathy for the nonviolent activists who use their own suffering as their primary means of promoting change. The philosophy requires that the nonviolent activists believe that the opponent has the ability to see the evils in his or her own actions and change voluntarily. This change must come about as a result of the opponent's free decision, not through coercion or force.

In sabotaging the property of individuals, corporations, and governmental agencies, the ELF has not displayed any hint of compassion or respect toward its opponents. Furthermore, the organization has never, in a communiqué or by any other means, indicated any belief that its opponents have the ability to voluntarily change.

I also began to consider the psychological intimidation that ELF actions aim to produce, which, while not belonging to the same category as violent acts that physically harm people, can reasonably be construed as violent in its attempt to force or coerce.

By early 2000, I had decided that it didn't make sense to me to describe ELF actions as nonviolent. I still supported, and continue to support, this type of action, but I felt it should be labeled differently. Furthermore, I felt that the group and the press office insisted too strongly that the ELF was nonviolent. With the limited resources available to the activists working to stop the murder, exploitation, and destruction of life on the planet, did it make sense to devote so much time and energy to the attempt to change corporate media's view and representation of a group like the ELF? Labeling is an attempt to control how others perceive the entity in question. In the case of the ELF, I am convinced that referring to the group as violent or nonviolent would not change the public's perception of it. To many people in this country, politically motivated property destruction is violence, even terrorism, and to refuse to admit this serves only to discredit the group. The nonviolence argument constitutes the main weak point in ELF ideology that the news media and the public seize upon. Refusing to play the labeling game and avoiding "he said, she said," "terrorist or freedom fighter," "nonviolent or violent" arguments frees up energy for the crucial task of educating the public on the atrocities committed by ELF targets.

Feeling hypocritical in my role as a spokesperson, I felt it was necessary to begin admitting publicly that the ELF was indeed committing acts of psychological intimidation. But rather than going public with my personal beliefs, I held them in and let them eat away at me through the end of 2000 and most of 2001. I didn't feel it was my place to contradict or publicly question the ideology and statements contained within communiqués sent by the ELF. After stepping down, I felt I was in a better position to recommend a reworking of the image the group presented to the news media and the public.

As I have said above, the growth and power of the ELF depended on increasing public support. Some may think that not labeling the ELF as a nonviolent organization would lead to a reduction in public backing, since many people hesitate to be associated with anything self-construed as violent. I propose, however, that ELF propaganda must not only convey the severity of the threat to life on this planet, but should be designed to communicate that a variety of strategies and tactics may be needed at this point to stop the destruction of life.

After I received my subpoena to testify before Congress in the ecoterrorism hearing, Leslie began reconsidering his decision to resign from the office with me. On February 2, 2002, he decided to resume his own spokesperson role and to go back to running the press office. Leslie wouldn't last long back in the saddle, however, as he quickly began to have many of the same realizations that had forced me to resign. In May 2002, Leslie stepped back down from his duties, and issued a lengthy explanation that expressed many of the motives that had also influenced me.[104]

---

104 Leslie's statement of resignation was printed in the Litha 2002 (June–July) issue of the *Earth First! Journal.*

THE FIRE
RAGES ON

*F*rom 1997 through 2001, the ELF inflicted over $40 million in damages on entities they identified as destroyers of the planet. During that time period, only five people were arrested and charged with any crime relating to the group. As a result of this amazing track record, the ELF was able to continually increase its number of actions and its geographic level of activity. Then came September 11, 2001.

While, undoubtedly, the attacks in New York and Washington did not reduce the threat to the environment, they did create fear and a shift in priorities among many Americans. As politicians and the news media demanded a unified nation in support of Bush, much of the country obliged. Inside the mainstream environmental movement, some groups, including the Sierra Club, even voluntarily backed off campaigns, fearing that the public might not support any activity that criticized the administration.

With instantaneous comparisons made between the ELF and Al-Qaeda by politicians and various mainstream media sources, public support for ELF activity was likely at an all-time low. Yet, since generating public support was only one of the organization's goals, in tandem with economic sabotage and psychological pressure, it is unlikely that the pervasive antiterrorism hysteria would have been enough to persuade members to reduce their activity. Nevertheless, there was a definite slowdown after September 11. And, in the wake of Leslie's and my resignation, no one seemed to feel compelled to take on the role of spokesperson for a group the FBI considers the number one domestic terrorism threat in the nation, or to publicly voice support for its actions.

As 2001 drew to a close, I wondered what would become of the ELF in the next year. With the Congressional Subcommittee hearing on eco-terrorism coming up in February 2002, I hoped the group would start the new year off with a bang, as it had done in the past. I so wanted the ELF to provide a show of force against the growing political repression and to demonstrate that even in the increasingly hostile political atmosphere, it was not backing down from its crucial environmental defense activity.

The first sign of life from the ELF in 2002 came with two actions near the end of January. On January 26, the ELF returned to the University of Minnesota for another action against biotechnology. A communiqué sent by the ELF to the NAELFPO stated,

The construction site for the new Microbial and Plant Genomics Research Center at the University of Minnesota had incendiaries left in the main trailer and two pieces of heavy machinery, including a bulldozer. Heavy damage was caused to the machinery and trailer by the fire, which then spread to the adjacent Crop Research building. The construction of this research building is being funded by biotech giant Cargill Corporation who develop, patent, and market genetically modified crops, making people dependent on GE foods. We are fed up with capitalists like Cargill and major universities like the U of M who have long sought to develop and refine technologies which seek to exploit and control nature to the fullest extent under the guise of progress. Biotechnology is only one new expression of this drive.

For the end of capitalism and the mechanization of our lives,

Earth Liberation Front

This was the second time in two years that the ELF had targeted a facility at the University of Minnesota. In February 2000, the group had damaged a greenhouse and destroyed transgenic oat research crops. This second strike, inflicting $250,000 in damages, was a definite sign of continued pressure on the university to stop its dangerous biotechnology practices.

The $20 million set aside to build this new biotech facility came from only two sources, the Minnesota legislature and the Cargill Foundation. In 1999, the Cargill Foundation donated $10 million—its largest grant ever—to help the University of Minnesota erect the Microbiological and Plant Genomics Institute.[105] As a proud supporter of genetically modified

105 Cargill has been donating to the University of Minnesota since 1969. Over this time, more than $16 million has been given to the school for various uses,

organisms, Cargill itself could have been chosen for an ELF attack.

Just three days later in Maine, the ELF struck again in a joint effort with the ALF against biotechnology and animal breeding. The following communiqué was released by both groups claiming responsibility for the January 29, 2002 action:

We are writing to inform you that there is a Biotech Park being built in Fairfield, Maine. We went there some weeks ago and put a sand/quickcrete [sic] mix in the engines, gas, and hydraulics of an excavator and a roller. These were the only machines there, plowing up the land, building bridges over creeks. So we left no trace so when the operators came to work the machines would run and then seize, costing big bucks. Now, we are letting the people know.

The park is being pushed by Paul Tessier, a representative of Fairfield, and others. It is in cohoots [sic] with Jackson Labs, which is the largest breeder of mice. They grow mice with human ears there! How sick! These people want the park to be an incubator to bring more biotechnology into Maine.

We oppose this for the following reasons . . .

Biotechnology is one more tool by the ruling class to control our lives and make more money. Only the rich can produce biotechnology and even if that wasn't so, we would want no part of it because it sees the wild as incomplete, or as lacking, needing manipulation. Our ancestors lived in harmony on this planet for a long time, now all of humanity's progress is making us sick. And we're gonna trust those that gave us cancer to create new technologies to cure it. No way!

We want to be left alone. No more development. We enjoy life here and are sick of businessmen coming in and trying to dupe us into trading the good life for wage slavery. People!!! Take action!!! The Biotech Park is on route 201 near Kennebec Valley Technical College in Fairfield. KVTC is in on it too.

primarily for agricultural, food, and environmental sciences. Cargill employs close to 600 University of Minnesota alumni, and the corporation's senior managers serve on ten University advisory committees.

Solidarity to those fighting against the greedy! ELF . . . ALF . . .

Together with all.

Jackson Laboratory, the major player involved with the new Fairfield Biotechnology Park, was at the time the world's largest research facility for mammal genetics.[106] With an annual budget of over $88 million, Jackson Labs supplied mice for research around the world, in addition to conducting its own experimentation in metabolic diseases, birth defects and aging, neurological and sensory disorders, cancer, and immune system and blood disorders. In 2001, Jackson Labs shipped out nearly two million animals to researchers around the world.

Kennebec Valley Technical College (KVTC) began discussions with Jackson Labs in 2001 to decide how the school could best meet the growing demand for employees at the nearby animal laboratory. Jackson Labs has pushed partners, such as KVTC, into "engaging high school students in the study of biosciences."[107] KVTC also volunteered to "use its network of high school contacts and its current Tech Program to identify promising high school candidates. These students would take courses at KVTC and if qualified, would be given summer internships at Jackson Labs."[108] Naturally, these summer internships would be designed to lead to regular employment.

This particular action, while limited in size compared to past ELF strikes, served to shine the national spotlight on Jackson Labs, Kennebec Valley Technical College, and the Fairfield, Maine, biotech park. Smaller actions such as these have, throughout the history of the ELF, successfully assisted in creating an atmosphere of uncertainty about where the group will strike next—a BLM horse corral in rural Oregon, a genetic engineering research project at the University of Minnesota, or anywhere there is profit-driven destruction of the natural

106 Andy Kekacs, "Fairfield biotech park part of 'the new frontier of medicine,' " Blethen Maine Newspapers, Inc., June 17, 2001.
107 "College offers programs in traditional, new fields," MaineToday.com, November 21, 2001.
108 "College offers programs," MaineToday.com.

environment. In this atmosphere, no one who is involved with the destruction in any location is immune.

Nearly two months later, in Erie County, Pennsylvania on March 24, 2002, the ELF torched an overhead crane in the Wintergreen Gorge that was to be used to complete a bridge project to connect Erie's Bayfront Highway to Interstate 90. In addition to the crane being set on fire, numerous trees were also spiked in the area to deter cutting. Damages to the crane were estimated at $500,000.

The ELF communiqué stated,

Trees Spiked, $500,000 crane and other equipment destroyed in Erie, PA

Nameless cells of the Earth Liberation Front have spiked hundreds of trees and destroyed Earth wrecking machinery in and around the Wintergreen Gorge in Erie, Pennsylvania. Both metal and evasive ceramic spikes have been randomly employed, high and low, throughout Wintergreen Gorge and areas extending several miles west/northwest. Workers should exercise extreme caution if attempting to kill these trees—they can now fight back.

Protective locks were cut and incendiaries successfully employed on several death machines, including generators and pumps. A 100-foot-tall, 60-ton crane worth $500,000 was also completely destroyed. Other machines were disabled and redecorated.

The unnamed cells took action to warn against bridge and highway building efforts that directly threaten the biological health of the Lake Erie watershed, and one of the region's most vital riparian areas (along with many threatened species that call it home). If an alternative is not chosen, we will be compelled to act again.

This action was not simply an attack on a developer, but was undertaken to communicate a vital message in the only language the industrial mega-machine can understand. The unimpeded destruction of biodiversity this frivolous project represents locally is, on a global scale, devouring all life from the face of the Earth and posing a direct threat to our very existence. Thus, we consider our resistance a critical matter of self defense in a heedless world gone mad. Businessmen and local government, beware. As long as profit is valued above life and ecological sanity, you will find no peace. If you build it, it WILL fall.

This was the first claimed action by the ELF in Northwestern Pennsylvania. In addition to the direct monetary damage inflicted by the crane fire, the Dick Corporation—a Pittsburgh based construction firm that had been awarded the $31 million contract to complete the bridge—felt compelled to hire a security service after the ELF attack. The cost of overdevelopment and environmental destruction in Erie County, thanks to the ELF, had become greater.

To many in the United States, both in and outside the movement, the most controversial ELF communiqué to date was issued on September 3, 2002. The communiqué appeared as follows:

The Earth Liberation Front is claiming responsibility for the 8/11/02 arson attack on the United States Forest Service Northeast Research Station in Irvine, Pennsylvania.

The laboratory was set ablaze during the early morning hours, causing over $700,000 damage, and destroying part of 70 years worth of research. This lesson in "prescribed fire" was a natural, necessary response to the threats posed to life in the Allegheny Forest by proposed timber sales, oil drilling, and greed driven manipulation of Nature.

This facility was strategically targeted and, if rebuilt, will be targeted again for complete destruction. Furthermore, all other U.S. Forest Service administration and research facilities, as well as all DCNR buildings nationwide, should now be considered likely targets.

These agencies continue to ignore and mislead the public, at the bidding of their corporate masters, leaving us with no alternative to underground direct action. Their blatant disregard for the sanctity of life and its perfect Natural balance, indifference to strong public opposition, and the irrevocable acts of extreme violence they perpetrate against the Earth daily are all inexcusable, and will not be tolerated. If they persist in their crimes against life, they will be met with maximum retaliation.

In pursuance of justice, freedom, and equal consideration for all innocent life across the board, segments of this global revolutionary movement are no longer limiting their revolutionary potential by adhering to a flawed, inconsistent "non-violent" ideology. While innocent life will never be harmed in any action we undertake, where it is necessary, we will no longer hesitate to pick up the gun to implement justice, and provide the needed protection for our planet that decades of legal battles, pleading, protest, and economic sabotage have failed so drastically to achieve.

The diverse efforts of this revolutionary force cannot be contained, and will only continue to intensify as we are brought face to face with the oppressor in inevitable, violent confrontation. We will stand up and fight for our lives against this iniquitous civilization until its reign of TERROR is forced to an end—by any means necessary.

In defense of all life,

Pacific ELF

The news media, understandably enough, focused attention on one particular sentence: "While innocent life will never be harmed in any action we undertake, where it is necessary, we will no longer hesitate to pick up the gun to implement justice, and provide the needed protection for our planet that decades of legal battles, pleading, protest, and economic sabotage have failed so drastically to achieve." To industry groups, law enforcement, and the media, this statement marked a major turning point for the ELF and the environmental movement.

Until the release of this communiqué, the ELF had consistently adhered to and promoted three main guidelines for its organization. One of these specifically stated that each individual and cell must take every precaution to ensure that no one was ever injured in any action. In following this particular guideline, the ELF's track record is flawless, as no injuries have ever been attributed to any of the group's actions. This new communiqué indicated that one or more ELF cells had reconsidered the nonviolence guideline, found it to be obsolete, and were now advocating for political violence, if and when necessary.

When I first read this communiqué, I was very pleased that ELF members had, perhaps, come to many of the same conclusions as I discussed in the previous chapters. Yet others—even many people who had previously supported the ELF—were less than thrilled with the new militant stance. The communiqué and its associated action were instantly questioned, and many in the environmental community were certain they had to be the work of agents provocateurs. As had been the case throughout ELF history, mainstream environmentalists argued that government or industry representatives had undoubtedly conducted this action and released the communiqué as an attempt to discredit the environmental movement in the eyes of the public. This view was also widely held and shared within the radical grassroots sector of the movement, including many who ideologically supported property destruction. While I personally believe the action was taken and the communiqué was released by a cell of the ELF that simply wanted to take measures a step further, the communiqué did bring up some very interesting complexities regarding the underground, anonymous cell structure of the group—namely how a group such as the ELF changes its ideology and/or operating guidelines. Since the group lacks a hierarchy and national meetings, and the cells are unknown to each other, it is difficult to imagine how an ideology or guideline could be altered. Additionally, since the group is organized around a particular ideology rather than any command structure, to change that ideology could very well mean changing the entire nature of the group.

Since ELF members cannot meet to change their guidelines, it makes sense for the members to continue to abide by the three primary guidelines as long as they individually believe the strategy is effective. Those who would like to take up different guidelines should simply stop operating under the ELF banner and form new organizations that encompass this ideology. As I alluded to in the previous chapter, I feel the addition of more extreme strategies is vital to protecting life on Earth, and I personally would support such efforts.

Indictments in Portland

As the winds of controversy surrounding this latest communiqué continued to blow, the national news media broke the story on October 18, 2002, that two logging protesters had been indicted for burning three cement trucks at Ross Island Sand and Gravel in Portland, Oregon. The incident, which occurred in April 2001, had been claimed by the ELF. This marked the sixth and seventh individuals in the United States to be indicted on ELF-related charges. Two Portland, Oregon area men, Jacob Sherman and Michael Scarpitti, were charged with four felonies, including obstructing, delaying, and affecting the movement of commodities in interstate commerce by extortion and violence under the Hobbs Act. Each man, if convicted on all counts, could face up to eighty years in prison and a $1 million fine. These were the first indictments handed down in the state of Oregon related to ELF activity.

Both Sherman and Scarpitti—better known as "Tre Arrow"—had been earlier indicted with two others in August for the burning of three logging trucks in June 2001. While this particular action was never claimed by the ELF, it was taken in protest of the Eagle Creek Timber Sale near Estacada, Oregon. The trucks, owned by Ray A. Schoppert Logging Inc., were to be used in logging this sale the very next day.

While Sherman and the other two alleged accomplices were taken into custody in association with this first set of charges, Scarpitti could not be found. Similarly, when the second set of indictments was issued regarding the cement truck fires at Ross Island Sand and Gravel, Scarpitti was still on the run, and was not captured until March 10, 2004. Arrested in Victoria, British Columbia, for allegedly shoplifting bolt cutters, Scarpitti was held in Canadian custody facing local charges and then extradited to face federal charges in Oregon.

The visible environmental community in Oregon condemned the June 2001 action. Cascadia Forest Alliance, the grassroots, Portland-based organization that headed the campaign against the Eagle Creek Timber Sale, denounced the act in the mainstream media. A spokesperson for the group suggested publicly that the logging truck fires had likely been set by agents provocateurs attempting to discredit the Eagle Creek cause.

When the news broke in August 2002 that four Portland locals had been indicted for the logging truck arsons, the environmental community turned again to talk of COINTELPRO. Those who knew or knew of Tre Arrow refused to believe he could be guilty of such an act. Many locals, especially those committed to state-sanctioned tactics, seemed to consider the logging truck fires a horrific act that only the worst demons could have committed.

In early November 2002, the FBI made public the first evidence of its case against Tre and the three others in a search-warrant affidavit filed in US District Court. This document alleges that Jacob Sherman went home after the logging truck fires with a car smelling of gasoline. Additionally, the FBI claimed that his eyebrows were burned while attempting to light an incendiary device.

According to the affidavit, Jacob's father, Tim Sherman, phoned the FBI the following morning to report his son's possible involvement. Jacob had allegedly borrowed his mother's car the night

before the action and then returned it early in the morning the night the logging truck fires were set. The FBI also claimed that Jacob, upon returning home at 3:00 A.M., told his brother to tell anyone who asked that he had returned home at 10:30 P.M. the previous night.

The document goes on to state that Jacob later told his girlfriend, Jacquelyn Caul, that he had set fire to the logging trucks. He added that he believed cutting down trees was wrong and that he and his accomplices had made a pact that if any of them were caught they would not squeal on one another. Caul allegedly shared this information with her father, a deputy state fire marshal.

The FBI stated that the case of the logging truck fires led authorities to charge both Tre and Jacob with the ELF-claimed cement truck arson. And the news of another ELF indictment quickly spread across the United States in the mainstream media, undoubtedly prompted by FBI press releases.

On February 21, 2003, Sherman pleaded guilty to burning the logging trucks and other equipment at two companies in 2001. Appearing to have had a change of heart, he told a local reporter for the *Portland Tribune* that he was "ashamed" of participating in the arsons. After his arrest, Sherman began immediately cooperating with investigators and implicated Scarpitti as the "ringleader" who had allegedly coerced Sherman into action. He was sentenced to just over three years in prison thanks to his friendly relationship with authorities. After his extradition to the US from Canada, on June 3, 2008, Scarpitti pleaded guilty to two counts of arson and was sentenced to 78 months in federal prison.

The few indictments in investigations of ELF actions up until this point appeared to have resulted not from the exceptional efforts of law enforcement, but rather from grave mistakes made by those allegedly involved with ELF activity. In the Long Island case, one of those involved unfortunately bragged about his involvement to schoolmates. The charges against Frank Ambrose in Indiana were dropped at the time, as the federal government had no case.

Then, in Portland, an FBI affidavit showed that one individual—Jacob Sherman—appeared to have made mistakes that jeopardized the freedom of himself and three others. However, due to the group's lack of hierarchy, its anonymous cell structure, and its organization based solely on an ideology, US governmental agencies were having a difficult time stopping the movement.

2002–2003 ELF Actions

In 2002 and 2003, the ELF claimed the following actions in addition to those mentioned above:

July 2002-December 2002: Richmond, Virginia

Nearly forty SUVs were treated with glass-etching cream, had their tires slashed, or were otherwise damaged. Graffiti and notes left at the scene included the letters ELF.

November 26, 2002: Harborcreek, Pennsylvania

ELF and ALF jointly set fire to a feed barn and its contents at the Mindek Brothers Fur Farm (4200 Shannon Road).

December 28, 2002: Northeast Philadelphia

Construction vehicles damaged with glued locks, sugar placed in gas tanks, disconnected hoses, spray paint, windows broken.

A sample house on Rhawn Street had its walls covered in spray paint, locks glued, and windows broken.

January 1, 2003: Erie, Pennsylvania

Four Sport Utility Vehicles destroyed and several others damaged at Bob Ferrando Ford Lincoln Mercury. Damages to the vehicles estimated at $90,000.

March 21, 2003: Superior Township, Michigan

A pair of houses were burned in an upscale suburban development. Graffiti left at the scene claimed the work as that of the ELF. Damages estimated at over $400,000.

March 28, 2003: Montgomery, Alabama

Vehicles at Navy Recruiting Headquarters attacked in protest of US invasion of Iraq.

April 9, 2003: Santa Cruz, California

Spray painted messages left on sixty SUVs.

June 3, 2003: Chico, California

A fire was set at the Sterling Oaks development. Water on the scene prevented the fire from causing extensive damages.

June 4, 2003: Washington Township, Michigan

Two houses burned in an upscale suburban development.

August 1, 2003: San Diego, California

Five story condominium destroyed by fire, causing an estimated $50 million in damages. Banner stating "If you build it, we will burn it, ELF'" was found at the scene.

August 22, 2003: Arcadia, California

Ten Sport Utility Vehicles were spray painted with "terrorist," "killer," and "ELF'" at Rusnak Mercedes Benz.

August 22, 2003: Duarte, California

Duarte Mitsubishi dealership building and approximately twenty vehicles were painted with "ELF" and the phrases "gross polluter" and "we [heart] pollution."

August 22, 2003: West Covina, California

A fire was set at a General Motors dealership, destroying and damaging several Sport Utility Vehicles including Hummer H2s. A warehouse on site was also destroyed by fire. Messages left at the scene included "I [heart] pollution," "American Wastefulness," and "ELF."

September 19, 2003: San Diego, California

• ELF targets three construction sites in protest of urban sprawl, causing $1 million in damages.

September 22, 2003: Martiny, Michigan

• Attempted arson claimed by ELF at an Ice Mountain Spring Water Company owned by Nestle.

October 6, 2003: Jemez Mountains, New Mexico

• Construction equipment belonging to the US Forest Service had electrical wires cut, tires slashed and windows broken by ELF

October 2003: Portland, Maine

• ELF slashed tires of 8 Boise Cascade delivery trucks and two trailers, glued locks and painted slogans across the building

October 24, 2003: Martinsville, Indiana

• ELF sabotages a Wal-Mart construction site, removing survey stakes, spray painting message on walls and vandalizing over a dozen pieces of machinery.

2004–2009 ELF Actions

January 22, 2004: Fayetteville, Arkansas

• Five Hummer SUVs are vandalized with tires slashed and slogans spray painted on the vehicles.

February 7, 2004: Charlottesville, Virginia

• ELF sets fire to a bulldozer and damages other equipment parked off Route 29, in protest of urban sprawl.

April 20, 2004: Snohomish, Washington

• ELF arson attack destroys two homes and burns two others at housing development, causing $1 million in damages.

August 3, 2004: Spokane, Washington

• ELF burns three Hummers at George Gee Hummer dealership.

December 27, 2004: Lincoln, California

• Attempted arson of three houses under construction at the Verdera Models construction site

February 7, 2005: Sutter Creek, California

• ELF set fire to the new Pinewoods apartment complex. Graffiti found nearby states: "We will win… ELF."

April 13, 2005: Sammamish, Washington

• ELF partially burns one of two buildings it targeted in a new housing development

July 27, 2005: Whatcom County, Washington

• Two houses under construction are damaged from arson. No claim of responsibility

September 11, 2005: West Old Town, Maine

• ELF vandalizes a dozen machines at the West Old Town Landfill.

November 19, 2005: Hagerstown, Maryland

• ELF claimed responsibility for four fires that burned new homes under construction in the Hager's Crossing subdivision.

November 25, 2005: Bothell, Washington

• Two pieces of construction equipment are destroyed by fire causing over $100,000 in damages.

November 29, 2005: Bothell, Washington

• Fire destroys one construction vehicle

December 14, 2005: Kenmore, Washington

• Two construction vehicles are burned causing an estimated $180,000 in damages.

January 16, 2006: Camano Island, Washington

• ELF torches a 9,600 square foot newly built mansion causing an estimated $3 million in damages.

January 31, 2006: Guelph, Ontario, Canada

• ELF burns a new home under construction and the communique stated the act was done "in the memory of William C. Rodgers 'Avalon.'"

June 27, 2006: Guelph, Ontario, Canada

• ELF sets fire to a new home under construction causing $200,000 in damages.

March 3, 2008: Seattle, Washington

• The Street of Dreams is hit with an arson attack burning four homes and causing an estimated $7 million in damages.

September 4, 2009: Everett Washington

• The ELF claimed responsibility for destroying two broadcasting towers used by the radio station KRKO.

EPILOGUE

*A*fter years of frustration in the investigation into the Earth Liberation Front arson attacks, authorities began to see some success in 2001. In addition to the takedown of the Long Island cell of the ELF that year, prosecutors were about to have a bit more luck in Eugene, Oregon. As discussed in Chapter 11, in June the year prior, shortly after a fire was reported at Joe Romania Chevrolet, Jeff Luers and Craig Marshall were arrested. Both had been under surveillance by local authorities who followed them to the crime scene. Even though the fire was put out with a fire extinguisher and only caused $28,000 in damages, Luers was facing thirteen charges and a hundred years in prison. In 2001, while Marshall took a plea deal and served four and a half years, Luers was sentenced to 23 years and 8 months for his role in the arson. In 2007, the Oregon Court of Appeals overturned Luers's sentence and reduced it to ten years.

The same year, shortly after a second set of fires were set at Joe Romania Chevrolet in Eugene (an act that undoubtedly lengthened the sentence Jeff Luers was facing for previously burning three trucks at the same location), Heather Coburn had discovered her truck was missing from its typical location outside her house in Eugene. She immediately suspected her housemate, Jake Ferguson, of taking the truck. The two had been in an argument the night before and she assumed he had taken the truck out of spite. Coburn called the police and reported the truck stolen; however, by the time local authorities arrived at her house, she had found the truck parked a block away. She decided not to move forward with the police report and instead filed a restraining order against Ferguson.

Coburn's friends were angered with her for going to the police, and one of them, Sparrow, went to the police station and asked to see the police report of the stolen truck and also a copy of the restraining order—all in an effort to determine just how much information Coburn may have given the police about the community. Sparrow's inquiry helped the Eugene Police Department in connecting Ferguson to Coburn's truck and then to the arson attack at Joe Romania that had occurred the night before.

This suspicion by law enforcement set the groundwork for empaneling a federal grand jury to investigate the Joe Romania arson, and even though many local activists were subpoenaed to appear before the grand jury, most refused to cooperate, causing the grand jury to stall for the next couple of years. However, in 2003, authorities struck gold without even initially recognizing it.

The Feds again contacted Ferguson and informed him that members of the community had fingered him for the Joe Romania arson. While they didn't have any hard evidence that Ferguson was involved, they brought him in largely on a bluff and convinced him they had enough evidence on him to send him to prison. They offered Ferguson a deal: fully cooperate with authorities and he'd be around to see his young son grow up. Ferguson agreed and ended up telling authorities about the Romania arson, but additionally—to their disbelief—about a significant number of additional arson attacks the ELF had caused through the previous decade.

One of the major components of Ferguson's deal was that he would wear a wire and travel throughout the country with the intent of meeting up with his old comrades and getting them to discuss their past crimes. So, during 2004 and 2005, Ferguson recorded conversations comprising thirty-five CDs of former ELF members talking with him.

Using Ferguson's secret recordings to obtain arrest warrants, on December 7, 2005, FBI agents arrested an initial six suspects associated with the Earth Liberation Front: Stanislas Meyerhoff, Daniel McGowan, Kevin Tubbs, William Rodgers (aka Avalon), Kendall Tankersley, and Chelsea Gerlach.

On January 6, 2006, the Department of Justice held a national news conference announcing a sixty-five-page indictment against eleven people suspected of being involved with Earth Liberation Front activities. In addition to the first six arrested, the indictment also included Joseph Dibee, Josephine Sunshine Overaker, Jonathan Paul, Rebecca Rubin, Suzanne Savoie and Darren Thurston. Eventually, the list would include Justin Solodnz, Briana Waters, Nathan Block, Joyanna Zacher, Jennifer

Kolar, and Lacey Phillabaum. The press release issued by the DOJ announcing the indictments referred to the group as "The Family," despite no one on the list recalling that term ever being used internally by the Earth Liberation Front.

While most of the second set of suspects were arrested in December and early January, four went on the run: Joe Dibee, Sunshine Overaker, Rebecca Rubin, and Justin Solondz.

Those in custody were met with scare tactics from prosecutors—cooperate or each face a lifetime in prison. Buckling under this pressure, many agreed to provide information against their co-defendants, while a few remained steadfast to their beliefs in noncooperation.

One defendant, William Rodgers—the mastermind of the 1998 Vail arson—committed suicide in an Arizona jail shortly after his arrest. He left behind the following note:

> To my friends and supporters to help them make sense of all these events that have happened so quickly: Certain human cultures have been waging war against the Earth for millennia. I chose to fight on the side of bears, mountain lions, skunks, bats, saguaros, cliff rose and all things wild. I am just the most recent casualty in that war. But tonight I have made a jail break—I am returning home, to the Earth, to the place of my origins. Bill, 12/21/05 (the winter solstice).

Within the following two years, nearly all defendants in custody took some sort of deal—either a cooperating deal with an expected reduction in sentence or a noncooperation deal where they would not have to provide evidence against others.

- Stanislas Meyerhoff received thirteen years in prison for the following actions: Toppling a Bonneville Power Administration high-voltage transmission tower near Bend in 1999 and seven firebombings: the Vail ski resort (1998), Childers Meat Co. in Eugene (1999), Boise Cascade in Monmouth (1999), a Eugene Police Substation (2000), Joe Romania Chevrolet Truck Center in Eugene (2001), Superior Lumber Co. in Glendale (2001), and Jefferson Poplar Farm near Clatskanie (2001).

- Kevin Tubbs was sentenced to twelve years and seven months in prison for his role in the following acts: the 1996 arson attack at an Oakridge Forest Ranger Station, the 1997 arson at Cavel West horse slaughterhouse in Redmond, Oregon, the BLM wild horse and burro facility in Burns, Oregon in 1997, an attempted arson at US Forest Industries in Medford, Oregon in 1998, Childers Meat Co. in Eugene in 1999, the Eugene Police Substation in 2000, Superior Lumber in Glendale, Oregon in 2001, Joe Romania Chevrolet and also a Clatskanie, Oregon tree farm, both in 2001.

- Chelsea Gerlach received nine years in prison for the following acts: Vail Ski Resort; Childers Meat Co. in Eugene, Oregon; Boise Cascade in Monmouth, Oregon; the Eugene Police Substation; Jefferson Poplar tree farm in Clatskanie, Oregon; and the toppling of a high-voltage Bonneville Power Administration tower near Bend, Oregon.

- Both Joyanna Zacher and Nathan Block each received seven years and eight months for their roles in the Clatskanie tree farm arson and the fire at Joe Romania Chevrolet.

- Daniel McGowan was sentenced to seven years in prison for his role in the Superior Lumber arson and Jefferson Poplar.

- Jonathan Paul received four years and three months for one act: the fire that burned the Cavel West horse slaughterhouse in 1997.

- Suzanne Savoie, likewise, was sentenced to four years and three months in prison for her role in the Superior Lumber fire and at Jefferson Poplar.

- Kendall Tankersley was given three years and five months for the attempted arson at US Forest Industries.

- Darren Thurston was sentenced to three years and one month in prison for his role in burning down the BLM's wild horse corral in California in 2001.

- Jennifer Kolar received five years in prison for her role in the 2001 University of Washington fire, Cavel West horse slaughterhouse, and Susanville Horse Corral, as well as an attempted arson at the Wray Gun Club in Colorado in 1998.

- Lacey Phillabaum was sentenced to three years in prison for her role in the University of Washington arson attack.

- Briana Waters maintained her innocence and was the only defendant in this group to take their case to trial. Charged with taking part in the University of Washington fire, the government's case rested on testimony from co-defendants that Waters acted as a lookout with a walkie-talkie for the action. Though Waters's attorneys demonstrated significant inconsistencies with the evidence implicating her, on March 6, 2008, a federal jury in Tacoma, Washington, found Waters guilty of two counts of arson and sentenced her to four years in prison.

- After living as a fugitive in Canada for six years, Rebecca Rubin turned herself in to authorities in 2012. She was sentenced to five years in prison for her role in the Vail Ski Resort arson, the horse release and fire at the BLM facility in Burns, Oregon, the 1998 attempted fire at US Forest Industries, and the horse release and fire at the BLM horse and wild burro corral in Litchfield, California.

- In March 2009, fugitive Justin Solondz was apprehended in China on drug charges and was sentenced to three years for narcotics manufacturing. On July 6, 2011, Solondz was extradited to the US and arrested in Chicago on conspiracy and arson charges. He was sentenced to seven years for his role in the University of Washington arson.

- Joseph Dibee lived for years as a fugitive in Syria and then Russia before being apprehended in Havana, Cuba in 2018. After his arrest, Dibee was held for twenty-nine months in addition to home custody. In 2022, Dibee was sentenced to time served.

- For all of his extensive cooperation with the government, Jake Ferguson received no prison time for his role in numerous Earth Liberation Front actions.

Up until this point the success by authorities in arresting and prosecuting members of the Earth Liberation Front had been limited to the Northwest cell of the group as well as the cell on Long Island. But in 2007, the Feds would finally make some progress with the Midwest cell of the ELF. That year, a man foraging for wood in a Detroit trash dumpster found writings from Frank Ambrose, along with a gas mask, an M80 explosive and other possessions. The man turned the materials over to local police, who immediately summoned FBI involvement. Upon questioning Ambrose, the FBI received full cooperation from him, even to wear a wire to record his wife Marie Mason as well as local environmental groups. With the evidence acquired from Ambrose's recordings, the government arrested and charged Mason with a string of arson attacks, including the $1 million fire at Michigan State University in 1999. The day after her arrest, Frank Ambrose filed for divorce. In 2009, Mason was sentenced to nearly twenty-two years in prison where she, now he—Marius Mason—resides today. Ambrose, for his extensive cooperation with the government, received six years in prison.

This brings the story to the case of Eric McDavid and an example of how far the government was willing to go to stop this movement. Eric was a twenty-six-year-old activist who met a woman in 2004 named "Anna," at an anarchist gathering in Iowa. Anna was actually Zoe Elizabeth Voss, a paid FBI informant posing as an activist. Anna became close with McDavid and would eventually convince him and two others to bomb various targets in California, including electrical power stations and cellphone towers. The plot by the Feds went so far it included providing the bomb-making instructions that were designed by the FBI, the transportation, a cabin in the woods fitted with hidden cameras, and even suggestions of potential targets for the new "eco-terrorist" cell. As Anna purposely became closer with McDavid, she lured him into this terrorism conspiracy with the promise of a sexual relationship once the actions had been committed.

McDavid was arrested in 2006 prior to any bombs being set and was convicted in 2007 of conspiring to use fire or explosives to damage corporate and government property. He was sentenced to nearly twenty years in prison. However, on January 8, 2015, McDavid was released after a judge determined that critical documents related to his case had been withheld by prosecutors. The documents, according to McDavid's attorneys, show a deliberate entrapment campaign waged by the FBI. In the end, McDavid served just under nine years in prison and, as for "Anna," she was only one of the estimated 15,000 informants the FBI had in the early 2000s assisting the government with its efforts to stop the Earth Liberation Front.[109]

•　　•　　•

So what can be learned from the story of the Earth Liberation Front and from the government's investigation into this radical direction action movement? Perhaps a lot. On a personal level, those involved sacrificed years of their lives in secrecy, conducting bold arson attacks, to then be met with even more years of prison sentences and significant fines. Surely, crimes were committed and resultantly, as expected, once caught, the saboteurs would face criminal penalties. However, most of the sentences for ELF members were far disproportionate to others of a similar nature during the same time period. The only difference was these individuals were engaging in direct actions to stop the destruction of the natural environment—a righteous cause but also one that put them at odds with corporations and a government operating in a capitalist society that had demonstrated it prioritized profits ahead of the environment. As a result, the sentences were long because the acts were politically motivated, and the government wanted to send a strong and clear message that actions such as these that stand to threaten commerce will not be tolerated.

109 Trevor Aaronson and Katie Galloway, "Manufacturing Terror," The Intercept, November 19, 2015, theintercept.com/2015/11/19/an-fbi-informant-seduced-eric-mcdavid-into-a-bomb-plot-then-the-government-lied-about-it/.

There is also the significant issue of the ELF members who ended up cooperating with the government in the hopes of reduced prison sentences. This began largely with Jake Ferguson and the assistance he provided to the FBI. But it continued once other co-defendants were arrested.

One of the most pertinent questions to be asked is, would the government have been successful in its Operation Backfire major case had no one—including Jake Ferguson—cooperated? Likely not. In addition to the toll the cooperation had on bringing down the Earth Liberation Front movement, the personal consequences of the cooperation were also catastrophic. Lengthy prison sentences up to twenty-three years each, many in supermax facilities, were handed down. Personal relationships between activists were destroyed. People suddenly hated one another. The environmental community disowned and even at times threatened those who turned state's evidence. Those out of prison with felony convictions and terrorism enhancements faced a difficult time finding work, mentally adjusting to the outside world, and struggling to figure out their roles in life after everything they had been through. And without a doubt, certain members of the FBI and US Attorneys office sat back with smiles on their faces, thrilled at their success, at the chaos they caused and at bringing down what they considered the number one domestic terrorism threat in the United States.

Another question that arises is what, if any, positive benefits came out of the Earth Liberation Front? Certainly there were a few examples of attacks, including the 1997 fire at Cavel West, that put companies entirely out of business. However, the majority of the targets were insured and were repaired or rebuilt, sometimes even larger than before. So on a purely tactical level, it's hard to say the strategy of the ELF widely paid off.

Beyond that, it is fair to say there was damage done, beyond even the group's intention. When the simultaneous actions occurred in 2001 against the University of Washington and at Jefferson Poplar in Oregon, the UW fire burned a valuable horticulture library. And the fire at Jefferson Poplar appeared to have been a mistake—the group was trying to target the previous company engaged in genetic engineering of trees. The company had been sold, and the new owners claimed to have ended any genetic engineering work.

There is also the notion that the ELF, unintentionally, drew a wedge in the environmental movement, one intentionally exploited by law enforcement, by making those concerned with the environment pick sides. Either you were in support of direct action and the ELF or you were against them. Division within movements causes weakness and ineffectiveness, and the FBI has utilized this phenomenon throughout its history (civil rights/Black power movements, antiwar movements, etc.). So, instead of one environmental movement supporting a diversity of tactics, there was a fragmented struggle with a lack of support for all segments.

At best, the Earth Liberation Front was a source of inspiration. It was an example of people being so upset at the powers that be ruining our world that they decided to do something different about it. They stepped outside of societal norms of what we are told to do, what we are allowed to do, if we seek to advocate for change in the world. The main problem with their strategy is that, for it to work, it requires— as history has shown—a strong, diverse, and open-minded mass movement, one that understands a diversity of tactics is required for any change to occur. And that movement didn't exist.

Whatever your view of the Earth Liberation Front and its tactics, one thing is certain, the environment is far worse off today than decades ago when the ELF existed. Whether it's climate change and its many impacts, species extinction, deforestation, plastic pollution, food and water insecurity, air pollution, or soil degradation, life on Earth is increasingly threatened. And as these issues are growing in severity, it is clear that whatever we have done up to this point, and whatever we are doing now to address these problems, is not working.

So, our job, if we actually give a damn, is to learn from history—what worked and what didn't, in specific circumstances—and devise a strategy utilizing every tool in the toolbox, including those outside of traditional norms and even legality to actually combat this environmental crisis.

Our lives depend on it.

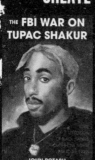